GoodTaste

How What You Choose Defines Who You Are

GoodTaste

How What You Choose Defines Who You Are

Peter Trifonas
Effie Balomenos

ICON BOOKS

Published in the UK in 2003
by Icon Books Ltd., Grange Road,
Duxford, Cambridge CB2 4QF
Email: info@iconbooks.co.uk
www.iconbooks.co.uk

Sold in the UK, Europe, South Africa
and Asia by Faber and Faber Ltd.,
3 Queen Square, London WC1N 3AU
or their agents

Distributed in the UK, Europe, South Africa
and Asia by TBS Ltd., Frating Distribution Centre,
Colchester Road, Frating Green, Colchester CO7 7DW

Published in Australia in 2003
by Allen & Unwin Pty. Ltd., PO Box 8500,
83 Alexander Street, Crows Nest, NSW 2065

Distributed in Canada by Penguin Books Canada,
10 Alcorn Avenue, Suite 300, Toronto, Ontario M4V 3B2

ISBN 1 84046 479 8

Typesetting by Hands Fotoset

Printed and bound in the UK by
Mackays of Chatham plc

For our parents:
Helen, John, Martha and Panayiotis

Acknowledgements

We would like to acknowledge Simon Flynn for his unwavering support for this project and his infinite reserves of patience. Ruth Nelson has been an outstanding copy editor, providing creative insight into the text at the points where the words crack, meaning breaks down, and ideas need to be set free – or at least rewritten.

We would also like to thank our children Peirce, Anthi and Yanni who have endured the writing of this book with joyful smiles of anticipation while being our source of inspiration to get it done.

Contents

CHAPTER ONE

Distinctions

> Taste is the basis of all that one has – people and
> things – and all that one is for others, whereby one
> classifies oneself and is classified by others
>
> *Pierre Bourdieu*

Taste swings open the doors of acceptance and it slams shut the gateways of opportunity by allowing others to make distinctions about us. It guides the working out of personal and social codes of conduct that render as readable our own aspirations. Good taste is an ideal – it determines the cultural value of what we do, say or think, the way we dress, eat or talk, what we own, whom we befriend. It consolidates our desire to belong in the public and private spheres where we live, work and play. Whether it be picking a brand of clothing, selecting a book to read or a CD to listen to, deciding on a career, or even choosing a mate, the conventions of good taste influence, temper and guide all facets of human behaviour. We cannot ignore this fact – no matter how hard we try. What is called 'good taste' has an intellectual and social history tied to human behaviour – manners, mannerisms and etiquette.

Taste seduces and tantalises. It fills us up with hope and drags us down in despair. Taste makes possible the dream of success and acceptance, but similarly entertains the nightmare of being shunned as a failure by those we wish to have standing by our side. In the best instance, we can become a model to others for the stellar choices we have made about how we look and act. When it is 'good', taste puts us on top – on the 'A' list – of a community. At its worst, it is a powerful source for ridicule that can turn our life upside down as it banishes us to the margins of society. Those unfortunate souls whose choices do not 'fit in' with a given community, mainstream or otherwise, must look elsewhere for acceptance through the appeal of similar cultural priorities, interests and preferences of everyday life. Taste involves classifying yourself and others so that you can try to find a common ground on which to be accepted for the choices you make, and, in the process, working out where you want to belong and with whom you have a collective bond. It is a kind of social initiation that marks everyone as someone to engage with or not.

Good taste makes distinctions of 'quality' along hierarchical lines dividing the highbrow from the lowbrow. Capitalist society, after all, is based on a system of classes. But extremes meet somewhere in a middle ground of taste we might call 'no brow', where choices are personal and eclectic. Regardless, that is, of any class we might belong to! Good taste relates to the creative and cooperative styles and habits we adopt and express as members of a collective and as individuals. The 'Aristocrat' and the 'Artiste', the 'Scholar' and the 'Musician', like all of us, belong to a culture that establishes standards to live by, ranking the good, the bad and the ugly of their group's practices. Any and all activities are subject to evaluation in the socialisation process we call 'being part of a community'. Everything relating to culture and human behaviour touches in some way on the standards of taste: how a person talks, what a person reads, watches, wears, drinks or even thinks (as it is indirectly indicated through behaviour) provides information about the quality of their sense of discrimination between good and bad. We all have an automatic reflex to categorise and synthesise all incoming information without necessarily maintaining any conscious awareness of the critical act. Some critiques are more sinister than others, but there is no escaping evaluation. The opinions that we form about things, actions and people offer credence to perspectives of taste as value judgements. Fads and trends begin because we all want to believe a diet drink will make us thinner and more attractive. If 'the pitch' is convincing enough, a judgement of value gains a following based on the power of positive suggestion. The bigger the group subscribing to a style or taste, the more generalisable and universalisable the definition of good taste proves to be. Sirloin steak is appreciated over stewing meat, vintage wine preferred over cooking wine; there is little disagreement as to the appeal of an item or practice that demonstrates a universally understood quality of good taste – one that is so familiar, it becomes idiosyncratic and narrow.

Not all tastes, however, are so easily appreciated. This is because many tastes highlight personal opinions as they develop through the looking-glass of a culture's ideals. The particulars of a group's evaluation of an object or action highlight what habits preoccupy them. Terms and phrases are born, adopted or adapted to accommodate where interests lie. Priorities establish a dialect in tune with the nature of a group's particular ideals. Phrases unique to the temperaments and styles of those in the judging pool reveal the idiosyncrasies a culture holds sacred. Evaluation relates to how radical, conservative, traditional and so on the fashions and philosophies of a social group prove to be. What is considered to be good taste differs because of the particular nature of the habits and styles of a group. Those who listen to Country Music, Classical, EMO, Grunge, Heavy Metal or Reggae are all definitive about what they deem as acoustically attractive and lyrically worthwhile in a song. Each group has its own standards of what is appealing or otherwise. The differences in the criteria serve to define the uniqueness of a style.

The crusty academics, inspired artisans, snub-nosed aristocrats, cool 'Hip-Hoppers', corporate types, bohemians and blue-collar workers all form examples of diverse groups that are drawn to specific systems of taste. Each group submits to personal and cultural priorities that lead to specialised codes of style and discrete visions of social success. Any way we choose to interpret it, the consequences of ignoring or 'playing up' the rules we use to classify ourselves and others make the quest for good taste a serious game: mainly because of the social distinctions that remain, thanks to the choices we make. Some aesthetic and intellectual choices are valued more than others, but there is always going to be plenty of room for competition through the play of innovation relative to quality ideals. Taste is like a stylistic contest between the 'good', the 'not so good' and the downright 'bad', where a practice wins out at the expense of another being rejected. There are always winners and losers, but the challenge is constant and dynamic, with the intervention of new players re-orienting the possibilities of where the game can lead. Good taste involves an awareness of the rules as they are played for winning admiration – not simply for participating in the game. Stylistic priorities are set up to legitimate every person's ability to discern between good taste and bad, whether or not one cares for the distinction! The top players of any class and culture understand the rituals of the game. Developing the skills of taste requires us to follow the principles of both science and art. In a game that is based on batting, you must understand the underlying mechanical elements of how to hit the ball before you can succeed. How you place your feet, hold the bat, look at the ball and swing are critical components of correct style. Nevertheless, you have to possess a proficiency at properly applying the dynamics of hitting to knock the ball around any part of the field you choose to. Batting becomes an art, rather than a science, when you are no longer limited by ability and can push your skill to higher levels of performance and understanding. Likewise, you must comprehend and be able to apply the rules of how to taste wine to enjoy the subtle nuances of quality vintage fully. How you let the wine breathe, hold the glass and check the colour, clarity and bouquet, as well as how the wine is left to swirl and aspirate as it sits, momentarily, on your palate before refreshing or swallowing, are all important components in the science of appreciating a superior product. However, being able to identify a bottle of 1921 Clos du Moulin Gewürtztraminer from a 1937 Clos des Grandes Murailles takes the skill of wine tasting to another level of expertise that makes it an art form. Good taste in any endeavour means understanding the principles that must be considered in order to execute it beautifully, with skill and understanding. The art comes into science when we know how to appreciate the correct application of skills and elevate them to levels of incredible proficiency! Those who want to attain the ideals of good taste just have to keep on trying to get it right. Using imagination and creativity to push the rules to the limit (once you have learnt them) gives birth to excellence that is always being reinforced or challenged by new ideas.

But there are also intangible forces like raw predispositions and talents that are inherited via the living examples of parents or acquired socially through participation in a community. These sources can provide any information needed to set out the blueprints for an awareness that can later blossom into a mature dialect in good taste. Personal experiences foster the essential ground for developing cognisant interpretations of what we like and why, based on understanding quality examples. Thus, we blaze new trails of ingenuity that stem from a knowledge of taste that has established in us mental templates of 'good' and 'bad'.

Taste shows others a version of who we are, or perhaps an image of who we would like to be, when the exercise to get it right is still a work in progress. It is an exterior vision, not necessarily complete, but a conscious pose achieved with attention to elements of style and grace. Taste preferences, simply put, express what we like from a selection of everything that is available in a culture as products and behaviours. What is consumed or performed by us, what we 'buy' and 'buy into' – Nike shoes, merino wool argyle socks, foreign films, fast food, German cars, malt liquor, self-help books, Gucci bags, Continental table manners, extreme sports, public television programming, Art Deco furniture, the selection goes on and on and on – all the things we say, own and do necessarily classify us for all the world to see. You could object to the arbitrariness of taste judgements that are based on simple and ever-changing observations. You could say, 'Appearances are sometimes deceiving'. And you would be right. But even though judgements of taste may be unjustified or unfair, we have little or no choice in matters regarding the opinions of others. The tendency to classify what we see, hear and experience is an automatic response, a reflex reaction. So, attention must be paid to the sense of taste and how it works through us, in society, as a meaningful code for understanding relations between people, the significance of their actions, and the material things that surround us in the world. It *is* possible to become more fully aware of what can influence perceptions of taste, and lead to judgements that make distinctions in the public eye between what is 'good' and what is 'bad'.

Consumer goods and cultural practices are not only 'products to buy' and 'behaviours to perform': each is a sign that conveys who we are, essentially by what is ours and what we do. Every object and action has multiple styles and forms to choose from. Some are considered tasteful, while others are not. Some are accepted as suitable, others are not. Which, of course, complicates matters greatly, because people are always watching for something or someone to comment on. Good taste involves making 'the right choices', or knowing how, when and why to navigate towards what is 'quality'. Propriety rules! Bad taste is the result of a serious deficit of understanding about what is valued, by whom, and at what time.

Making Statements

Embroidered denim bell bottoms, once again, sit low on the hips of pre-pubescent teenagers and aging baby boomers alike. Navel gazing is a global pastime from Japan to New York. Tattoos are abundant – popular for no good reason other than the fact that they are believed to be fashionable expressions of individuality, regardless of how abundant they are on everyone else's well-engraved bodies. Now, at this very moment, while some hapless teenager who is getting a cool Sanskrit tattoo on the small of her back cringes through the pain with a teary-eyed smile, her head nodding dizzily in time to the driving beat of Aerosmith's 'Walk This Way' as her friend watches closely, waiting breathlessly to go under this *serious* flesh artist's needle, good taste is being tested. But not because tattoos are in

7

'bad taste'. Quite the contrary: they are the epitome of good taste in the pit of anti-establishment culture zones.

There is a tattoo for everyone. Although having the same tattoo as someone else could be like a symbolic form of incest if it was not to establish some kind of social cliqueing. This is a taboo of taste reserved only for gang members, Marines, secret societies and sports teams. It's like a cross tattooed on the sole of a Satanic cult member's foot in the Middle Ages or a battle verse emblazoned in Latin on the rippling forearm of a battle-scarred commando. In this case, the tattoo is a sign whose real meaning and significance is shared only by the common experience of a select few. The ritual aspect of the tattoo as a rite of passage and proof of belonging within a community is more important here than the tattoo as an art form or a personal expression of voluntary deviance from 'the norm'. These are the main reasons why tattoos have been popular with the members of contemporary middle-class society – especially with the 13th Generation, the Gen Xers, who chant the mantra of individuality, rebellion and freedom while finishing the last courses toward an MBA and what was thought to have been a lucrative career in Stock Portfolio Management, Mergers and Acquisitions before the last technology sector meltdown.

Despite the contradictions between 'buying in' and 'selling out', tattoos are most certainly also in good taste with the late rebel teens of today. Tattoos sustain an attractive symbolism, like a butterfly breaking from its cocoon as it changes the pattern of its surface. The wings of a youth unfold with the engraving that serves to initiate a world away (from mum and dad). Adulthood and freedom of choice are branded onto whatever body part best serves to convey the message. Tattoos are multiplying on the economically thriving bodies of people who are not sailors, strippers, hookers, bikers, convicts or circus performers. Worries about the future state of laser tattoo removal technology are forever brushed aside. Who knows whether the world will still exist at an unforeseen time in the future, or whether tattoos will still be in good taste as a fad of the distant future? An alien phyto-animal culture made up of the DNA of extinct Earthly species could rise thanks to the nuclear testing of rogue nations to vanquish humanity, once and for all.

By the same token, the idea of a pair of turned-up trousers should not cause anyone to break out in a cold sweat. But it can and has – it's definitely not a symbol of good taste in the fashion scene of today. Historically, however, and for some time after the introduction of trousers as we now know them, men would commonly roll up the bottoms by hand to keep them out of mud and water. The advantage of the knee breeches worn in the 18th century was the fact that the hem was so high off the ground that they were not likely to be soiled. The stockings worn with knee breeches were much easier to launder than trousers. Good taste was thus created out of the very practical initiative of saving on the energy needed to wash a pair of trousers. Today, in the concrete urban metropolis, we aren't concerned with trekking across muddy, unpaved city trails. Turn-ups are a matter of stylistic preference – not a practical way to keep trousers cleaner. In the early 1890s, the sporting country look with turn-ups was first tailored onto trousers, but even at the time, when the fashion was introduced, the response was far from positive. There was an uproar in the Houses of Parliament when in 1893 a certain Viscount Lewisham broke with the tradition of never turning up trousers and shocked the oldest and best-respected of statesmen by wearing turn-ups. However, by the early years of the 20th century turn-ups had become an accepted variation on regular trouser bottoms, most significantly for the younger generation of well-to-do entrepreneurs and professionals. The older male population, however, did not adapt well to the new tastes of a younger generation. T.S. Eliot immortalised the dilemma in 'The Love Song of J. Alfred Prufrock', in which the aging, anti-heroic protagonist wonders: 'I grow old, I grow old. Should I wear the bottoms of my trousers rolled?'

Real people who are aging don't need that kind of pressure about insignificant things that do not add to or subtract from the quality of their lives. They should wear what they like in the time they have left and not care a fig about the fashions of youth cultures. And the bravest and most self-assured of elderly males do! Specifically, in West Palm Beach, Florida, which is perhaps the home of the most innovatively radical of retirement communities with respect to defying fashion norms. Dissension is what high-waisted, intricately plaid, double-knit polyester trousers held up with a white belt over winged-tip golf shoes are all about. They are protesting against the limits age puts on the mind's capacity for creativity in fashion by stretching the boundaries of good taste. Some may choose to call this idiosyncratic form of dress that nauseates traditional aesthetic sensibilities 'tacky leisure wear'. Especially when it is topped off by a striped polo shirt of contrasting Day-Glo hues, a squarely fitted baseball cap and the conspicuous glitter of a gold Masonic ring worn on the right little finger below a self-monogrammed medic alert bracelet. The outfit displays a total disregard for the cultural logic of any and all dress codes that Western society has experienced to date. This seemingly haphazard combination of incompatible patterns, colours and accessories that breaks all the rules of attirement is not, however, without reason, nor without imitation. The 'West Palm Beach look' is reproduced by the subculture within this locality and outside of it across North America as innumerable armies of elderly gentlemen in retirement communities show their disdain for the restrictions contemporary fashion puts on their God-given right to self-expression in old age. These octogenarian rebels selflessly put their bodies on public display to make a point against popular styles that are being imposed upon them against their will. It is as if their clothes are screaming out what they themselves cannot say, what a younger culture obsessed with popular taste does not wish to hear: 'Growing old is punishment enough. Let us wear what we want!' This polyester-based anti-fashion statement merely provides a way to break the silence of a troubled mind and give its pain a creative voice and identity.

To be considered 'in style' or 'in fashion' gives the desirable cachet of good taste and alters the way we are perceived as human beings. But clothing, style and fashion should not breed psychosis – an incurable envy and glorious paranoia in the quest to be *like* others yet to distinguish ourselves *from* others. Nor should they nurture the misery of a fearful and debilitating self-loathing, when it comes to matters of choice discerning good taste. If we want to feel miserable about our bad taste, a quick trip to Las Vegas – the kitschy city of drive-through marriages and complimentary shrimp cocktails – could accomplish this quite nicely, and is preferable to the self-induced psychological violence that we live through every day thanks to the fear of having a poor sense of style and fashion. The pain of it all and the horror! Simply put, we care about appearances and being *in fashion*. Why?

Clothes have meaning. They tell the world about us! So what if we experience lapses of judgement in good taste to be dressed similar in style to everyone else? When we are all wearing the same thing, no one will notice just how unnatural some clothing looks despite its popularity.

For taste to be considered 'good', it has to relay the sense of one's having the ability to discriminate between choices that are available to us by presupposing that: all things are not of equal worth and value. Some things are more appropriate and acceptable than others depending on the situation. Extreme inappropriateness would be bad taste. A gift certificate for a round of electrolysis sessions at 'The Hair Razor' is not a good choice for a Valentine's Day present to your fiancée. No amount of roses would help your pre-marital relationship to fully recover its romantic lustre from that taste *faux pas*. There would always be nagging doubts about whether or not the aesthetic appeal of your mate is forever diminished in your eyes. Even the hint of a moustache shatters the ideal of womanly beauty, while a hairy back undercuts the mystique of male vigour by suggesting a bestial nature. If you feel your fiancé needs the treatments, there is a more tactful way to broach the subject and a more appropriate time to do so, since Valentine's Day is an occasion for celebrating the attributes of the person you love, not suggesting how you would like them to change to suit your tastes. Especially since the presence of excessive hair on the body or face, male or female, is really a matter of biology and personal preference. DNA and taste.

No Man (or Woman) is an Island

From the decisions we make about what we say and do, to the things we select to consume and own, we provide information about ourselves to be judged by others within a community. Because it is a public expression of individuality and similarity, taste demands a social critique, a judgement as to whether it is 'good' or 'bad', that is decided by a dominant culture within a group or society. Let's call it an ethos. It is a moral imperative or 'critical consciousness' that beckons a response from others – whether we want it or not! We have to live with the consequences of obeying or disobeying the norms of that ethos in order to be part of a community, a society, a culture. Which is where the problems of taste begin and end: with you and me and the world we live in with others.

The French sociologist Pierre Bourdieu was right! No judgement of taste is innocent. The point is one of distinction: similarity with a difference. It is a question of preference and style, or the subjective interpretation of taste made by an individual person. The problem is not only how to draw attention to the fact that we have a sense of good taste in common with that of others, but how to exhibit a unique sense of style that is personal, yet acceptable with current trends by mirroring and refining aspects of them. To be tasteful is to willingly submit ourselves in some part to the guidelines, systems and codes of taste dominant within a culture. It is a blind obedience, more or less. Otherwise, the danger is that we will not be looked upon as being part of the cultural spirit of the times, its *Zeitgeist*, and therefore will be beyond interpretation and understanding – an outsider. 'No man [or woman] is an island', to paraphrase John Donne. Psychologically, everyone needs the reassurances of others, a confirming gesture that we as individuals are on the 'right track' with respect to the cultural and historical conventions of good taste demanded by a general will steeped in tradition.

Selecting a social group to 'seamlessly' bond with has to take place through opportunities to make connections that are real and authentically motivated by personal values and judgements. Only then can refining taste towards a specific style be successful and satisfying, simply because it is genuine and not the result of a pose – not fake. Styles are the challenges posed as an initiation rite by a group. A heavy diet of *The National Enquirer*, fast food and Pamela Anderson's hand-me-downs wouldn't serve as good initiation fodder for Hillary Clinton's first choice in a social companion. Tastes divide and conquer between high and lowbrow manners and mannerisms. They help the social graces of etiquette to be carried out successfully within a community. Tastes are thought to be consistent with socio-economic factors that help to define the aesthetic options and choices we have in common with others, i.e., income bracket, home design, hairstyle, hobbies, level of fitness, education, fashion sense, preferred cuisine, religious beliefs, political orientation, musical appreciation, literary preferences and so on. All of these factors, in every facet of our lives, convey the potential areas for compatibility within specific communities of taste. It is not that there are no differences between individuals, but a social clique happens because values are based on a consensus of stylistically compatible tastes. People in a community or class experience solidarity because there is agreement about what they find attractive, a sharing of common interests. Spontaneous evaluation of one person by another is the basis for recognising similarities that lead to compatibility. This process discourages socially 'unmatched' relationships, while encouraging potentially well-suited ones. Yet, these judgements can be naïve, formalised into nothing other than the social language of likes and dislikes. An upper-middle-class woman who adores spending money on *haute couture* and fine dining, likes to play tennis and follows homeopathic remedies would not feel at ease spending time with someone who believes it is best to save everything for the impending future, detests shopping and sports and firmly believes that naturopathic medicine is more 'hocus pocus' than scientific solution. The discordant taste preferences would make it difficult for these two individuals to identify subject matter to discuss. Such a situation would lead to uncomfortable moments of silence based on taste differences. There might be something to say, yet little to agree about. Taste peculiarities on a personal scale often determine whom we can spend time with on a social scale. Good taste demands consensus on what is attractive and pleasant by many, sometimes most, members of a community. Knowing that others agree with you provides a support system that validates tastes. Without an audience there can be no on-going public discussion about taste.

Every person and object is evaluated and classified relative to a group identity. It is taste that aligns aesthetics to subjects who possess similar affinities and needs. Finding shared dispositions generates communal social identities. Where there is a consensus of taste and many people can see it as attractive, the values and choices we have in common with others become respected cultural ideals, status symbols and a passport to acceptance. A superfluous and conspicuously unnecessary fad like the endlessly popular board game 'Trivial Pursuit' can unite by way of the play activity and emotional release it offers – not necessarily the usable knowledge gained from the experience. As the title suggests, the intellectual pursuit is 'trivial'. The satisfaction lies in the challenge we feel to play a game that allows the popular culture distinctions of the knowledge we possess (or not) to be shared with others: taste exists only as a group dynamic. But we can play with its sense of seriousness, especially when it is the game of choice for a society. Without social interaction there is no regulating body to determine the importance or quality of an idea. It is an egocentric enterprise that completes its cycle only in the admiration it invokes. Without a living scale from which to evaluate the quality of an idea or style, there is no way to consolidate or fully determine the value it holds. A display of discriminating judgements reveals what a person finds to be appealing. A viewing public is required to validate the effort of an idea or style. Searching for an attractive and fashionable outfit is futile if it is only going to be worn around the house. Wearing 'Versace' to clean out the garage, or to work on your home computer while waiting to make dinner, defeats the purpose of the effort to invoke a sense of good taste. That is, of course, unless you are one of the privileged few who can recklessly indulge in such fashion treats without the need to complete the aesthetic labour by receiving social admiration for the cumbersome financial imposition made. Taste exists as relevant on a personal scale and conversely is sustained through an audience required to consume and evaluate it. The process involves establishing group affiliations. We pursue practices and tastes that culminate to their full good taste potential when they take place within comfortable public settings. An act ridiculed by a specific individual or group can amount to social suicide.

Seeing and being seen, judging and being judged are all requirements of daily living. Unless of course you choose to live a life in exile, a life like Robinson Crusoe stranded on a desert island. Or Tom Hanks, who gets washed up onto a deserted tropical island during his role in *Cast Away*. In this slow-moving but convincing movie, the protagonist, deprived of any human social interaction on a deserted island, begins to speak to a volleyball that was washed up onto the shore in the same manner as he himself was after an aeroplane crash into the sea. The volleyball becomes his sole companion. He paints a face on it and gratefully engages in conversations with it on every topic, from his plans for the future after being rescued to pleasantries and superficialities about the weather. Near the end of the movie, while trying to escape the island, Tom Hanks experiences the heart-wrenching pain of losing his only friend to the perils of a tropical storm. The loss of his volleyball, this sports toy companion of five years that is no more, brings him to the verge of madness. In this movie, the fictional and potentially ridiculous but still very much convincing relationship created between the castaway and the ball companion suggests the deep-rooted human need for social bonding and recognition. Where interpersonal opportunities are impossible, the mind makes up for what is lacking in reality by creating fictional opportunities for social interaction. Socialising validates our ideas and self. Bouncing our feelings off another, to see what kind of response we will get back, acts as a gauge that determines the soundness of our perspectives and tastes. The 'good' ideas will be adopted, borrowed or shared. A culture industry will be produced. For example, good taste relates to the durability of a fashion movement in a social context; this, in turn, determines fashions in music, food, literature, theatre, architectural decor, recreational activities, etc. Fashions that interest a culture are what identify fads of good taste – quality for the times. What originally begins as a creative idea becomes popular when the majority of a cultural group sees it as a meaningful option to take on. Every taste choice works within the dynamics of a constant tension between the person and the group. The personal is validated by the plural and the plural is validated by the personal. Even a self-made recluse – a street person – makes a taste choice by choosing to be isolated from the material world. The statement is intentional and understood through a social audience. The recluse interacts only to feed, clothe and exercise within the parameters of other people's perception. The 'anti-establishment' ideal demonstrates a deplorement of social and cultural fashions, rituals and expectations but in so doing defines an attitude that maintains a group identity and tastes of its own. An intentional rejection of other cultures is visible and relevant only because it exists within those cultures. Even attempts to show bad taste demonstrate a style of indifference, thus creating legitimacy for the style itself for others who share the same pained disappreciation of expectations relating to taste.

Tastes offer social family ties, of a sort, for those who can successfully coordinate styles, attitudes and hobbies that culminate in a group appreciation. A family brings a sense of security, a place to belong. Similarities in the taste pool work to facilitate compatibility. These are the tangible landmarks that signal a common grounding before conversation even takes place. Simple material cues can make or break the feasibility of a union: the style of a person's shoes can indicate whether a more meaningful relationship can be considered. Classifying through discerning similarity in tastes is real – quickly summarising a person's foot apparel tells you how important they consider comfort, exercise, material quality, funk, fashion. High, low, grungy, elegant, sports, establishment, anti-establishment: the clues are enormous. A hairstyle is worth a thousand words, and preferences in music can define the edginess of the cut. Style directs choices. Making the cut means orchestrating a vocabulary that expresses the essence of a community and what means 'great' to them. Good taste is adopting and adapting to define the best of their own, relative to the styles, practices, values and morals that influence the preferences. The diversity of possible labels for group identities – the 'goth' or 'nerd', the 'snob', 'skinhead' or 'yuppie', the 'sloane' or 'metal head', for example – bears witness to the number of choices and alternatives that allow others to offer judgements towards the development of our standards of good taste. An appreciation of a cultural style must be authentic for a genuine understanding of the group values to be taken on and repeated, over and over again, thus naturally influencing our choices and behaviours. Impostors or 'posers' would not sustain a heartfelt sensitivity to the quality choices of a culture or community. The affiliations need to be sincere or the tastes conveyed will confuse the styles and intentions. Personal selections reflect what value and meaning people, practices and things have for us. We sometimes sacrifice or adjust the personal for the sake of group affiliation. Reflecting a relatively accurate picture of our personal tastes provides a comfortable network of social groups to rely on for co-membership in a community of taste.

Miss Manners

Don't get this wrong. Individualism is a desirable personality trait in the Western world. Where would liberal free enterprise, capitalism, multi-national corporations and the global economy be without it? Free will sparks novelty and the creation of new tastes and desires. Capitalism sells innovation as the freedom of cultural expression, or the democratic right to own the latest, greatest, 'bestest' thing – be it technology, goods, services – in order to be able to display openly your good taste to the world as a tangible commodity of human ingenuity. Cultural clout with a price tag. The never-ending array of choices regarding what we will want to own and what we will decide to avoid helps others to classify us by what Thorstein Veblen called 'conspicuous consumption'. Taste determines exactly where we rank in the social structure. It shapes what kind of person those who are 'above' and 'below' us – or even of 'equal' stature – think we are. Every possession and behaviour serves as a cultural indicator of taste that reflects the extent of our acceptance of value systems representing a general culture that cuts across social groupings. Others can read us by the objects we possess, the topics we discuss and the actions we perform. We will accept some tastes imposed upon us without argument by justifying them as the result of a commonly held sense of principles or shared opinions – mostly because there is a desire expressed for familiar behaviours and similar artefacts that grows out of the necessity to get along with and understand others on a cultural and social level. At times, there are just happy convergences of taste. Like the baby boomers with middle-age spread who are lucky enough to be in a position where loose-fitting, wide-leg styles are very much in fashion, since one of the contemporary forces driving the 'baggy' clothing styles of youth culture is Rap and Hip Hop. Those who share the public spaces of a community build comparable preferences over time that run parallel to each other and serendipitously intersect at times for very different reasons. The mutual dependency of commonalities and difference allows a society and culture to thrive and not remain static.

And yet, taste judgements are also relative to the specific values of subcultures that we inherit, or opt to adopt, based on where we come from and where we want to go. Distinctions and choices have to be made once again. The problem is that we can have many affiliations and identifi-cations. Let's consider the problem of manners, mannerisms and etiquette to illustrate the implications for cultivating taste.

Holding up two fingers in the shape of a 'V' for Victory used to be a favourite gesture of soldiers. But the hand sign can also be interpreted as a call for peace. The Victory gesture was co-opted by American Hippie subculture during the 60s to protest against the Vietnam and Korean Wars. In the UK, turn the gesture around, with the back of your hand facing the person you are signalling to, and you have all the makings of a fist-fight. The gesture is obscene like the proverbial 'bird' or middle finger salute in North America. Manners and mannerisms of distinction are an integral component of good taste for any group, be it a dominant culture or a subculture that has or had a definite anti-dominant cultural 'identity' like the Hippies. Gangs have a detailed, complex vocabulary of hand signs that seem like innocuous gestures or stylised poses to the untrained observer. Yet, the reality of what these mannerisms might signify is quite different. Hand signs are meaningful gestures used to convey messages. In part, they are an expression of subcultural bravado and a unique form of identity building that gives each gang member a sense of belonging and self-respect. Hand signs allow for public communication to be carried on via a secret language of symbolic gestures without words. Allegiances are acknowledged. Enemies taunted. Gang members 'throw' hand signs at each other to make a point. Friendly or not. When hand signs clash, worlds collide and violence begins. Manners and mannerisms are related to civility because etiquette governs the nature of human relationships around which cultures and subcultures are defined. Watching a 'Gangsta' Rap video by IceCube, Dr Dre or the now deceased TuPac Shakur gives one a very skewed image of how hand signs work to express a real identity beyond the media image. Good taste is wrapped up in Adidas tracksuits, basketball shoes and thickly braided gold rope chains holding up the diamond-encrusted shape of a giant dollar sign, $, that symbolises upward mobility and freedom from oppression. The life of leisure. The reason behind the use of hand signs in almost all Gangsta Rap videos is related to the marketing of an image, not the expression of a street identity. IceCube, Dr Dre and TuPac were never gang members. The widespread imitation of pseudo-gang poses is not an authentic and genuine expression of Hip Hop taste rooted in the origins of street gangs. White teenagers did not start wearing Tommy Hilfiger until it penetrated the ghettos of America. The cachet was its 'street cred', not the designer label. Even now designing houses and running shoe companies test-market clothes and shoes on the schoolyard basketball courts of inner-city USA by giving out free products to youths of a lower socio-economic background. Taste testers work alongside pimps, prostitutes and drug pushers to see if they can get kids hooked on new trainer prototypes or T-shirts. But just because the clothes and shoes are free does not mean that the teenagers will wear them. That is why the products are test-marketed in the inner-city neighbourhoods; to see what the potential commercial impact will be on the real customers who will buy them. If kids will not wear free clothes, there is no point manufacturing items and spending millions on advertising products that will sit in warehouses gathering dust. To white middle-class teenagers, Hip Hop attire is more or less a trendy fashion costume, a politically benign form of dress catering to a cool image not rooted in the same socio-political and economic circumstances of everyday life as are experienced by the black inner-city youth. It would be quite bizarre to watch public school students in a crested jacket, school tie and shirtsleeves throwing gang signs to each other during a supervised visit to Cambridge University Law School on 'Career Day'. Where is the genuine 'street cred' in that?

We have to question the authenticity of manners and mannerisms that are not grounded in experience and history. The rules of etiquette and politeness are designed to mitigate the negative consequences of actions performed in real-life situations. What we call 'good manners' come to be the moral cement of a civil society. Years of repetition do not seem to wear them out of practice as the expression of cultural habits required to convey a gentle respect for others. The ideal of 'good manners' speaks to the human desire for codes of conduct that will allow a society to grow peacefully and prosper without violence. Creating distance between people by offering models of predictable relations between ourselves and others in public gatherings reduces the chance of conflict. The cultivation of refined manners in any culture or subculture is built on the notion that eliminating extreme or unexpected behaviours allows for more positive social relations through the demonstration of mutual respect. We tend to follow the moral exercise of keeping 'good manners' as though there were merit to these rituals simply in themselves, without a need to question their logic and usefulness. In the United States, the syndicated column 'Miss Manners' – a.k.a. Judith Martin – dispenses advice to millions of readers on just about every topic involving human interactions from romance to bad breath. The commentary is decisive and shrewd. A reader asks a question about inviting an ex-boyfriend to her nuptials; 'Miss Manners' usually answers without pulling any punches and provides suggestions and commentary like: Go ahead, but expect to see your betrothed's ex-girlfriends at the ceremony, itching to make him think twice about taking the plunge – not a positive way to start married life. The finer points of planning a wedding are sometimes addressed, and myths are dispelled: for example, the acceptability of telling guests what to purchase by way of a wedding list that forces them to pick out gifts that they don't necessarily like; the belief that, although a required practice, the married couple need not send 'thank you' notes for up to a year; or the notion that an envelope filled with money is the best wedding gift because it pays for the pricey, 'excellent meal' to be served at the reception. The purpose of etiquette training is to take the guesswork out of how we should properly act by providing a regimen of good taste in manners that readers can emulate and put into practice.

We must blindly subscribe to manners for our faith in customs and rituals to be reaffirmed. In that way, a social rapport between people that demonstrates good taste is established through a display of cultural codes in action. Sometimes it is impossible to question traditions of acceptable behaviour and parents must take TV time away from their children when they cannot otherwise succeed in reinforcing the importance of proper manners. Every time someone says 'Thank you', the expected response is 'You're welcome', only because it is polite to say 'You're welcome'. But what exactly is the person welcomed to? That is a mystery. The phrase 'You're welcome' might well have begun as a way to encourage or welcome the reciprocation of a considerate action or gift. However, it has become more of a conversational gambit, a bit of lexical give and take, in the form of a stock response or throw-away expression, used as verbal filler after a trade of goods and acts of kindness. By contrast, this Anglo-Saxon-based formality still has real meaning in some non-English-speaking countries. In contemporary Greece, for example, you barely hear the words 'Thank you' mentioned in public, except in personal situations. There is a feeling that having to thank someone every time you are offered a service or given change back from your euro is an excessive appreciation. It introduces into routine exchanges an obligation to reciprocate some sort of kindness that the culture wishes to avoid. Merchants and patrons prefer to slam coins down hard on the counter before anyone obliges the other to return a favour in the future. If you say 'Thank you' after buying a loaf of bread, the expected response might be 'Thank you for what? Do you owe it to me? Get out of here!' Who are we to question the codes of everyday 'polite' exchange used and sanctioned through years of a culture's history? These practices may reveal the kind of 'civilities' that are native to a society, though not the reasons behind the actions themselves. Not all behaviours that suggest good taste in manners have an obvious purpose. Why say 'Bless you' at a sneeze? Folk superstition variously explains it as a blessing to prevent the devil flying in your mouth, or your soul out of your nose. But it seems the custom actually originated with St Gregory (540–604), the story being that he enjoined its use during a pestilence in which sneezing was a mortal symptom (sneezing was also a crisis symptom of the black death, as evidenced in the line from the nursery rhyme, 'Ring-a-ring-a-roses': 'atishoo atishoo, we all fall down'). But although the phrase had some logic to it originally, it no longer holds any meaning, and its use now is quite arbitrary. What if the expression to honour a sneeze was 'Go call Nelly!'? Or 'God is dead!' Would it make any difference? Etiquette is arbitrary, even ritualistic, and although it is important for maintaining the stability of the social sphere, it can often make little sense relative to what one might believe personally. Seeing that we live in an age when religious convictions are a point of uncertainty, why exactly should 'I' be the one anointing the other with a blessing – and for a sneeze of all things? Perhaps there is a god for small things that we take for granted. Accepting the conventions of tastes means not giving a second thought to the way manners are applied. Nonetheless, instruction in etiquette is never neutral; it has the developing force of habit. Like drinking orange juice out of a glass instead of the carton at home, even when no one is there watching you.

Socially agreeable manners are supposed to convey good taste. That occurs when the display of etiquette is in tune with the behavioural norms governing human relationships established by a culture or subculture. Because the influences of race, class, gender, sexuality and ethnicity are not the same for every individual, the terms for conducting ourselves in the company of others must be plotted out in advance according to the situation. We take our behavioural cues by reading the context, then decide what is appropriate or not, and quickly apply that store of knowledge to the social circumstances. Etiquette requires education. Tastes are revealed in an impression of sentiments and choices that are vying to be noticed by the public practices of a social group. A charcoal-grey Hugo Boss suit with matching white shirt, gold-striped tie and brown shoes worn to an executive dinner party of a huge firm would match the designer apparel displayed by the corporate leaders. The outfit would be noticed, even if not commented on directly – the looks of approval would certify it to be an appropriate fashion choice for the occasion. Taste is what enables and forces us to judge between choices. Invited to the dinner by his potential new boss, the Hugo Boss man verified to others like him that, when the occasion arises, he has the executive savvy to dress like the best of them. Being a quick learner with an ability to scan and plan appropriate gestures and comments on the spot can similarly help with successful acquisition of other manners introduced by an important occasion, familiar or not. Constructing a personalised filter to determine how credible choices will be, based on identifying established etiquette, when set in front of an audience, saves face before a bad taste mistake is made. Consider, look and listen before you try the strokes is a wise chestnut of advice in matters of taste. When in unfamiliar waters, you have to learn how to swim or the fluorescent life jacket will be sure to give you away. Associations have to be appropriate in order to convey the respected habits of a group identity.

You won't walk with a demeanour like a politician if you are a member of the Rap music scene. The way P. Diddy stomps, leaps and bounds across a stage to rhyme into a microphone about settling his lawsuits has little stylistic rapport with how Colin Powell would walk up to a podium to deliver a speech at the United Nations on the bilateral disarmament of countries in conflict. Both would reveal 'bad taste' if they were to take on the manners and mannerisms of the other and be serious about it. Styles please or displease depending on the intended audience. An individual becomes competent in defining a group's stylistic moods by assimilating appropriate practices and gestures. The challenge that is being met, as well as the praise and respect garnered from others, reinforces the value of the effort. Tastes reflect approval from the world we chose as our own, relative to what the site-specific expectations of a given situation are. These again are based on who we are and what expectations society makes on such a person. Specific affiliations limit the options that can be comfortably considered.

Age, similarly, restricts the code of conduct that may be followed in relation to a style of taste. You wouldn't expect to see a 50-year-old woman skipping down the street like a child, even if she did still have the inclination and the supple knee joints to do so. Even more to the point and perhaps a bit more traumatic, in all seriousness, you wouldn't anticipate seeing a 70-year-old grand dame wearing a Britney Spears-type snake-theme outfit to her granddaughter's school fundraiser – no matter how well she had maintained her shape through years of constant exercise: pilates, yoga, jogging and a regime of healthy eating. Stylistic practices and behaviour are culturally coded and what is appropriate relates to age regardless of whether you are sliding up or down the scale in years. Taste is the result of choices and actions that constitute our personal makeup, and it expresses our public profile through a vocabulary of styles and manners we believe are suitable for specific occasions. The very meaning and value of everything we choose as ours varies according to the context in which it is placed. Prince Charles' royal regalia are exquisite examples of finely crafted and rare materials combined with the expert tailoring of many generations. The wardrobe items are illustrious and prestigious cultural assets specific to an age of European monarchies when showing 'good taste' in the construction and design of majestic robes was conceived to be necessary for their social and political purposes not as clothes, but as a ceremonial symbol of the governance of Britain and the wealth of the nation. If he were to wear these priceless artefacts, however, anywhere other than to formal aristocratic or 'court' functions, in an attempt to impress the crowd with his princely outfit, he would risk being labelled as having no sense of the occasion, and therefore, as lacking judgement in taste. Good taste means making choices that help us fit into the social systems which best express who we are while simultaneously showing an understanding and respect for the community of people we interact with. In this way we identify what best meets our needs as well as the needs and expectations of the group we are associating with.

Erasmus of Rotterdam, the greatest classical scholar of the 16th century, wrote a guidebook to manners that was a bestseller for three centuries after its date of publication, circa 1530. Entitled *On Civility in Children*, the manual details what respectable behaviour is for the Renaissance period. Although we would find some of Erasmus' advice strange today, many of the suggestions are relevant to the 21st century with respect to good taste:

'If you cannot swallow a piece of food, turn around discreetly and throw it somewhere.'

'Do not move back and forth on your chair. Whoever does that gives the impression of constantly breaking or trying to break wind.'

'Turn away when spitting lest your saliva fall on someone. If anything purulent falls on the ground, it should be trodden upon, lest it nauseate someone.'

'Do not be afraid of vomiting if you must; for it is not vomiting but holding the vomit in your throat that is foul.'

'Do not blow your nose with the same hand that you use to hold the meat.'

Erasmus intended these rules to be best instilled at an early age as a catechism on good manners for children. The education of youth will always serve as a major influence in predisposing human beings to particular ways of responding to social situations. Like Aristotle, a tutor in the ways of the world to the young Alexander the Great, Erasmus knew that the strongest impressions upon us seem to be made in our early years when our young minds are still uncluttered by competing perspectives of right and wrong. Even now, the most valued of lessons taught in primary-school classrooms along with basic literacy skills are those that have to do with social manners and cultural tastes. By the end of kindergarten, every child knows what it is proper to do in public and the behavioural qualities that are valued by others as 'good': cooperation (no fighting), politeness (saying please and thank you), patience (not pulling toys out of anyone's hands), avoiding distasteful habits (picking your nose, peeing your pants, swearing) and courtesy (sharing your possessions, smiling). Any education system reinforces the distinctions of manner and taste approved by a culture.

Many rules discourage certain behaviours, but not all are readily explainable or defensible. Putting shoes on a table is supposed to bring bad luck to the household in some European cultural traditions. Consider this scenario described by a friend: 'The look of open-eyed distress on my grandmother's face as she moved, quicker than her old frame would typically take her, to remove the shoes I had absent-mindedly placed on a kitchen table is an image that, even after the passing of many years, imposes an influence on me. According to my grandmother, shoes must never be laid to rest on a table top – bad luck will fall upon those who foolishly dare to make the connection. A slight sense of anxiety still comes over me if and when I happen to make the so-called "mistake". Not because I believe there would be any bad luck, as my grandmother so feared, but because the etiquette, which her lessons impressed upon me, has left me uneasy to even consider the option.' What is bestowed upon us in our formative years and takes the form of youthful lessons creates lasting impressions that can fade into the sentimental recollections of an older self during the influences of another generation. These habits are often replaced through contact with alternative ways of thinking and responding as we mature. But still, the original traces remain that bring to mind the traditions and expectations we grew up to understand, before maturity served to dispel some of the ghosts that accompanied our cultural traditions.

You can take the individual out of the culture, but the culture will still show through in the sentiments and mannerisms that make up a person's heritage. Etiquette from outside of a strictly Western environment better illuminates the relative nature of what defines good taste for each of us. Cultural baggage does not allow a European tourist of Danish extraction, temporarily displaced on a voyage to Beijing, China, to fully understand the tastes and customs of the local population. Guidebooks for travellers are one way to help provide the prior knowledge required for a visitor to get by socially in a new country. A North-American man travelling to India urgently needs to brush up on a few new codes of conduct if he plans to be accepted by his potential new in-laws. Without any awareness of the particular rituals of good taste at play in a first meeting between a suitor and 'the parents', there could very likely be insurmountable difficulties in proving that he is a polite, honourable, well-intentioned and respectful man worthy of their daughter's hand in marriage. Not to mention that the lack of a cultural vocabulary will serve to exacerbate the fact that he hasn't learned the language yet. The in-laws, however, who speak no language other than their own, could expect at least a minimal fluency in matters of etiquette that make the man's tastes compatible, comprehensible and friendly towards their own. Even a small gesture that would put both the suitor and the parents at ease and give them both a common ground to work with is recommended. Sitting down to enjoy a dinner of dishes consisting of fragrant sauces poured over rice could result in a misunderstanding between the participants when proper eating manners are not reasoned out, agreed upon and followed. The potential son-in-law – not knowing how to eat sauces with his hands as his Indian hosts are expertly doing – asks for a fork. The hosts are clearly insulted. Their traditions abruptly questioned, the young man's smooth initiation into the family is suddenly uncertain. It should have been understood that in India eating with your hands, sauces and all, is good manners. Nothing comes between the food and the person doing the eating. No metal spoon or plastic fork interferes with the taste of the food. In the West, the principle guiding table etiquette is consideration for the people sitting beside you; whereas the Indian dining rituals are founded on the idea of purity as opposed to impurity. Hands are washed at the table, before, during and after the meal, between salty and sweet courses. Yet, you have to know how to eat confidently with your hands. The food is scooped up carefully onto the thumb and first two fingers of the right hand and into the mouth, allowing the pleasure to be extended to a tactile experiencing of the food.

In Western cultures, cutlery exists to intrude on the sensual experience of eating. It has been used in some form or other when serving or eating food since the European Renaissance. With the introduction of the fork, after the Crusades, as well as the cultivation of new crops that resulted in a variety of original cooking techniques and recipes, Western eating manners evolved. Plates, as we know them today, gradually replaced soup bowls made of wood that were meant to be shared by two people at each meal, along with drinking goblets and 'trenchers' – or stale bread squares – that were used to hold food and later given to servants or the poor who were always in search of more nourishment. Louis XIV of France was the first person in Europe to require that guests be served with a full place setting of a rounded knife, a four-pronged fork and a spoon, thus establishing the Western etiquette of always using cutlery to consume foodstuffs – especially wet and saucy ones. Polite eating in an Indian style, with your hands and licking the residual matter that you were not able to bite into, makes for what could, in Western society, be considered a mother's worst nightmare.

The Parent Trap

Formal and informal education teaches us how to make distinctions between 'good' and 'bad' public behaviour according to the idiosyncrasies of our heritage. Traditions thus reflect what we have learned about conducting ourselves in social situations. Often, they never come into question when passed on as 'in-bred' ideals that influence the preferences we have. The 'guy next door' loves the outdoors and works in construction. His parents both adored taking him on walks to beautiful mountain lakes when he was young. There they would spend their days swimming and eating. It is not terribly surprising that the activity should still hold a special appeal. An interest in handiwork is again inspired by the examples of an 'honest day's work' set out by a father who cherished the child he was unintentionally to influence. The work that his dad had shared with him through his own occupation in the trades fuelled the son's interest in building things. Seeing the beaming face of his father's pride in showing off the skill of fine craftsmanship when a job was done cemented the choice of career for the man, as a boy, and provided an ethic of hard work and honesty that would influence him throughout his life. The opportunity and manner were provided; the progression and choice made easy. Then again, if the 'guy next door' were the son of a Mafia don, he would most probably interpret the meaning of 'an honest day's work' in a radically different way. His father – having preferred a life of extortion and racketeering to 'rake in the dough' – would not give a second thought to the moral implications of giving his son first-hand insight into a world of 'stiffs swimming with the fishes' or 'Sicilian neckties', as the eventual successor to the head of the family. Business is business. Nothing personal. The sins of the father are passed on to the son. Many individuals have followed the ideals, manners and tastes of their parents.

The easiest to identify are those whose careers have brought them into the media spotlight as taste-makers and cultural creators. Picasso's father was a painter who encouraged the young artist to learn difficult painting techniques that enabled him to easily create images of amazing realism that the young Pablo would eventually turn on their head by collapsing three-dimensional perspective into the plane of cubism. Liza Minelli inherited Judy Garland's throaty voice, the ultra-feminine manner of her magnetic stage presence and her taste for pills and alcohol. Gustav Klimt, the Austrian ornamentalist painter, was one of seven brothers who were all to initiate careers as artists and engravers. George Clooney might never have acquired the taste for entertaining had not Rosemary Clooney been a popular jazz singer. Natalie Cole, having inherited the golden windpipes and the confidence to go it alone in the jazz world, took to heart the example set by her father, the great Nat King Cole. Lalia Ali, daughter of the pugilist, philanthropist Mohammed Ali, has made a name for herself as a serious contender in the world of female boxing. Kate Hudson projects a reticent grace and beauty that radiates the confidence of her superstar mother Goldie Hawn. Gwyneth Paltrow conveys a respect and admiration for her mother, Blythe Danner, who inspired her efforts to achieve excellence in the field of acting. The list goes on. Children do not make for exact blueprints of their parents' taste and mannerisms, but the influences can be counted on many occasions where the similarities stand up to be noticed. Connections are easily found. Personalities, education and even friends can unconsciously conspire to influence and alter the direction of the paths that anyone chooses as a life's calling. It can be understood that the options for 'making something of yourself' are made easier when the trail to follow is made crystal clear with a living model right by your side guiding you through the path of least resistance and homing in on inherited attributes and predilections. Observing the manners, tastes and desires of those closest to us offers a system for success that is always there, ready for the taking, no matter what field of endeavour.

No wonder that it is easier for children of professional parents to be channelled into executive 'white-collar' careers. Acceptance into a big-name university is typically easier for students whose parents have 'BIG' written all over their accomplishments. These children are given all the educational and cultural advantages of an upper-middle-class household. Not only because of money. These children will most probably attend the best schools and are taught the 'soft skills' that offer them the 'cultural capital' required to fit in with the successful sectors of society. That is because their parents are economically and politically influential – avid consumers of high culture who know how to use their store of cultural capital advantageously in social situations to succeed at getting what they want. Their children are sent to school where they are expected to read 'the classics', speak and write 'correctly', espouse the 'right thinking', learn 'acceptable' social graces and eventually know how to swim in a sea of prosperity with other potential big fishes. Achieving a larger-than-life career is easier when the adolescent road of bad intentions is paved over and smoothed with precious stones that reflect the preferences and habits of the parents. The ideological and economic network in place increases the likelihood of securing its reproduction over time. But that is not to say that individuals coming from working- and lower-middle-class worlds cannot climb the social ladder and achieve success.

Upward Mobility

That educational systems and upbringing reinforce distinctions of taste, there is no question. And a privately funded education is certainly more discriminating than a publicly funded one, for the simple reason that the paying customer wants results and has a very large say in the outcome to produce a satisfactory product. But that does not mean that your future is necessarily mapped out for you because of the books you read at secondary school or because the working-class household in which you were raised placed more emphasis on practical, useful knowledge as a means to getting a well-paid job than on developing a sense of good taste in literature or art. There are many who have gone from humble and middling beginnings to penetrate the echelons of a higher cultural and social status. In the course of a lifetime, real life gives you a practical education in how to apply taste distinctions gleaned from hardship and experience and allows plenty of opportunity for successes and failures.

Oprah Winfrey exists as a familiar case in point. A child born out of wedlock, Winfrey began life in the poverty and suffering of a Milwaukee ghetto, her childhood ridden with misfortune. She spent the early years of her youth being passed from one care giver to another – from her grandmother she was sent to her mother, then to a children's home that could not house her. At age nine, Winfrey was raped, and later as a teen she suffered repeated abuse by family members. By fourteen years old, she had given birth to a premature baby that later died. Winfrey later described this moment as traumatic, but the bitter lesson of a second chance she desperately needed in life to make amends with her demons. On a downward spiral of sexual promiscuity and experimentation with drugs, Winfrey's life took a drastic turn for the better when her father took custody, brought her to Nashville, Tennessee, and enrolled her in a local high school. There she realised an interest in public speaking which resulted in her getting a job as a student intern at a Black radio station. Winfrey later entered Tennessee State University where she majored in Speech Communications and Performing Arts. During this time, she won the titles of 'Miss Black Nashville' and 'Miss Black Tennessee'. Afterwards, she sought out and found a position at a Nashville news station as a 'street reporter'. Winfrey's emotional attachment and personal investment in the stories she covered was not considered appropriate for a 'serious journalist' who was expected to report the news dispassionately and objectively. She worked on a number of morning television talk shows, eventually landing a job as host of a faltering local talk show, 'AM Chicago', that she turned into the hottest show in town during 1985. Winfrey was an unqualified success and found her professional and personal niche. In 1986, she landed her own talk show – 'The Oprah Winfrey Show' – which was named the number one talk show in the United States later that same year. The programme has been on the air for thirteen seasons and has garnered 30 Emmy awards.

Oprah Winfrey has become a culture industry in herself. Let us not forget she is as much a commodity as she is a person, lending her name as a trademark to organisations and companies to promote products she endorses and worthy causes. A taste-maker who can influence an entire country with a few well-placed words delivered on a subject that is near and dear to her heart, she is the daytime tele-guru of the masses, a high priestess of self-help and an arbiter of good taste regarding everything from losing weight to the importance of finding spiritual redemption. Not only does she show the American people real-life stories about how difficult it is to live life in the post-urban jungle of disposable morals and convenient relationships, but she also gives them intervention techniques to help them take control of their lives and overcome adversity. 'The Oprah Winfrey Show' has paved the way for spin-off counselling shows such as the psycho-babble-filled 'Dr Phil' that are the antithesis of Jerry Springer's brand of adversarial culture trash and bad taste: a voyeur's paradise of bizarre tales of betrayal and deceit usually ending up in endless four-letter bleeps, trampled cameramen and the two ex-girlfriends of the same ex-convict turned Minister, who are suing him for palimony, pulling out each other's hair. To her credit, Winfrey has not only focused her popularity on building a publishing empire and a production company that earns billions of dollars a year. Some of it is put to good use to demonstrate good taste in moral fibre through establishing non-profit foundations, scholarships and other philanthropic fundraising activities like 'Oprah's Angel Network' designed to help the poor and disadvantaged through activities such as donating homes to selected underprivileged families. Winfrey became instrumental in establishing a national database of convicted child abusers that is made available to parents and communities across the United States. 'Oprah's Book Club' supports the fight for literacy education and spiritual awakening by introducing the public to inspirational stories that in the opinion of its members make for good reading, great literature and valuable lessons about the human condition. Any book she endorses becomes an instant bestseller. In 1998 Oprah Winfrey was honoured as one of the 100 most influential people of the 20th century. Today, she is a far cry from the troubled little black girl that barely survived the onslaught of violence and shame that is the cultural product of poverty so prevalent in the urban centres of the United States.

There is no question that Oprah Winfrey has overcome the traumatic experiences of exploitation and subjugation that constituted her childhood and threatened to limit her personal and social development to nothing more than a life of wasted potential and delinquency, if she lived that long. She has become a media icon, a role model, an inspirational leader for those seeking to achieve something more than what the limitations of life's circumstances often afford them. One of Winfrey's mottoes has been, 'I always feel if you do right, right will follow.' An admirable maxim, no doubt. The level of success she has enjoyed is witness to her doing a lot of things right. And yet, despite the moral visions of social justice and fairness Winfrey espouses, there are those who criticise her accomplishments as self-aggrandising and exploitative. The negative commentary relates more to how the message is put forward on her talk show than to what is said. There have been questions about the ethics and taste of displaying people who are undergoing personal tragedy on national television and probing the open wounds of their emotions and personal lives on camera. Is the experience cathartic for the individual or is it a form of cheap voyeurism intended to raise audience ratings? Or does it do both at the same time? It is difficult to tell exactly. Sometimes the life stories on some talk shows have been contrived by unscrupulous guests or producers. There is always a question about authenticity and whether or not the story is being told for someone's monetary gain. Which brings up the issue of making sure that the coverage is responsible: knowing whom the programmes will influence and how. Winfrey and other talk show hosts tend to pontificate and preach to an audience that is looking for guidance and epiphany in the form of a universal solution to their problems. They operate from a general moral attitude about what is right and what is wrong that is universalised. The free advice is received in the same spirit as a sermon and becomes a type of popular religion of self-help to be doled out to the viewing masses whose demographics are paralleled by those of the talk show audience. Elvis has his own church, so why not a 'Church of Oprah' complete with velvet icons? She is more than just an influence on needy individuals. Winfrey represents a system of values and tastes that have a very distinct moral character, especially when she often interrupts interviews to speak her mind in a very self-assured and inflexible way. There is little room for disagreement and her advice is taken seriously by millions of people in 132 countries as far flung as Singapore, where the show is syndicated. The question is: How do we know this advice is right for everyone? Just because we see stories on a talk show that touch the emotions, is this reason enough to begin to change our lives in accordance with someone else's moralities and tastes? Because of someone else's problems? We have spent a lifetime becoming the person we are.

Oprah Winfrey is an exemplar of how the social mobility of taste works. She is the embodiment of someone who rises above horrific circumstances to make something better of their lives, simply because they envisioned the reality of it happening and were determined enough to follow through. This fairytale story makes for a perfect parable of a journey toward 'the good life' that passes from the utterly grotesque to the spectacular. It illustrates human potential achieved in a way that is meaningful for an individual person, though not necessarily the way to go for everyone. The moral dimension of good taste reigns high as one of Oprah Winfrey's most obvious desires and accomplishments. Helping others to help themselves to a better life is an admirable vocation, a remarkable one, in fact. But how can one provide self-help to others? Oprah Winfrey, the underdog, beautifully assimilates herself into the tastes and morality of her own accomplishments as a woman of enormous wealth, upper-middle-class taste and faith. And while she could be a model to emulate, the distance she has covered – from under-privileged urban youth to cultural icon – is huge, and many do not know how to make the transition from watching television quasi-evangelism to creating a new life story. Others do not want to. It helps if you know what it is that you are looking for, what you want, and how to begin to get there within the freedoms and constraints of your own life situation. People like Anthony Robbins, Deepak Chopra and Oprah Winfrey are motivational speakers. And while they do help some who buy their books, audio and video tapes, CDs and DVDs and attend their seminars, how personalised can a program of action be that deals with everyone in the same manner and offers the same advice for success to all? The journey toward the positive transform-ation of mind and body cannot begin wholly with the suggestions of a motivational speaker or a talk show host, but has to start from within oneself.

Oprah Winfrey has invented herself as a mouthpiece for conservative middle America. Madonna has chosen to become quite the opposite. But just as there is only one Oprah, there is only one Madonna, despite many imitators and 'wannabes'. Madonna has frequently demonstrated tastes and manners that are less than savoury to a general public morality – often influencing, anticipating or setting pop culture and fashion trends and flouting cultural taboos in the process. Through her wide range of real-life experiences, a steely determination and long-range vision, Madonna has extended her style and tastes beyond the connections made from her middle-class Italian upbringing in Pontiac, Michigan. After leaving home on an academic scholarship to pursue an education in the performing arts, she dropped out of the University of Michigan Dance

Program to carve out a career rather than spend time at school. Madonna was confident and resolved to take on the world with a vengeance that was not going to subside until she achieved nothing short of success. It has been said that she wanted to be more popular than God. Arriving in New York City, in July 1978, with 35 dollars in her pocket, Madonna displayed the 'blonde ambition' that was to be the title of an album she would record in 1990. Success, fame and fortune did not come right away. Madonna worked in a variety of jobs, including stints in fast food chains, eventually finding her way into dancing companies and singing groups. After she signed a record deal in 1983, Madonna was on the way to blazing her own trail as a dance artist and taste-maker.

The tough and rebellious youth soon became internationally recognised as an exciting new cultural icon. Madonna was immediately known as a shape-shifting provocateur, a diva whose deconstructed images of a submissive femininity worked well to reflect the tensions present within a female identity. Among teenage girls, Madonna's songs and videos catalysed support for the struggle of women to take power over their lives. The message of emancipation was wrapped up in an ethic of fun. The images Madonna cultivated most certainly embodied the cultural contradictions of a rebellious and carefree life that was called irresponsible by proponents of 'good values' who stood against a radical individualism for women not encumbered with the psycho-religious trappings of middle-class morality. Although her self-titled first album established 'the Madonna look', *Like a Virgin*, released in 1984, was the album that solidified her musical influence, popularity and identifiable sound. The rise of video disseminated her fashion, morality and tastes worldwide. Using this new medium to full artistic advantage and ideological effect, Madonna revealed no inhibitions about playing with religion and sex – the two most sensitive subjects from which cultural taboos are drawn. She created memorable statements in picture and song about teenage pregnancy, romantic love, spiritual awakening, obsession, religious faith and a wide array of other socially evocative subjects that challenged middle-class values. She experimented with gender stereotyping and images of female sexuality in ways that outraged the moral sensibilities of taste among the more conservative members of the media and society. Madonna took to wearing lace bras, see-through lycra camisoles, torn clothing and bustiers as outer wear. And she played on the associations of her name by matching the outfits with large decorative crucifixes hanging around her neck, assorted beads and baubles, and seemingly endless supplies of plastic bracelets around her arms. All of these allusions were wrapped up in the disturbing combination of woman as 'virgin', 'whore' and 'mother'. She was a Freudian field day for less-than-secure men and women that could cause tremendous insecurity about gender, social relationships and sexuality. She was not at all the traditional image of the supine woman created and supported by a patriarchal culture along with its negative moral judgements on sexually and ideologically liberated women. The fact that Madonna was a role model for teenage girls was troublesome for some traditionalists. Especially given the 'Express yourself; Don't repress yourself' philosophy she espoused and reinforced through her appearance and music. Yet, Madonna was being imitated so widely that she was expected to take responsibility for educating impressionable kids about the dangers of the moral implications of the behaviours and tastes she exhibited. A fair criticism. However, Madonna claimed not to endorse any lifestyle, but rather to describe alternatives. The song 'Vogue' takes as its motif the image and practice of 'vogue-ing', a term used in gay culture to suggest a pose that is inauthentic: a superficial aesthetics of visual taste that supports an illusion of identity constructed by choice – like a man being in drag. The term alludes to the fact that homosexual men often consciously conceal their true identity to avoid moral scrutiny. 'Vogue-ing' is a way to try on different personas in an alluring way without the risk of having to live up to an image for ever and simultaneously erase your own individuality. Because she hides behind an exhibitionistic flair for the dramatic without being trapped in a traditional moral and sexual role, Madonna has been described as a gay man trapped inside a woman's body. So, the notion of 'being in vogue' is a most apt and revealing description. Indeed, Madonna's appearance can be construed as all surface, a controlled and crafted illusion, oscillating between the masculine and the feminine that is in all of us. In this way, she is like a mirror reflecting a multiplicity of styles and tastes that are constantly coming and going in a state of flux.

Even though the image of a Mardi Gras carnival queen did not live up to her name, Madonna became a sex-symbol of sorts – though not without some risqué antics. On the 1985 *MTV Video Awards*, Madonna performed the song 'Like a Virgin' wearing a half-cut wedding dress and rolling around on the floor singing suggestive lyrics about being 'touched for the very first time' that highlighted the playful tensions between sexual innocence and carnal experience. Her style of dress echoed the moral paradoxes of human nature that were suggested through her actions. Such blatant and provocative displays of controversial sexual mores resulted in her video 'Erotica' being relegated to midnight viewing, with all sorts of disclaimers by the video jockeys warning viewers that explicit sex scenes were coming. 'Justify My Love' so shocked MTV executives with its sado-masochistic images of semi-clad straight and gay lovers engaging in acts of domination and bondage that the network deemed it religiously and sexually offensive and banned it from its programming rotation outright. The video for 'Like a Prayer' immediately outraged religious groups worldwide shortly after it was released because, they argued, it portrayed holy symbols in a blasphemous way: the sight of burning crosses juxtaposed against a white altar upon which Madonna was making love to a black saint, who had been transformed from stone statue to living flesh a short while before, was surely emotionally and spiritually provocative. Critics either loved the video for its artistic adventurousness and aggressive moral posture or they detested it because of the unorthodox mixture of sexuality with religion.

Madonna has revelled in exploring the ambiguous or darker spaces of taste that are not so obvious or comfortable, framing the raunchy side of her fears and dreams as a woman in symbolic ways for all to see. In a very controversial book entitled *Sex*, Madonna exposed herself totally to the world through explicit images of what she claimed were some of her most intimate desires and erotic fantasies. Again, the viewer was invited to be a voyeur into a variety of exhibitionistic behaviours that were intended to astonish and jar the traditional sensibilities of good taste. We see Madonna: dressed as a school-girl in poses that look like she is having sex with two boys; passionately kissing another woman; or hitch-hiking totally naked on the side of a highway. A mixture of low and high art styles, the book exploited some well-worn erotic fantasy clichés, yet it showed Madonna's willingness to test the boundaries of what is considered a normal life of good morality. Her staying power as the 'Queen of Pop' has been accomplished by a simple formula – 'Sex Sells'. We cannot argue, however, that she does not have an uncanny sense of the aesthetic and is a very talented singer and song writer. Above all, Madonna as an artist embodies and symbolises the hidden passions perhaps lurking in each of us and the latent power we all have to reinvent ourselves, to expand the horizons of our tastes and desires without guilt, to strike less familiar or new poses and to try on different personas so as to grow by taking risks. The old Madonna is not the Madonna of today. That is why it is still difficult to pin her down.

Madonna has succeeded in displaying a variety of tastes as refined as her celebrity occasions in different settings. She desperately wanted to play the lead in the movie version of the musical *Evita* – a story depicting the life and triumphs of the infamous first lady of Argentina who came from a modest upbringing to capture the heart and imagination of a country. The president of Argentina, however, refused to allow the filming of the piece at the royal palace if Madonna was to play the role. He could not allow the raunchy 'material girl' of disputable tastes and dubious accomplishments to play the role of the beloved Evita. Determined to get the part, Madonna organised a meeting with the president, who was resolved to turn her down. As the story goes, Madonna arrived at the presidential palace in Argentina and after spending a full day with the president, she successfully managed to change his opinion of her. With elegance, beauty, grace and intelligence, she proved herself 'fit' for the part.

It would be all too easy to revile Madonna as a petty diva with shallow preoccupations and bad taste, doing inappropriate things at inopportune times in unfitting situations to get publicity. Yet, through her work, she has reinforced the necessity for a non-judgemental attitude toward others. Even if Madonna has disturbed tastes that are part and parcel of a conservative morality, her drive and power to raise social consciousness on thorny issues (e.g., teenage pregnancy) and celebrate differences of identity and culture cannot be questioned. As the 'Party Girl' image has died down, her support of various humanitarian causes has been noticed. If there is an urgency to a message, such as the fight against AIDS, Madonna has tended to use her fame and celebrity status as a powerful medium through which to expose and publicise it. Her latest artistic venture that crosses over into the realm of politics is a video from her album *American Life* that indirectly comments on the brutality of war. The message is aimed at the Bush administration and the cruelty of the war on Iraq. Madonna has joined many influential recording artists, actors and celebrities in breaking the silence on the conflict as a critical observer of how politics and persuasion work towards sanctioning violence to support the American dream of prosperity that excludes so much of the world. Out of respect to the soldiers, the video was not released during the war because it contained graphic scenes of bloodshed and mutilation suffered by Iraqi women and children. There were well-founded rumours that the footage would never be shown by American television networks. But even hearing about the video (to be released later in a cut version) created intense media scrutiny on the reasons behind the conflict and placed the singer on a collision course with conservative critics who questioned her patriotism.

Madonna has chosen to hide very little about what she has traded for fame by way of rejecting the lower-middle-class mentality of her youth, but instead has used herself as a willing model to reveal an individual uninhibited by the limitations of social structures on morality and taste. Yes, Madonna is rich and famous. Yes, she has defied the moral restrictions society puts on good taste to make a career, but also to make a point about what she believes is right. Madonna serves as an example of the many who have risen from one class to another on the arms of personal integrity and faithful convictions at the pain of offending others. Whether you like her or not.

Can't Buy Me Love

What is considered good taste is relative to the culture or society in which we live. Where upper-class tastes are the dominant ones in society, if lower-class people want to be successful at climbing the social ladder, adopting these dominant tastes will help them, simply because they are more popular. But making the 'jump' from low and middle culture to upper-class culture regarding good taste is very different from being better off financially. It involves a determination to learn how to interact with people in a different way. The learning curve is huge for this sort of metamorphosis and many do not feel comfortable making a complete transition. For this reason the nouveaux riches and famous often hobnob with the upper classes of old-world money and aristocracy, to gain legitimacy and respect, as well as to be one of them. Regardless, their own-world influences often shine through this social facade. It can be simpler, in these cases, to find others who share a common social heritage, but who have similarly climbed to fortune based on excellence in their accomplishments. This allows the tastes of the 'lower-brow' ways to still be enjoyed without condemnation – eating pizza instead of escargot, using street vocabulary not pretentious language, and not over-dressing. It's all about maintaining a cultural comfort zone. Good taste reigns to provide quality control and assessment even when it relates to less than ostentatious social trappings – there is good pizza and there is bad pizza. It helps if you know what it is that you are looking for.

It is difficult to thrive socially and ideologically in places that one has never seen or experienced first hand – tastes and all: 'schmoozing' members at an exclusive golf club as potential buyers; 'doing lunch' with the CEO of a major corporation; meeting a foreign dignitary; brokering a business deal in an overseas country. Pulling out a wallet, carefully counting your store of cash, and then giving it to the waiter as if you were giving away your first-born child might indicate that you were a fish out of water in that most important moment of the entrepreneurial fine dining experience co-opted by the corporate world – paying the bill without visibly wincing. Others around you who *were* ready to do business with your company would note, of course, that unspoken etiquette had been breached, since the obligatory 'Platinum' corporate credit card was not given and the receipt signed after barely even glancing at the total. The same would apply if you began to tally the total and ask each person at the table what they had ordered, then asked for a menu to cross-reference amounts charged between the bill and the advertised price, asking in the process if anything wasn't 'on special'. While this behaviour *might* be appropriate among friends going out to a movie, we have all seen how the closest of friendships have been tainted by the lurid implications of being accused of 'not paying your fair share'. Relationships sometimes never fully recover. In Israel, it would be unthinkable to split a bill. The offer would be a great insult to the host that made the invitation to break bread together. In many European cultures, more time is spent devising ways to pay first without your companions knowing that the account has been taken care of until it is too late. The strategy effectively avoids any tug of war and hard feelings at the end of a meal. Such a seemingly trivial manner and gesture as 'paying the bill' is an even more important proving ground for *Homo economicus*. It allows the business communities to defuse the questions of worth and profitability that constrain the making of deals. Without having experienced the unspoken rules behind the etiquette of 'treating the customer to lunch', there is always the fear of making poor decisions that will alienate us from the individuals we most want to impress for fun and profit.

Taste choices open us up to classifications that tell others who and what we value and also reveal the peer groups by which we want to be valued. As social creatures, we search for behaviours that support the ideas and ideals we feel inclined to convey. To prove the worth of an attitude, we try to assimilate and appropriate tastes that are similar in behaviour to those we admire. Trying them on for size, we begin to understand the complexity of dispositions which make up the human conditions for taste when introduced to new people and their realities. As the sets of choices we have to make become more involved and varied, we start to suspend the tendency to respond naïvely to possibilities. Our basic survival needs are fed and nurtured by an unwavering security in the decisions that we take. This need for reflection on aesthetic preferences and choices becomes clear in the ever-changing conditions of our socially complex existence, which is further complicated by the marketing of taste on all media. The reality is that we must learn to assimilate and consume in a discriminating manner. Choices not only serve our basic needs but also define our membership of communities of knowledge and taste that convey to ourselves and to others who we are.

Having an aptitude for learning how to adapt your demeanour and behaviour to unfamiliar codes of conduct, by trying them out and then making them your own, can help to redefine and refine your personal tastes and manners to suit the 'finer distinctions' required for some situations where the definition of good taste is not negotiable. In this way, individuals have broken with the strict conventions of class and taste to reinvent themselves above and beyond the experience of 'their station' in accordance with what worlds become available to them through successful careers.

There is a long line of films that explore the subject: extending from *My Fair Lady* starring Rex Harrison and Audrey Hepburn to *Educating Rita* with Michael Caine and Julie Walters, *Maid in Manhattan* featuring Ralph Fiennes and Jennifer Lopez, and *Sweet Home Alabama* casting Reese Witherspoon and Patrick Dempsey. The story lines are strikingly similar, but move in different directions. The male protagonist falls in love with a woman based on an image of female beauty he takes for granted, expects, or is complicit in creating, either by design or by error. Then he realises he is wrong, at which point the differences are bridged or not. Each story can be reduced to a variation of the plot archetype seen in the classical myth of Pygmalion as it was originally set out by Ovid in the tenth book of the *Metamorphoses*. Pygmalion, the Prince of Cyprus, was an overzealous but disillusioned sculptor who tried to create an ivory statue of the ideal woman. He named the creation Galatea. The statue was so beautiful that Pygmalion fell in love with it and prayed to the goddess Venus to bring Galatea to life. Venus granted Pygmalion his wish and the couple lived happily ever after.

George Bernard Shaw modified the myth, popularising its social implications, in his play *Pygmalion*, which was later adapted as a musical and then a film as *My Fair Lady*. In his version, the story becomes a parable that explodes the myth of the relationship between class and manners, and between cultural refinement and good taste. Professor Higgins wants to show that he can take a Cockney flower girl, Eliza Doolittle, off the street and, with some intensive training in phonetics and etiquette, pass her off as a duchess to unsuspecting guests at a society ball. He succeeds. In the process Higgins falls in love with Eliza, yet cannot bring himself to express this love because he still sees Eliza as a flower girl, and always will.

In *Educating Rita*, the Pygmalion myth is turned around somewhat. The alcoholic professor of English Literature who tutors a Liverpudlian hairdresser, Rita, watches her take on the manners and demeanour of a cultural snob as she begins to distance herself from the people she once loved. Education causes her to question the behaviours and tastes of the working class she inhabits, mostly made up of the pub dwellers whom she becomes ashamed to call her family and friends. Rita cannot bear to be around the people of this world any longer. After a while, she leaves her husband in search of more suitable companions and the freedom of an enlightened existence far away from what she perceives to be the cultural decay of the working classes. The professor deeply regrets what he has done to the unique personality, charm and well-adjusted life of his student and this realisation creates an emotional rift between them despite an obvious attraction to each other.

In *Maid in Manhattan*, love conquers all, albeit with difficulty. A well-known Kennedy-like politician, heir to a political dynasty and with rising senatorial aspirations, mistakenly walks in on a New York maid who is occupying an adjacent hotel room and mistakes her for a guest, rather than an employee. She does not immediately correct his assumptions, even after he asks her to dinner and a relationship develops between them based on the false impression. Urged on by her co-workers and friends, the maid, more or less, deceives the politician about her real identity and background using all of the assets at her disposal. He eventually discovers the truth, but blind love allows him to overcome any negative perceptions of her as an opportunistic working-class mother and bridges the class conflict that threatens a happy union. Like Cinderella, the maid rises above her socially imposed station to defy fate and become a model of inner beauty and taste, rescued from domestic enslavement by a handsome princely figure who sees the worth of her heart and smile.

Sweet Home Alabama is about what happens when a woman who has escaped her blue-grassy Southern roots to reinvent herself as a successful fashion designer in New York goes home to a backwater town to ask for a divorce from her country-bumpkin husband. Her impending marriage to a Manhattan socialite, the son of the mayor, depends on it. Having lied about her humble origins, she is worried that her fiancé will find out she is not the daughter of a wealthy plantation owner. He eventually does, and calls off the engagement on account of her deception. Even though the wedding is back on after her fiancé reconsiders his decision and asks for forgiveness, she begins to have second thoughts about the impending marriage after spending time with the people she grew up with, including her husband. She starts to see that she may have been wrong to reject her past out of shame and embarrassment for her country roots. In the end, she goes back to her husband who has made something more of himself than she thought he was capable of, having founded a glass company that produces designer stemware and art. She always saw him as a 'good-for-nothing red-neck', and could not imagine that he would amount to much other than a 'beer drinking Bubba' with no aspirations besides hanging out at the local saloon on Saturday nights getting drunk. The irony is that while she was trying to hide who she was, he kept a respect for his cultural roots intact while attempting to find out who he could be, and still proved her wrong. She did not expect to see him as a changed man and was blind to the possibility of his success and the evolution of his taste.

The Pygmalion myth as it is related by Ovid and dramatised by Shaw and these popular films, speaks to what is called 'the self-fulfilling prophecy'. Once an expectation is set, we tend to act and respond in ways that are consistent with that expectation and confirm it, even if it is not accurate or true. And so people's judgements of us do not always correspond to the reality of what lies behind impressions. Yet, original expectations still tend to influence final opinions despite a reality that is quite different. All of the films mentioned above work to both reinforce and overturn the principle of a self-fulfilling prophecy by showing how our appearances and actions do make a difference to how we are perceived and treated. Sometimes, if the judgements are just plain wrong, the cost is dear and amends have to be made. There are deeper reasons to value, respect and distinguish individuals other than the manners, mannerisms and etiquette they exhibit. Taste cannot account for the true worth of the human spirit. There is more to the experience of living life well than social acceptance of the choices we make. You have to be true to yourself about what you value and why. However, the reality is that good taste defines and categorises us in a positive way according to a hierarchy of classes. Even though any judgements describe only surface appearances, the reasons that we have for placing value in someone are always related to the initial impressions that we have about a person's behaviour, appearance and understanding of how to act and 'fit in' in social situations where particular codes of decorum are expected. *Good taste is making the right choices in the right places.* If one displays cultural refinement, a better life with greater respect from peers and a 'better class' of friends, acquaintances and lovers can follow. In short, developing a sharper sense of etiquette and proper codes of behaviour according to the human contexts we desire to encounter holds the promise of social competence and happiness. Others define who we are by what we say, how we look, what we own and what we do. The hope is in the possibility of transforming oneself into someone able to make connections with people on any level of interaction. Then others will treat you in the appropriate way because of the choices you make – with distinction.

CHAPTER TWO

Fashion Deficit Disorder

> Fashion is a thing so intolerably ugly that we have to change it every six months
>
> *Oscar Wilde*

Think of: the mini-skirt, the thong, the tie-dyed T-shirt, suspenders, leather vests, wide-bottom or hip-hugging trousers, sequins, rhinestones, cubics zirconia, the mood ring, straight-leg jeans, silk jackets, the fur coat, faux suede, velvet hair bands, flowered denim, the ascot, the necktie, tweed coats, top hats, berets, the fedora, platform boots, cowboy boots, stiletto heels, snakeskin belts, plastic 'jelly' shoes, the corset, the bustier, petticoats, slips, smocks and dungarees.

What do these articles of clothing have in common? Other than the fact that, in your day-to-day life, you have most probably worn some of these garments. And perhaps still do. Each of these items of dress has managed to seize the day of its own stylishness – and not. Every garment or accessory, at some point in time, has been enviably *in vogue*, or hopelessly *out of vogue*.

All of us, without exception, have experienced feelings of loss, emptiness and betrayal caused by merely looking into the bedroom closet. Some have felt the mocking patience of that wide-lapelled, checkered blazer. Others have sensed the fatal attraction of those badly scuffed white pumps. Pieces of clothing waiting – hoping that the time will come when they will be proudly worn again, some day. No one is a stranger to the waves of sickening alienation and paralysing self-doubt that often come with the task of having to choose 'the right thing' to wear in the public eye.

Of course, this most private of shaming rituals that we suffer by having qualms about our good taste in clothes is a common reaction for us as human beings – and a very natural response to the potential disgrace of revealing to others the true extent of our 'stylistic adversity'. Especially if the psychological effects of an instant of indecision about what clothes to wear are only momentary, a fit of fashion madness or amnesia – not the lasting emotional by-products of the guilt resulting from an irrepressible nostalgia to put on last year's dog. But the sense of insecurity and mortal dread we may feel because of an overwhelming desire to dress fashionably is not rational. It is just a complicated glimmer of muddled emotions and fear due to a lack of expertise when it comes to showing the world that we have good taste in clothes – that we are not stylistically challenged.

Clothing choice is based on a 'looks good' or 'feels right' sentiment. Since taste judgements are the products of individual and peer-group formations, the expression 'dress for success' has multiple meanings and nuances according to the context. The typical male 'office worker' – a term that takes in everyone from bank tellers to lawyers – prefers the suit, while his female counterpart often dresses in jacket and skirt. Dark blue is the preferred colour for both. It conveys a serious attitude and respectfulness without being too sombre and off-putting. Black is the colour of death and mourning. Bank managers should not look like undertakers or waiters; you would not give them your money with any confidence if they reminded you of your own impending mortality or an outstanding bill waiting to be paid. White-collar workers, in fact, become the human extension of 'suits' in action, drawing their personal and social identity from the symbolic power of the outfit that defines who they are in relation to a job. The qualities that are associated with this piece of clothing are transmitted to the individual and an aura of professionalism is created through appearances. You would never see a criminal lawyer pleading a case in jeans and a short-sleeved T-shirt. Any judicial system and self-respecting association of legal professionals would not allow it. The prospect of good lawyering is tied to an image of competence established through the wearing of 'proper attire' because the lawyer is publicly accountable to uphold the law, in either defence or prosecution, and must look the part. Counsel's appearance has to engender confidence in their abilities and a trust that all efforts will be made to see justice is served, in the judge, defendant and jury, as well as the spectators. Given that human lives hang in the balance, the least one should do is be willing to dress up for the public display of jurisprudence. Because the solemnity of the proceedings requires a strict code of decorum, the accused must also wear formal clothing that does not comment on their guilt or innocence. Courtroom image management consultants were hired by O.J. Simpson's lawyers to mould the look of their client in the hope of getting a fair trial, or at the very least not prejudicing the jury. In essence, fashion plays upon the use of clothing as symbols to create images that represent ideas like masculinity and femininity, power and dominance, insecurity and self-confidence, guilt and innocence, and so on. Even though outer appearances are decorative illusions not necessarily relating to personal attributes of character, it pays to understand how others respond to the way we dress. Are we unconsciously promoting a look that would characterise us in a certain way? – 'wealthy'? 'intelligent'? 'homeless'? 'conservative'? 'radical'? Usually, stereotypes are reinforced because fashion is most effective in communicating well-defined categories of meaning that have a cultural history.

Clothes evoke emotional impressions that are originally aesthetic, non-linguistic attitudes. A leather jacket elicits different feelings from a cherry-pink blouse. But then the emotional reactions must be given salient categories of meaning that relate to social stereotypes. Who would be most likely to wear a cherry-pink blouse, a biker or a housewife? Knowing how to read clothing as signs involves being a quick learner with an ability to scan potential social situations and plan recognisable cues for others to respond to appropriately. It also demands the cultivation of fashion sense that filters out good choices from bad ones. With the proper attention paid to detail, we can more or less predict how others will respond to a style of clothing worn on a particular occasion or event given the circumstances. There are only two ways to acquire this skill, unfortunately, and both entail becoming a connoisseur of taste in fashion: the first involves trial and error; the second requires getting some help from a mentor or guide.

Learning through practical experience is not a new idea. Charles Sanders Peirce and John Dewey popularised it during the 19th and 20th centuries. Trial and error is really a type of discovery learning or a 'practice makes perfect' approach. The stakes are high, however. You have to be willing to make mistakes and to learn your lesson by negative example. This method is fine and dandy if the situation is not risky or life-threatening. There are, however, non-forgiving learning environments. Defusing bombs comes to mind. Another is assessing the correct length of skirt to wear.

Laver's Law

James Laver – a costume historian and a past 'Keeper of the Robes' at London's Victoria and Albert Museum – assessed the surly turns of fashion and their relationship to society by creating a 'Timetable of Style'.

Laver's Timetable of Style

Indecent	10 years before its time
Shameless	5 years before its time
Daring	1 year before its time
Smart	**In fashion**
Dowdy	1 year after its time
Hideous	10 years after its time
Ridiculous	20 years after its time
Amusing	30 years after its time
Quaint	50 years after its time
Charming	70 years after its time
Romantic	100 years after its time
Beautiful	150 years after its time

'Laver's Law' says fashions have cycles of popularity in which the cultural value of clothing can be charted according to the passing of time. Society, of course, fixes the worth of human finery with respect to contemporary taste. Public memory is short, but fashion's memory is even shorter. Taste follows suit, as Laver's 'Timeline' shows us by illuminating the lifecycle of style. Once the shock of novelty wears off, so to speak, an item of dress is accepted, becomes popular, enters the fashion mainstream, leaves it after a while, and then becomes a historical artefact marking the time of its passing. If that is the case, according to Laver's guidance, the reappearance of the miniskirt today as a retro trend can be considered a phenomenon somewhere between 'amusing' and 'quaint'. Not funny exactly, but still eliciting a smile, perhaps of contentment and overfamiliarity.

First popularised in the mid-60s, the miniskirt created a cultural and fashion uproar. Hems had been steadily rising since the 1920s. Movements promoting the emancipation of women demanded the disappearance of physical restrictions on the female body in the name of social equality. But so did the climate of global upheaval. Women had to enter the workforce in greater numbers to compensate for the loss of men to military efforts during the First World War. There was no other choice if civil life was to continue. Women were recruited as chauffeurs, land labourers, bus drivers, elevator attendants. The sexual revolution of labour began innocently enough with the sudden abolition of the corset as well as the multiple layers of underskirting, flounce, lace frills and bustles that characterised women's dress during the 19th century. Freedom of movement was more important than an ostentatious complexity of style. The full-length dresses that had cloaked the Western female body for centuries began to disappear after the First World War in favour of shorter skirts cut boldly to the knee which revealed the legs and enabled women to work more comfortably than before. The erosion of class barriers in post-industrial society offered the promise of upward social mobility. In the 1920s, the bourgeois mentality that valued individuality, conspicuous consumption and competitive difference was supplanted by a mass-labour culture. The purpose was to rebuild after the ruins of war. The ideological climate and economic reality thus supported the idea of keeping the workplace open to women as a permanent feature of modern living. This development tested the traditional gender boundaries between males and females. But it also meant that more and more women could take advantage of the right to work to achieve greater social freedom and equitable treatment through prosperity, not simply to perform a patriotic duty or to keep the economy stable in post-wartime. Fashion changed permanently to accommodate the new lifestyle of the modern working woman. No longer was it dishonourable to acquire a livelihood. So, shorter skirts, trousers and less restrictive clothing became acceptable female attire that reflected the changes in attitude toward gender roles. The post-war era brought an optimistic spirit that was reflected in the liberal designs of women's clothing which was quickly becoming mass-produced rather than commissioned from *couturiers* who were traditionally the arbiters of good taste in fashion.

'Ready-to-wear' has displaced 'made-to-measure'. Gone are the days when a suit or a dress was bequeathed to a loved one after the death of its owner because the manufacturing of clothes was a complicated technical achievement that made quality garments an expensive proposition. Because of mass production and the proliferation of competing fashions, clothes are cheaper. Tailoring is a matter of science, now that art as technology has taken over the fashion industry. The invention of man-made fibres and sewing machines has revolutionised the making of clothes by allowing designer factories to churn out garments in cheap labour markets. Despite the quantity of clothes and styles on the market, or perhaps because of it, consumers are now more knowledgeable, discriminating and sensitive to different tastes. To make a good impression, it becomes fundamental to know who the spectators will be, what they will be looking for, and when they will be watching. The goal would be for a community of taste to applaud the value of your efforts and not be ambivalent about appearances because of price or brand name. Consequently, one has to be competent in reading both the stylistic trends that are predominant and the fashion moods of a group that puts them into practice. There is no lack of advice available in celebrity, lifestyle and pop culture magazines written for men and women. *Glamour*, *GQ*, *Cosmopolitan*, *Esquire*, *Vanity Fair*, *InStyle* and *People* are only some of the publications that offer their readers useful fashion tips, along with critical commentary on 'what's hot' and 'what's not'. Look through any one and you will see: 'seductive women' lying in satin pyjamas on a sumptuous bed with a handsome lover; 'care-free women' wearing sun hats and sandals, frolicking through a field of flowers; 'sophisticated women' stepping out of a limousine in a formal evening gown for a night at the theatre; 'successful women' donning a power suit and glasses, ready to do battle in the concrete jungle; 'maternal women' wearing faded jeans, playing with children and enjoying the role of care giver. You will also see: 'outdoorsy men' sporting a few days' growth of beard, earth-tone shirts and cotton twill trousers on the porch of a log cabin overlooking a lake; 'business men' reading the stock page, gauging their multitudinous investments and the complex state of their finances with studied enthusiasm; 'athletic men' in designer togs, watching their serve break the concentration of a feeble opponent; 'romantic men' with cardigan slung over the shoulder, hugging their sweetheart on a dusky beach like there is no tomorrow; 'family men' playing football with their kids on the front lawn of their humble abode. These images are fashion models in every sense of the word. They try to tap into the experiential world of consumers by offering portraits of style dressed up in vignettes of real life. We can imagine ourselves and our lives in any one of the images. The models in these magazines could very well represent any and all men and women. Good taste, it could be said, reflects community approval from those who occupy the same worlds that we choose to call our own.

A nun venturing out on a dinner invitation in the traditional black gown and habit that her sisterhood would be proud of cannot achieve the same appraisal for her outfit as the leggy damsels hanging out at the wine bar waiting to meet someone. The moral inspiration behind the full-length frock is a very important factor in forgiving its stylistic shortcomings for the secular world. A nun's habit is designed to cover up any and all skin, except the face and hands, which might result in the nun being thought of as a physically attractive woman, not as a servant of God. The purpose is to prevent the flesh from inciting and reacting to the erotic impulses of others. The same principle of suitability would apply to the clothing of the women looking for companionship, but in a totally different direction. The spiritually liberated damsels are at the wine bar to attract attention and admiration for their feminine form; therefore, their dress would be provocative in cut and style, placing more emphasis on revealing the 'erotic capital' of various parts of their anatomy – arms, legs, neckline – that are designed to arouse the attention of admirers. The result: a flurry of meaningful looks, flattering comments and drinks being sent over to them by potential suitors in search of an introduction. It would be ridiculous, even blasphemous, to think of the wine-bar damsel inhabiting the chaste confines of a monastery. Likewise, the nun would surely be overwhelmed, if not upset, by the forthright exhibitionism and intellectual coquetry of a singles bar. Neither scenario would be in good taste if settings were to be reversed, given the site-specific nature of fashion codes as they relate to particular events and situations. Each scenario implies discrete ideological and behavioural consequences of fashion choices. Good taste means making choices that help us fit into the social systems that best express who we are, while simultaneously showing an understanding and respect for the community of people we interact with. In this way, we identify what suits our needs as well as meeting the expectations of the social group we are associating with in order to be unequivocally accepted by its members. Learning how to weigh clothing choices with an experienced eye becomes the objective of fashion sense, especially when trying to impress upon others that you have good taste. Gaining an appreciation of amount and proportion are keys to success. There is nothing worse than excesses of form and design that draw attention to style for its own sake by providing a cartoonish caricature of fashion. Bad taste is not knowing when there is too much of a good thing.

Given its long and contentious cultural history as a clothing accessory introduced to 'beautify' women during the Victorian period, the corset allows us to understand how the amount of exposed cleavage and unnatural proportions affect fashion trends and social behaviours. But is it tasteful? If we use Laver's 'Timeline of Style', the corset in itself is a thing of beauty, being conceived and designed more than 150 years ago. And yet, we don't see it worn often today outside of specific contexts of dress. Some feminists have railed against the corset as an instrument of physical oppression against women, serving only to objectify them in sexual roles. They point to the fact that bourgeois women in the Victorian era dressed in a way that inhibited their motion and curtailed their ability to contribute to society through work. Heavy skirts, tight-laced corsets, flimsy footwear and elaborate headgear were designed to constrain the female body and make it a symbol of economic prosperity. Thus, women were made subservient to males who had the pecuniary power to remove them from the world of work. Fashion here performs not only a decorative role, but a social function for the bourgeois class as status seekers concerned solely with cultivating good taste through the exhibition of their buying power. The exaggerated proportion of the female form as an hourglass shape thus becomes a symbol of leisure and wealth, not to mention male dominance and the social and sexual bondage of women. As the quasi-mythic stature given to the tiny waist became more popular, it led to the rise of eating disorders and obsessive diet regimes that were adopted to keep the female form in such a shape. Despite the beauty of its design, it has been argued that the corset is in bad taste because it enabled men to subordinate and objectify women in well-defined sexual roles – to treat them like beautiful objects and chattel rather than respect their individuality and right to self-expression as human beings. Over time, women have turned the tables on men, however, and the corset has become a means for expressing sexual liberation and female autonomy in the boudoir. It is worn out of choice in private, not out of necessity in public.

Platform shoes are another interesting example of excess of proportion and amount taking over the logic of use. The invention of 'high heels' is the culmination of a long cultural history of footwear rooted in questions of social acceptance and stature. What we know as the contemporary platform shoe was popularised during the first half of the 70s by glam bands KISS, The Tubes and Elton John as well as Funkadelic rhythm masters George Clinton, Earth, Wind and Fire, and Sly and the Family Stone. Nevertheless, the elevated soles of yesteryear alter the mobility of today's well-informed consumer. The average height of audiences at rock concerts and the general population seems to have increased sharply over the last decade with the decline of the sensible shoe – no doubt along with greater incidences of twisted feet and broken ankles. Platform shoes, pointed shoes and high heels are again an orthopaedic surgeon's nightmare. Men and women are riding high on the heels of fashionable footwear.

Everywhere square-toed, platform boots still peer out sheepishly under wide-bottom trousers. And the pointy tip is again becoming easily found as a fashion statement of its own, at least for the most up-to-date and discriminating buyers of fashionable footwear. The pointed toe is making a serious comeback in women's formal footwear thanks to high-heel aficionados Jimmy Choo and Manolo Blahnik.

Most contemporary consumers of 70s cool are not aware that the platform shoe was immensely popular from the late 1400s to the middle of the 17th century. The 'chopine', as it was then called, consisted of an 'overshoe' worn on top of a smaller, finer shoe, to protect the daintier footwear from dirt and mud. Usually made of cork or stacked wood, the platform was covered with velvet. Some chopine soles reached the height of 30 inches. Legend has it that the platform shoe originated in medieval Venice as a precautionary measure against adultery. Along with various other mechanical sexual deterrents like the chastity belt, stoning and public castration, some women were forced to wear excessively thick-soled chopines by their jealous husbands who deduced that if a woman could not move quickly enough, she would always be under a watchful eye and could not have an affair. Linked with sex and gender, the chopine became a status symbol because it elevated and separated the elite female from the rest of society. People literally had to look up to a woman wearing the footwear, and she could happily look down on them – even though she had to have no uncertain amount of help walking down the boulevard. Consequently, the chopine signified luxury, wealth and social standing in relation to women. At the same time, however, the excessive height of the platform displayed the female body prominently as a possession to be worshipped and had. Prostitutes wore chopines to call attention to their worldly virtues and assets. Associated more and more with sexuality and scandal rather than high society, the platform shoe gradually became a fetishised fashion and was worn less and less in public outside of Venice.

High heels – the podiatrist's aphrodisiac – were derived from the idea of the chopine as a more practical way to heighten and elongate the female body without limiting normal physical functions – too much. It is rumoured that Leonardo da Vinci invented high heels at the end of the 15th century. But that is legend. The first to try this new fashion on for size was the vertically challenged Catherine de Medici who wore two-inch-high heels to the altar in 1533. Transplanted from Italy to France, she enthralled the court with the serpentine sway of her walk, the graceful poise of her elevated stature, and a female sophistication that was the envy of every noblewoman. Another moment of historical significance was Marie Antoinette ascending the executioner's scaffold in high style wearing two-inch heels. Gradually, though, high heels fell into disfavour until their revival in the 1930s. The Victorian Age popularised flat soles of inconspicuous height – the 'pump' – because modesty was the desired attribute for the era. Female footwear supported and eased walking without drawing attention to the feet. The high heels of the 1930s were platformed but, unlike the chopine, did not consist of a monolithic sole. The 1950s brought the introduction of the stiletto and a very pointed tip, which has resurfaced as a must-have for any fashionable woman following the trends of today. In the 1970s, to be fashionable or 'hip', the soles of male and female shoes had to be at least two inches with a five-inch heel. Some platforms were hand-painted with moons and stars, featured rainbows or were sprinkled with glitter. Others even contained live goldfish in clear, detachable containers that formed the supporting sole of the shoe.

There was no limit to the creative potential of decorating a large surface as if it were an identity banner to make a statement about yourself. The 70s were, after all, the 'Me Generation'.

The F-word

Finding yourself in fashion requires the confidence to be able to choose clothes well in the face of the potential for stylistic adversity. The ability to make a rational appraisal of the possibilities of dress that are suitable to a social situation – be it formal or informal – is what a good sense of taste demands. Fashion choices have to be connected to real-life contexts. An *ad hoc* mixing of styles does not go very far toward recognising the required connection between social expectations and personal preferences. Individualism conveys, at some level, an indifference to the collective sense of judgement that good taste demands, inspires and carries forward into the public sphere. If the aesthetic beauty of clothing does exist in the eye of 'the beholder', then 'the beholder' must share or at least understand the motivations behind a style of dress to appreciate its appropriateness and desirability. An 'unsociable' or 'off-putting' form of dress that is unflattering and has more negative than positive social connotations attached to it must be called 'unattractive'. Good taste must maintain the capacity to be desirable to a general audience of social observers, big or small. Conflicts in judgement are inevitable. This realisation goes a long way to explain the existence of fashion trends.

Clothing alternates between *chic* and *passé* in that cycle of socially regarded and acceptable dress that we call fashion. Fashion calls for a critical evaluation of the public appearance of the individual through clothing: that is, for a measurement of social character as judged by the stylistic appropriateness of one's way of dressing in relation to the conventions of taste popular at the time.

Class systems are established according to hierarchies that separate those governed by the harsh dictates of physical labour from those who enjoy the excessive values of monetary wealth. Fashion has traditionally been associated with the body and not the mind. It is a luxury, not a necessity. That is why the concern for fashion has been considered a frivolous pursuit, or at least a non-productive one, for the labouring masses who have neither the time nor the money to worry about the minutiae and excesses of dress. When the body is hard at work, how can it be possible to think about pampering the body, to make it look and feel good simply for its own sake, despite the everyday grind of work? Fashion belongs with leisure and luxury to those who have the peace of mind to enjoy it. Not to mention the disposable resources. The word fashion refers to the pleasures of adorning the body because there is time and reason to do so for purely aesthetic reasons, not always practical ones. Fashion then becomes an art and a science of sorts, an experimental study in the process of design; not to be confused with those involved in the study of science. Think about those notorious intellectuals, Albert Einstein for example, scholars too busy enjoying the complexity of their beautiful minds and unique brains to worry about petty concerns like appearances. Material concerns distract serious thought and stifle intellectual creativity. The unkempt style of Einstein's hair has achieved a cultural status of its own as a metaphor of the genius's lack of concern for public judgement. The cerebral asceticism of 'the thinker', like the material abstinence of 'the worker', forbids the excess and frivolity of being in fashion for its own sake. That is, shaping, moulding and reconstructing the body in fabric simply for the enjoyment of it. For that is surely what fashion is about, especially if we consider the etymology of the word, tapping its cross-cultural sources of meaning.

'Fashion' originally comes from the Latin verb *facere*, which means *do*, *make*, *create*, *acquire*, *cause*, *bring about*, *compose*, *accomplish*. This was translated into Old French and Middle French as the nouns *fazon* and *façon* respectively. Later adapted into Middle English as 'fashion' (a transitive verb), it retained the Latin emphasis on *doing*, *making* or *shaping* that marked its original meaning. In the 16th century, the word *fashion* begins to take on a social sense of significance as 'a special manner for making clothes'. Today, *fashion* is primarily a noun, and refers to the mode of dressing, manner of speech, etiquette or style adopted by a society or culture for the time being. Wearing fashionable apparel provides a relatively easy way to fit in with the greater part of everyday society. It is a safe way to flaunt our personal anonymity in a big city of strangers and yet to be viewed, more or less, in the same way as others so as to be accepted by the community at large. Being 'in fashion' is to openly display the similarity of our good taste in a social context by using clothes. It is a matter of showing that we know what appearance is appropriate and desirable to others without having to say a word about it.

If fashion has a language, it is spoken through us and by us in the form of clothing. Meanings are expressed both consciously and unconsciously through what we choose to wear, how we decide to wear and display it, and what is said about it by ourselves and others. Personal taste does play a role in all of this. But that may be part of the problem of recognising good taste. Following fashion trends becomes a matter of course in living a social life, but the experience is rationalised as if it were a result of free choice. We forget that good taste is an acquired sensibility. Fashion may guide our choices, but clothes speak us – tell others who we are, what we do, what we like. 'Fashion victim' or 'fashion pioneer', 'clone' or 'stylist', 'poser' or 'original', 'designer slave' or 'no logo': at one time or other everyone has had to make a choice regarding dress. The decisions, of course, are not easy. The language of fashion then becomes the 'F-word', f*****n. The trauma of 'coming out of the closet', so to speak, manifests itself in at least two ways through human expression. On the one hand, as the fear of not being accepted by our peers. On the other, as the trepidation of being shown up by others. Both scenarios require defence mechanisms to protect against the deflation of ego. Fashion and style – the lack of either or both – hold the promise of humiliation, a very public death of sorts, essentially because the survival of the ego is always at stake. The expression, 'I could have died of embarrassment', contextualises the experience.

The effects of being reviled publicly for wearing a particular attire, or not, can be illustrated by a dream that many have experienced, but few would readily admit to outside of intensive counselling and psychotherapy. Picture this: there you are, sitting in a classroom, panicking, trying to finish a test before the time runs out and the teacher utters those final words of doom: 'Everyone. Put down your pencils please.' You look up at the clock. Again and again. It gets closer to the end of the school day. As the teacher paces the room, up and down, up and down, along the neat rows of desks, she watches for cheaters. You feel guilty. You are not cheating but *you* think *she* knows that *you* haven't studied as well as you should have. You try to concentrate, feverishly trying to complete the test. The bell rings. The teacher commands the class to stop writing. You finish scribbling your last sentence. The teacher stares hard at you in disapproval as she collects the papers. You feel pangs of guilt again, but are satisfied. The class is now engaged in conversation about the test. Slowly, the students, your friends, begin to rise and move toward the door of the classroom. As you get up, you hear the class beginning to laugh softly. Looking around, you see awkward, embarrassed looks on their faces, sly grins and stifled nervous squeals of amusement. The titters turn into deafening roars of laughter and guffaws. You want to laugh, but you don't know what the joke is. 'What's so funny?' you ask. No one can answer, they are laughing so hard. You look around the room at the circle that has now formed around you, searching desperately for a friendly face. Instead, you find only monstrous grimaces of joy. 'What's so funny?' you ask again. This time they all point: 'You!' – the word crashes around in your brain. You look down, totally unaware that you are wearing your mother's feather-trimmed, baby-blue silk pyjama bottoms, under your favourite red T-shirt, until someone screams it out to you, to everyone: 'You look ridiculous!' At which time, those with whom you were speaking in polite company only a few moments ago are laughing hysterically, uncontrollably, at the sight of you. You become horrified as you realise what has happened. In your rush to get to class on time, you forgot to look at the trousers you pulled on. Searching for a place to hide, you find nothing but the faces of gawking strangers smiling lasciviously at your misfortune. You want to crawl away and be forgotten; to die a quick and dignified death with your own clothes on. Then you wake up. To the beginning of a bad hair day.

Since fashion and style are always poised between modesty and exhibitionism, the contradictions are frightening because what is considered normal and desirable in one instance can be irrational and painful in another. For example, it is natural for members of the same football squad to wear identical clothing, whereas two women wearing the identical dress to a social occasion would be disastrous. The quality of 'sameness' that is desirable in the context of a team sport aimed at achieving collaborative goals is to be avoided in a situation where the purpose of clothing is to make a distinct impression by displaying an individual sense of style and uniqueness within certain guidelines of formal attire. One has to be aware of the cultural boundaries of good taste and of how the fashion choices we make define who we are for others.

The colour of a dress should not be a good reason for impugning a woman's character, but clothing and personality are intertwined. We don't need to hear a love-crossed Sting singing a torchy punk ballad to Roxanne, effectively begging her 'not to put on that red dress tonight'. We can take a hint. A red dress might be an innocent mistake, a bad choice of clothing. Or an impetuously misguided fashion statement perhaps intended to ignite the flames of passion, to challenge the stability of a sexual relationship. However, even before the days of Daniel Defoe's depiction of the upwardly mobile vixen heroine Roxanne who went from walking the street to a life of luxury, red has been a traditional colour of choice for sex-trade workers. The term *scarlet woman* – originally found in the Bible, Revelation 17 – became fashionable in Victorian England when 'respectable ladies' wore subdued colours such as grey and brown so as not to draw attention to their sexuality. 'Women of ill repute' wore bright reds, greens and blues to signify their availability for sex. The phrase 'scarlet woman' is seldom used today, and then mostly in a tongue-in-cheek manner. Prostitution districts are called red-light districts because of the lighted lamps the girls used to put in their windows to show they were open for business. The practice is still used today by sex-trade workers where the world's oldest profession is legal. Symbolically, the red dress ranks right up there with the fluorescent light on the front porch. Roxanne should know better. Culture determines the values of our responses to colour, giving them social and therefore symbolic and ethical meaning beyond the essence of their own chromatic qualities, so to speak. The mathematician Alfred Tarski once said that the proof for the logical link between appearance and reality can be encapsulated in the statement, *snow is white if snow is white*. Truth, quite literally, is in the eye of the beholder, who makes conclusions that are justified through language. This means that, depending on the context, Roxanne might well be taken for a woman of easy virtue because she has a 'red dress on'. The idea might seem impertinent, shallow, or even obvious as a *cliché* or stereotype of the sex-trade worker, in the light of this decoding. Clothes do make a difference to the social measure of humanity, no matter what (the) age. Appearances and identity are related in the symbolic imagery of the public mind: 'You are what you wear!' Right or wrong, clothing allows others to make judgements about who we are and where we fit in with society. The ethical propriety of what we do is scrutinised simply from the way we dress. Fashion redeems our sense of good taste and makes it understandable to the rest of the world, showing others that we know what appearance is appropriate and inoffensive to others at a particular time and place in history.

Perhaps we are taking all of this a bit too seriously – reading too much into the meaning of the 'F-word'. But the language of fashion tells us otherwise. Allusions to death and violence have unconsciously crept into the language of fashion as a way to inoculate ourselves against the repressed fear of rejection or mockery. How many times have we heard people using images of violence when referring to fashion sense, personal aesthetics and the appearance of others?: 'I wouldn't be caught dead wearing that alpaca jacket!'; 'I would give my right arm for ... [insert the desired attire: a Versace suit, a diamond necklace, a Rolex watch, Gucci shoes, etc.]'; 'That watch fob is to die for!'; 'She is a knockout in stilettos!'; 'My heart stopped when I saw him in that thong'; 'The man looks dynamite in that pinstripe!'; 'a fashion victim'; 'a slave to fashion'; 'clothes off the rack' (the medieval torture device); 'a sharp dresser'; 'if looks could kill'; 'drop-dead gorgeous'; 'a killer outfit!'; 'that dress bombed'; and the emphatic 'DRESSED TO KILL'. The language of fashion is driven by a dark side: performance anxiety and the fear of rejection. The danger of not actualising the objectives we want, fulfilling the needs we have and attaining the objects we desire brings about aggression – a natural human emotion that once externalised gives rise to images of violence, death and dying that express frustration and recall the proverbial Freudian 'death wish'. Along with the search for principles of achieving pleasure, Sigmund Freud called the death drive a primal human instinct. The language of fashion – the words and concepts we evoke to talk about it – reflects the internal tensions associated with not achieving good taste and not being welcomed into the world for who we are. It is not a question of physically dying as much as it is a metaphorical question of rebirth or transforming oneself into a beautiful creature, like a caterpillar becoming a butterfly. We can read the dark side of the language of fashion in the manner of a Freudian slip. The needs, wants and suppressed desires of the ego are revealed through the words used to describe images of style and fashion. A fear of exposing to the world the possibility that we have bad taste comes through in the ways we talk about clothes and how others look in relation to what is fashionable. The psychological profession has given this fashion-induced psychosis a name, *vestiophobia*: the fear of clothing.

For some, the notion is absurd. How can clothes harm us? They are inanimate objects created at our discretion. We use them; they don't use us! We make clothes; clothes don't make us! Or so the story goes. Consequently, there should be no mortal dread at the thought of putting on, let's say, an exquisitely embroidered, multicoloured silk caftan. The experience should be savoured sensually, aesthetically, morally, and most of all, emotionally. It should make a woman feel attractive and good about herself! Make her happy – not depressed and suicidal. But there is more to it than meets the eye of the beholder, consumer or fashion critic. The caftan is back 'in vogue'. At least, that is what the fashion designers are hoping and praying as they have been trying to sell the 'modern woman' the idea of wearing a Middle-Eastern style of loose-fitting tunic that dates back to the days of Babylonian antiquity. The caftan is being marketed as a sexy artefact of ethnic culture 'whose time has come again'. A funky alternative clothing choice to the boring blouse or stale shirt. The caftan may be alien to modern Western experience, yet we are shown in magazines across North America and Europe that it is now relevant to today's casual, yet busy, urban lifestyle. Not a fashion relic. The caftan is usually seen draped over the bodies of 'full-figured' women who would have used its tent-like capacity as a low-order form of camouflage to conceal physical imperfections from excessively prying imaginations. But now we can spot it luxuriously floating down the sensuous catwalks of Yves St Laurent, Fendi and Gucci. Fashion works in mysterious ways to rehabilitate the caftan and legitimate the fashion options of even plus-size wardrobes. It plays on the dreams and desires of the consumer to divest the garment of the stigma associated with it as 'overweight wear'. Frightfully thin fashion models are making the caftan a seductive article of clothing in the West. It has become a bold fashion statement rather than the consequence of always having seconds from the dessert tray at *La Grande Pêche*. From Whoopi Goldberg to Gwyneth Paltrow, celebrities of various forms have been spotted in caftan-like garb. The mystique of stardom fuels the desire to possess and display an item of clothing. Those old caftans from the 60s are coming back out of the closet and being worn without the stigma of obesity. A sleeker, more close-fitting and sheerer version of the caftan now reveals all the nooks and crannies, hills and valleys of the female form, instead of hiding them under billowing layers of an industrial-strength fabric. But a traditional sizing is still available, if you want it. For the emaciated and the robust alike, the caftan is coming back in vogue with sartorial vengeance. At the moment, the fear associated with this piece of clothing is being repressed in social consciousness by fashion image-makers. The caftan is thus rehabilitated. Like a Rubens painting, burgeoning body mass can again be flaunted, the overflowing and robust female figure can be celebrated, and made to look appealing, tasteful and desirable in the eyes of others. Once the stigma of weightism has been temporarily divested from the billowing and cavernous outlines of the caftan that suggest vast interiors of dense space, it becomes an attractive article of clothing and not a red flag for joining a weight-watchers support group. Fashion dictates our self-perception through the public eye of the beholder. Taste is likewise a socially constructed aspect of distinction with respect to dress. Otherwise, why on earth would an article of ethnic clothing indigenous to regions of Mesopotamia circa 3500 BC be desirable to the typical Western city-dwelling woman of the 21st century who does not have to hide an overzealous cultivation of love handles?

Fashion Deficit Disorder

With the alphabet soup of newly discovered syndromes that are waiting to be authenticated by the medical profession, we might as well give the needy condition of unrequited taste in clothes an identity and worry about legitimising it later. Thus, Fashion Deficit Disorder or FDD is born.

FDD can have many psychological manifestations and physiological effects, but the major symptom is the lack of attention to clothing details that reveals the absence of 'style intelligence'. Having no sense of colour coordination or awareness for analogous patterns counts as a symptom. Wearing a red and green ensemble reminiscent of Christmas wrapping paper is as bad as wearing stripes with checks, or polka dots. Another common feature is difficulty in identifying clothing forms and shapes that are complementary to particular body structures. A high-collared shirt under a double-breasted blazer makes the short man seem dwarfish, wide and cartoon-like. Elmer Fudd comes to mind.

An inability to identify different styles of clothing that are an inherently bad idea magnifies the effects of Fashion Deficit Disorder. Who could argue against the opinion that puffy, turquoise taffeta-sleeve dresses should be reserved for bridesmaid attire? How else can the wedding guests (and the groom) be persuaded that the bride is significantly more beautiful and desirable than the other women in her entourage? Skirts for males is another example of a really bad fashion idea. I am not talking about cultural forms of dress that are indigenous to a geographical area, historical period or ethnicity. There is a difference between the kilt, the sarong or the dohti and current variations of the 'male skirt' that have been designed by Jean Paul Gaultier, Paul Smith, Dries van Noten, Vivienne Westwood and Yohgi Yamamoto as artistic showpieces of alternative masculinity for a consumer fashion market controlled by Western sensibilities. In the hot and arid climates of the Middle East and North Africa, the jellaba evolved out of the environmental necessity of keeping the body cool, and not from the desire to promote the idea of a unisex clothing style. The geographical and historical location of the garment itself authenticated its cultural use and value. We cannot say the same thing about the male skirt that was re-introduced to the Western fashion scene during the mid-70s as a revolutionary clothing style for the 'New Man'. Some designers were reacting against the staid rules of men's fashion, others were searching for another way to achieve good taste in male clothing without the traditional features of masculine attire. Yet the motivation for the male skirt was primarily aesthetic rather than the result of a grassroots cultural movement. There was no public demand that began with the desire of the 'ordinary' man to wear a hemline. David Beckham, Prince Charles and David Bowie may well have been spotted in cheeky little numbers that espoused the benefits of laser electrolysis, tanning spas and regular exfoliation, but just how often do we see a man running about town in a skirt during the course of the day? For all intents and purposes, the male skirt is a fashion anomaly out of step with modern times in urban Western society – a historical artefact forced upon an unsuspecting public. If it had taken hold during the 70s as a subcultural trend with a critical mass of active supporters, the male skirt could have been a masculine equivalent to bra burning, which was an act of fashion defiance that permanently altered gendered dress codes and was a groundbreaking symbol of independence for the Women's Liberation movement. The male skirt could have radically redefined traditional notions of masculine taste and identity. It did not happen. So, the male skirt can be looked upon today more as a postmodern artistic statement to showcase designer talents and creativity than as a useful piece of clothing. An exhibition curated in 2001 at the Victoria and Albert Museum around the concept of 'Men in Skirts' drives home the point quite nicely. Celebrities and members of the gay community as well as Punks and Grunge enthusiasts modelled outfits such as the 'Utilikilt' (a 'rough and ready' pinafore for the workman who needs more than just a snazzy uniform) and baby-doll dresses reminiscent of the floral ice-blue gown Kurt Cobain wore on a magazine cover as a radical challenge to the stereotype of the rock star as macho sex god. The problem with the male skirt for the 'New Man' was quite simple really: not many men wanted to set their trousers aflame, except for Jimi Hendrix maybe. Even less wanted the right to wear a skirt. The majority of women did not care for it either. Mainstream society wasn't at all receptive to a public form of cross-dressing that feminised men and held masculine pride up for ridicule. Let's face it, the 70s were not a golden era for Gladiator chic or polymorphic male character types like the 'sensitive guy'. Vietnam put an end to the illusion of the noble warrior and disco fever upheld the image of the cheap Casanova in gold chains and tight trousers. The male skirt never really took hold of the contemporary fashion scene at the time and it still hasn't today, despite its obvious echoes of cultural forms of dress like the kilt, the sarong, the dohti and the toga.

FDD also reveals itself in the lack of compatibility between the choice of clothing and the event to which it is worn and displayed. Social expectations govern dress on any occasion. A low-cut, halter top and ripped-up, oil-washed jeans worn to the office on 'Casual Fridays' may be a comfortably cool look on a hot summer day and will get you noticed by normally aloof management types and co-workers. However, the outfit could also detract from your professional reputation as a 'serious worker' depending on how low the neckline plunges. You don't usually see a lot of exposed flesh around even the most casual of office spaces. The 'Puritanical Work Ethic' rules the white-collar business world. Arms, legs, necks and torsos are almost completely covered in the modern office so as not to distract anyone from the task at hand: to make loads of money in the most efficient way possible. The fashion dilemma of 'career wear' is not the clothing itself, but the suitability of the style to the situation in which it is worn. A 'G-String' doesn't have a moral attitude – people do! We must remember that. Taste judgements are made by people and cultivated by societies and cultures. The difficulty comes with what can potentially be interpreted about personality because of the meaning we as a society attach to clothing styles in different contexts. Social psychologists have found that it takes approximately 90 seconds to 'size up' another person and make initial judgements about their character, right or wrong, simply from appearances and not dialogue. Whether we want to or not, the limbic system of the brain reacts to visual stimuli on an emotional level and we begin to draw conclusions without reflecting on what has been seen and said until much later. First impressions are powerful, reflex-determined reactions that are highly primitive in nature. The limbic system that forms the second level of the brain (or the *paleopallium*) is a vestigial remain of the survival systems used by all mammals to distinguish the agreeable from the disagreeable. Fifty-five per cent of first impressions are based on appearance, which includes clothes along with grooming and personal mannerisms. Aesthetic judgements lead naturally to inferences about character and personality. The tone and pitch of voice account for 38 per cent, while only 7 per cent of first impressions are determined by what we have to say. Even if the public judgement about you as a person is incorrect, it will be difficult to erase the negative impressions your tastes have made. Fashion Deficit Disorder is not a life or death health emergency; nevertheless, it can definitely be a terminal social disease and a professional nightmare. Despite the medical community's all but total ignorance of FDD, the media have highlighted the effects of Fashion Deficit Disorder as a pathological condition of consistently bad taste to be overcome at all costs. But there are specialists to whom we can turn for help.

Fashion critics can be and are relentless in judging the value of clothing forms and practices on a social scale. Each and every year, we are bombarded with 'authoritative lists' of the best- and worst-dressed celebrities, our most famous of human beings – and also the most envied. Celebrities include movie stars, musicians, television personalities, royalty, sports figures, writers, fashion models, politicians and convicted criminals (who could belong to any of the aforementioned groups). Their voices, faces and bodies have been made instantly recognisable by the televisual media apparatus, which makes them intriguing to no end as universal entities different from you and me and yet the same. Fame is the defining feature of being a celebrity, and has critical importance in explaining why 'Best Dressed' and 'Worst Dressed' fashion lists hold any interest for us at all with respect to good taste. The public wants to know about the private lives of media stars – where they go, what they do, what they wear, who they see and why. Not simply out of a curiosity to catch them out in bad behaviour, but to reaffirm the reality of their participation in the human condition by getting behind the persona of stardom and the cocoon of secrecy to the actual individual, warts and all. The making of a celebrity may be based on a publicist's marketing illusion; however, it has very real effects on the world that are reported as cultural phenomena by tabloids, fanzines and newspapers, not to mention television, which is part of the new information age with its total recall and immediate projection of the life world to viewers across the global village. All is fair game when it comes to documenting and exposing the lives of celebrities, from diet to dating, friendships to fashion. They are the living, breathing images of the success and good taste that almost everyone secretly desires and envies – the unimaginable wealth, boundless fame, beautiful lovers and all the accoutrements that go along with it (parties, exotic 'getaways', no waiting in queues at restaurants). Nothing in the celebrity world is beyond scrutiny. This type of voyeurism makes us feel good about ourselves and our day-to-day predicaments as we can see the rich and famous involved in real-life problems and situations that the 'common folk' experience, including dressing appropriately. The celebrity fishbowl also creates a reason to seek 'more' from our ordinary lives, to nurture a feeling of envy that is pushed by the desire to have 'better' material possessions and perhaps cultural clout. Seeking 'greater' satisfaction in this case means having 'higher' aspirations – or redefining our personal sense of taste in accordance with that exemplified by the lifestyles of the rich and famous. The purpose is to defeat the 'feeling of emptiness' that we would not have known was there, crippling our existence, if the media hadn't alerted us to just how 'full', 'meaningful' and 'rich' the lives of celebrities are compared to our own. Great personal discontent often accompanies the clarity of a marketing vision of reality and its staged depiction of taste judgements. And this is the desired outcome of an effective advertising campaign that makes its viewing public crave and consume over and over again in an effort to keep up with fashion trends.

The consumer is the focus of over 2,000 advertising messages a day. Approximately 15 per cent of those are celebrity endorsements. It would make sense then that the 'Best Dressed' and 'Worst Dressed' lists act as vehicles to market taste and huckster fashion to the masses of adoring fans with varying amounts of disposable income. It is as if the aura of celebrity pervades the clothes that are being advertised and magically transfers its qualities, good or bad, from the person to the thing being sold, then on to the consumer. Here is how the marketing of fashion works through the celebrity: Star X is in Town Y to attend an opening or promote a movie. A publicist who has been hired by a fashion designer to generate interest in a new clothing line keeps tabs on the comings and goings of celebrities around the world. Knowing that Star X is in Town Y, the publicist offers an invitation to the designer's shows and parties. The celebrity fashion juggernaut is now rolling. Star X would benefit from the media exposure, but also likes the other perk: *the free sampling of couture*. After some delicate negotiations involving the celebrity's manager, stylist and astrologer, a mutually satisfying agreement is struck. Having accepted the offer, Star X is sent a generous assortment of the designer's clothes in exchange for attending the events. It is an amicable pact. Not all of the clothes have to be worn as long as the designer's name is mentioned to the press as the purveyor of the celebrity's outfit. That way, everyone is happy. As the complimentary limousine that the designer has hired for Star X pulls up to the runway, the paparazzi shoot the arrival of the celebrity and 'the walk' down the red carpet in a veritable frenzy of flashing bulbs, screaming fans and the hydraulic rewinding of cameras. The photos are barely digitised before they are sent to *Vogue*, *InStyle*, *People*, *Glamour*, *Vanity Fair* and *GQ* via modem. The designer and the celebrity have a good thing going here, thanks to the media and the public's insatiable appetite to consume images of the rich and famous. Nobody loses.

The media machine survives on capturing the workings of celebrity no matter what the situation, and then sells a supremely plastic and idiosyncratic vision of 'success' on to us as consumers by commercialising products endorsed by celebrities. Authenticity doesn't matter as much as the manufacturing of a glamorous image that is managed to the hilt. Let's not forget, celebrities hire publicists and fashion stylists to concoct a public persona through appearances. The Attractiveness Quotient, or 'AQ' rating, of a celebrity is tied to how the celebrity is perceived in the public eye. Exposure is not enough. Celebrity seduces us with the promise of showing us perfection and the possibility of frustrating our expectations of ordinariness. By giving us examples of how the rich and famous look and dress, the media are actually performing a public service – helping consumers to counteract the debilitating effects of FDD in the never-ending quest of human beings for good taste and aesthetic perfection by offering styles of desirable dress to emulate as well as hideous fashions to avoid. We see shadowy stills of alarmingly handsome men in dark poses, wearing finely tailored suits created by designers with names that sound too perfect: Prada, Versace, Boss, Cerruti, Armani, Dior. The images seem to be saying: 'Just think how the world would react to you if only you dressed like James Bond, 007, Rolex and all.' We see airbrushed pictures of long-legged divas with hourglass figures, preening and smiling lusciously through ruby lips to no one in particular except a camera that mercilessly takes in every bodacious curve, healthy nook and immodest cranny. These cameos of a womanly beauty both terrify and tantalise a mortal female population with a stiff challenge: 'Be like me. If you can.' It is not that all celebrities are more beautiful or fashionable than every person who is not rich and famous. Having attractive physical characteristics and dressing them up does help achieve the desired effect. Big full lips and perfectly formed curves are aesthetically enticing features, but taste is always fickle and forever changing in the public sphere. Remember Twiggy or Elle MacPherson? Total image is more important than the separate parts. As much as we have been conditioned to think that all celebrities are 'beautiful people', nothing could be further from the truth. The external image potentially hides a reality that could be radically different. The media both expose and hide the truth. A fascination with seduction drives the cult of celebrity, and plays on the negative effects of Fashion Deficit Disorder by supplying the public with endless images of good taste. The media don't worry about morality as much as ratings or controlling the art of persuasion. Fame doesn't necessarily need to be characterised as 'good' or 'bad' to be effective as a marketing tool for selling fashion. Only taste has to be. Which explains the fact that after her notorious fifteen minutes of fame during 'The Clinton Affair', Monica Lewinsky enjoys a successful career as a designer of trendy handbags. Infamy does not always hamper the marketing of taste as long as Fashion Deficit Disorder continues to plague us.

Clowns of Fashion

Novelty is what drives fashion in today's mass-market consumerism: the desire to have something current, something new, not something borrowed, something blue. And with the pleasure of consumption comes a seductive illusion that drives the fashion industry, just as the fashion industry drives the taste economy. Novelty constitutes freedom from the past. But nothing lasts for ever. The risk of obsolescence frustrates customer satisfaction and leaves the consumer wanting more. In order to meet the demand for newness to satisfy the cult of novelty, the turns of fashion are inexhaustible. Yet, to be perceived as being 'out there' alone in the wilderness of style and fashion is to be morally defenceless, even in a capitalistic democracy where anything goes as long as it can be marketed and sold. The reasoning behind our choices is exposed to public scrutiny according to the cultural logic of the times. The German philosopher Immanuel Kant puts it best: 'It is better to be a clown of fashion than to be a clown without fashion.' A culture accepts only what it recognises and tolerates only what it does not abhor. So, for Kant, the transitory ideals of fashion are a necessary evil that one must take into consideration and live with, or accept the consequences of a social distinction outside the norm, i.e., the notoriety of belonging to a sub-culture. Fashion, thus, is not always about good taste, but also about identity politics and creating a sense of belonging for yourself and a way for others to accept your difference.

To be considered 'fashionable' is to be given the same level of social distinction as others in a community. A passing nod of blind tolerance given to you on the street by someone you don't even know – no more, no less. That is the reward for wearing clothing similar in cut and style to everyone else. Imitating the clothing influences of the day secures us a place in the contemporary visual motifs of a community and its general culture. Fashion offers a relatively easy way to 'fit in' with the greater part of everyday society. No questions asked. By dressing like everyone else, fashion provides a safe way to flaunt our anonymity and safeguard our personal independence in a big city full of strangers.

Clothing earns you the democratic right to be part of an idea of community. As far as appearances go, on the surface, you could be anyone and anyone could be you, even if it means existing as another shiny cog in the wheel of a well-oiled social and economic machine. It is as though wearing fashionable clothes confers a good-taste seal of approval on the individual as part of a community at large. But acceptance does not come without paying a price: losing your independence to fashion.

CHAPTER THREE

Food Porn

Food and sex are human nature

Chinese proverb

I know what you are thinking: 'Surely you jest! What does food have to do with porn?' Food is about eating, porn is about sex. But, as we shall see, these two basic instincts, food and sex, are closely linked in a number of ways, and the phrase 'food porn' will prove extremely helpful in our understanding of good taste in food.

But what does food have to do with porn? A fair question, considering that the standards of good taste in food are not typically associated with the 'adult' appeal of porn. But the rise in heart rate, increased blood flow and general feelings of arousal that occur when mouth-watering dishes are set before us with names like 'Caramel Rum Delirium Cake', 'Gratin of Creamed Potato Fingers' and 'Hot Spicy Pork Loin' are enough, you would think, to make the connection clear. Indecently appealing desserts understandably referred to by names such as 'Chocolate Demise' or 'Chocolate Phantasmagoria' are 'the last word on a consuming passion' as Marcel Desaulniers presented it in his book, *Death by Chocolate*. There is an obsession to encounter the physical pleasure that comes with eating. Unable to speak, in the rapture of a mouthful of chocolate ganache blending with toasted pecans, sugar butter crust and melting triple-cream ice cream – all inhibitions dissolve as they are replaced by the sensuality of the moment. The experience melts away, but the memory remains. Fantasy-flavoured foods, often recklessly high in calories, stimulate us, flooding our senses with gratification. Taste buds register and remember the satisfying feeling. Sugar Cane Smoked Duck Breast or a not so *haute cuisine* dish of fresh halibut Fish and Chips – the fish perfectly battered and the chips freshly crinkle cut, wine vinegared and sea salted – can provide a pleasant feeling as the food enters our body through our upper orifice, a sensitive organ that registers exceptional enjoyment. Flavours penetrate the taste buds, eliciting an uncontrollable declaration of happiness – UMMMM! Moans spontaneously escape when the palate is satiated from a satisfying bout of eating. The encounter goes beyond words, and dreams do come true. Eating offers moments that transport the individual beyond the worries of everyday life. Ecstasy achieved through a deliriously sensual experience: there is an obvious similarity between the illicit – sex – and the licit – food: worlds of temptation and pleasure collide. Even in memory, an amazing eating episode revisited registers an increase in heart rate as the salivary glands moisten in reminiscence of the mouth-watering encounter.

The sensual appeal of food has spread like wildfire in the cultural vernacular of recent memory, conjuring up not-so-subliminal images that display gratifying culinary masterpieces in ways that boggle the mind's eye and titillate the palate. References to the erotic similarities between the equally gratifying physical pleasures of eating and sex are everywhere. The suggested erogenous appeal of food most certainly fuels disgust from fundamentalist factions praying for temperance in the 'traditional' display of recipes. Erotic exhibitions relating the pleasure of food to the pleasure of sex are everywhere. The 'indulgence industries' of cruise lines, luxury hotels and fantasy vacation packages openly declare that they are in the business of selling pleasure. It has become clear that physical gratification is the 'stock concept' they use in promoting all services. References to sensual satisfaction have a seductive appeal, and the adverts suggest that people's cravings for the quality comforts of life will be gratified.

Advertising, the 'dream industry', repeatedly exploits the pleasures of the *corps* by associating the physical pleasure of the body with the products being promoted – and particularly so in adverts about food – because, quite simply, 'sex sells'. A Pizzaville ad that has been aired for years on Canadian radio cleverly uses the connections between food and sex to make its jingle memorable. The last six numbers of the line you call for 'take out' or delivery are '36-36-36'. In itself, there is nothing out of the ordinary about it, just repeated digits – to make them easier to remember. However, the commercial is being narrated by a gentle Cockney English voice. You quickly realise that the character is quite naïve. Every commercial begins with the line, *'It was a rainy day in Pizzaville'*, but contains references to pizza that can be taken 'the wrong way' – other than intended by the narrator. The advertisement is promoting the fact that the pizza is a mouthful. Huge. But in one commercial you hear the narrator telling a story about the time he offered his mother-in-law a slice of pizza by asking her if she wanted to wrap her mouth around sixteen mouth-watering inches, at which point she slapped him and called him a 'cheeky bugger'. He doesn't know what he did wrong. When the narrator gets around to giving the audience the phone number, '36-36-36' becomes 'free sex, free sex, free sex', but it is offered up with such an inoffensive, natural air and naïve quality that it brings a smile to your face when you realise how cleverly the reference was pulled off.

Advertising no longer relies strictly on airbrushing pictures to infuse them with subliminal sexual references. An advert endorsing a gourmet blender is captioned 'Famous chefs naked with their blender'. The picture takes you aback. A chef is naked, holding only a blender erect in front of his 'nether regions'. The phallic symbolism is clear – there is a satisfaction to be attained by the quality merchandise the chef has been endowed with. A second caption reads, 'I have two heroes: Jerry Garcia and whoever invented this thing'. The reference is to the blender that the chef is flaunting. The chef's 'mean' machine offers memorable experiences similar in quality to the emotional resonance of the music of a legend. Jerry Garcia makes the music, his blender makes the magic. But getting naked with it? A chef is measured by the potency of his blender. The proof is in the pudding. The physical pleasure of eating what the blender is capable of offering, metaphorically represented by the anatomical part it replaces, can gratify the palate – in a big way. Could the symbolism be any clearer? The erotic, sensual appeal of high-quality food, thanks to tools that are handled well, is not about temperance and disdain for physical satisfaction: chefs are in the business of selling pleasures, stimulating appetites and gratifying desires. Big or small. Any chef worth his blender has hedonistic aspirations for good taste in cooking, where dining is intended to harmonise, vitalise, rhapsodise and soothe the restless soul, to 'turn the customers on' to whatever flavour the satisfaction is being sold in. And if sex sells food, then so be it – eating good food simply for pleasure rather than sustenance indulges the senses. Would you look at the size of that blender?

Without sex and food the human race could not survive.

The body demands the fulfilment of its biological requirements, sometimes defined by psychologists as 'base
instincts'. These continuously drive the ego's will and duty
toward acts motivated purely by the desire for self-
preservation. Abraham Maslow identified a hierarchy of
human needs. Appetite for food and sex and the need for
water, air and sleep must be satisfied or we will feel
irritation, discomfort and illness. These undesirable feelings
motivate us to satisfy our base needs. Maslow calls these
'physiological needs'. A society thrives and its population
grows in times of plenty, pushed by factors that create the
conditions for expansion and renewal. Food and sex
constitute essential elements of nature that sustain and drive
human life by providing the means to fight off death and
secure the legacy of a future generation. The argument has
been made by social anthropologists from Joseph Campbell
to Clifford Geertz, who have documented the profound
influence of food and sex on the mythic structure of human
consciousness. Without a stable source of nourishment,
there would be no natural foundation sustaining the
biological dynamism that over and over again gives rise to
the glorious reproduction of the human species. The structure of all social institutions – the family, the State, even the
educational system – is built around the necessity of
securing food and sex for the very practical reason of
ensuring the survival of humanity. So, it is quite fitting that
they be joined in a celebration of the sense of good taste.
Neither money, ideology, nor organised religion comes close
to having the same ability to weaken human willpower as
food and sex. And when they are combined – look out!

Once these primary needs have been adequately satisfied
we go on to establish a sense of comfort and security in our
surroundings. The second order of 'needs' that Maslow
identifies is the securing of a safe existence. Whether it is

growing up in an abusive environment or experiencing the devastating hardships of war, having to look over your shoulder lest the bogeyman is there leaves an individual with no time to be preoccupied by anything but the conditions of their immediate existence. It goes without saying that if you are vulnerable and unprotected – in the midst of a dangerous battle zone – it isn't going to be the best time to be looking for a new friend and lover or, for that matter, a piece of cheesecake. At this point, anything beyond survival is reduced to a ridiculously insignificant stature. It is only when a person can fulfil basic food needs, and is safe and secure, that they can actualise the yearning to find others to bond with over a 'butterscotch ambrosia torte'. If safety or hunger is an issue, this third level of needs cannot play first fiddle to staying alive. Feeling safe motivates a disposition to consider the pleasure of falling in love or of forming a close relationship with a roast beef sandwich. Who or what is 'in' and who or what is 'out' is settled on the basis of cultural trappings referred to as 'tastes'. Whether it be a burger or a lover, the better the quality of taste, the more appealing the food or the person will be. Anything that is qualified as 'good' stands out as attractive, simply by the nature of the definition. Since 'love' involves giving and receiving, and receiving something that is really fine is always better than getting something that is really not so fine, good taste begins to be factored into the process of establishing friendships and falling in love. It also doesn't hurt as a stepping stone to achieving Maslow's fourth hierarchy of needs that is perched above 'love and belongingness', and is proudly called 'self-esteem'.

Gaining competence or mastery of knowledge or skills accesses this level, which facilitates social ascent into a group or community. When a person becomes very good at grasping the principles of a discipline or practice, they can then demonstrate this understanding to receive praise from anyone who is interested in noticing. An individual who masters food preparation and flavour coordination can impress guests simply by way of a perfect pastisio sauce. A champion skateboarder will blow away spectators with awesome, superhuman feats, on, above, around and below the board. The talent displayed exists as a veritable source for achieving self-esteem. Knowing the countless subtleties that make interior decorating, cooking, painting and even courtship a kind of science in its perfection offers the observer a pleasure that establishes respect for the competence attained. Self-esteem, then, follows naturally into Maslow's highest level on the holistic hierarchy – 'self-actualisation'.

Self-actualisation involves having the confidence and maturity to realise objectives that direct personal goals. Individuals must be true to their own nature to achieve 'peak experiences' that ultimately externalise internal desires. Stances adopted in matters of taste offer opportunities to assert one's own ideals in a social setting. These distinctions constitute selections that challenge norms. A Parisian chef has chosen to include as a personal trademark for his line of chocolates an assortment of cheeses covered in chocolate. He has gone where others dared not venture and created an intriguing new experience for himself, his profession and his clientele. The personal commitment to be what you want to be and go where others go or even beyond where others have gone makes experiences personally meaningful. It is here that creative geniuses can strike out towards new horizons of good taste.

The most essential basic needs such as food and sex must first be satisfied if there is to be any hope of arriving at the higher-order needs and desires: love, self-esteem and self-actualisation. The stages of development progress from achieving a sense of physical and emotional security to experiencing a feeling of social belonging through accept-ance. The ego must be both well fed and secure in its construction of a personal and public identity in order for it to be ultimately ready to experience self-actualisation, whereby life is given direction and therefore meaning on a personalised scale. Maslow believed that human beings pass from one level of 'deficiency needs' to the next until they reach the highest forms of subjective awareness and happiness through acts of their own volition and choosing. Self-actualisation is really the key to self-fulfilment – satis-faction of physical desires the first stepping stone. At the highest level, 'needs' turn to 'wants'. The ego has the confidence and power to freely engineer and guide its own actions toward achieving personal goals and tastes through which the meaning of existence is defined. Nevertheless, the base motivating forces of food and sex can be stronger than the need to create a mental picture of success in order to help us feel good about ourselves. For this reason, it is quite easy to see why food and sex are not considered higher-order pursuits, but are nevertheless interrelated and need to be satisfied. They are basic drives that are similar, if only in the pleasures and pains they are both capable of producing.

The connotations and mental images produced by the phrase 'food porn' present some 'unique' challenges to the rational mind: this phrase could make eating a hot dog an ethical dilemma – simply because it might bring to mind the easy associations to be made between food and the anatomy. No matter what blinkers of Freudian analysis we may willingly put on to succeed at interpreting the hidden meanings of figs and melons in terms of their physical resemblance to forbidden erogenous zones, the similarity exists in the physical appearance as well as in the tactile pleasure of consuming the fresh fruit. But these simple and facile associations, without intellectual depth and moral sophistication, are of no real use to us in defining what the boundaries of culinary good taste and its effects upon us as a society of obsessively neurotic food addicts might be. Sure, a banana is phallic, and yet so is the Eiffel Tower as it pierces the undulating phosphorescence of the silky moist Parisian skyline. Even a teeny, weeny pencil that we manipulate each and every day to spill an uncontrollable fountain of words onto the pages of a daily calendar has the shape of male pudenda. (Some of the greatest philosophers – such as Jean-Jacques Rousseau and Jacques Derrida – have identified parallels between writing and masturbation as the spending of human spirit.) Psychologists determine our psychic make-up from the way we interpret ink-blots, dreams, etc. Sexual clichés go a long way toward explaining both why bananas are not often eaten by adults, especially women, in mixed company, and why people flock like lemmings to see the Eiffel Tower or any other perpendicularly erected, man-made structure of great height and girth. But these overtly sexual comparisons, no matter how titillating, reveal nothing about the aesthetic value and appropriateness of each object regarding the nature of its intended function. We have an innate tendency to notice how forms resemble each other, and thus to make associations between them that give them symbolic meanings. But always reaching for the obvious limits the depth of our imagination to a recitation of stock responses. The power of new sources to create meaning is drastically reduced, thus resulting in the most banal and hackneyed of interpretations. 'Food porn', as a term that will help us define good taste in food through its antithesis, has more to it than this. We will come to it later. First we need to look further into food – at the tensions between pleasure and guilt, between sin and liberation, which it embodies.

You Are What You Eat

In prehistoric times, long before gourmet kitchens produced the 'food porn' we know today, the 'natural', 'normal' and 'expected' foods would have consisted primarily of raw fruits and vegetables, and meat cooked over an open pit. The sensual appeal of the first ripe, juicy apple accompanying a warm summer breeze would have seemed like heaven on earth after a long winter of frozen water and sun-dried fruits. Berries, turnips, nuts and carrots more than satisfied the raw sensuality of naked tastes. But with the advent of formalised cultural cuisines, a hierarchy of culinary acrobatics accomplished by manipulating raw ingredients made the expectations of a meal much more complex. The appeal of the earth's simple treasures was lost to the buttering and basting of natural flavours accompanying the tasting of refined versions of the original ingredients. Cooking, like every art form, has its own set of rules. Flavours intended to please the experienced palate mean dishes full of blissful gratification. The treats that chefs churn out to surprise and satisfy the sensitivity of the palate are a far cry from boiled meat and potatoes. A simple diet of uncooked grains and fruits does sustain survival; however, it no longer achieves much of a sensual climax when compared with cultural kitchen masterpieces made by the hands of an expert. Shepherd's pie, baked carbonara, baklava, steamed ginger fish and apple pie have stood the test of time as favourite cultural pleasures.

Cuisine has developed into a highly complex affair, which is no longer simply about eating, but has become endowed with social rituals and significances. Certain foods and ways of eating are appropriate to certain situations, and entirely inappropriate to others. The kind of food set before a managers' meeting will quite clearly signify what kind of company the managers run, through the kind and quality of the food and place settings. A meeting for the executive board of a multi-billion-dollar corporation will differ from a meeting for the managers of a popular doughnut chain. Reversing the settings would make for a ridiculously difficult proposition. The items that flaunt the fabulous frills of the corporate world would intimidate the doughnut group. The common simplicity of the doughnut managers' lunch meeting would earnestly insult the traditions of the expected executive 'atmosphere'. A few choice questions can further illustrate the specificity of tastes that reveal the comfort factor of certain groups' rituals. What are you most likely to find at a dinner for parents sponsored by a boarding school that houses the offspring of royalty? Tablecloths made from custom-woven Liddell linens or plastic checkered no-slip table sheets? Seared beef shoulder tender with couscous and citrus-onion marmalade or stewed chilli with green peppers and double-butter garlic bread? Chocolate marzipan torte or jelly with whipped cream? Would the meal be a sit-down affair served on fine china, or would all the foods be placed in great communal vats on a table under a sign reading 'Best Buffet in Town!'? Would each course be served at its own designated time, in small manageable amounts, or would each person line up to put as much as they liked of too many dishes onto their plate? What choice of eating utensils would guests be provided with: multiple forms of silver cutlery for specialised uses covering each distinct course, or a plastic knife, a plastic fork and a plastic spoon? If the answers to the above questions are obvious, then the message is clear. The content and presentation have to fit the context appropriately. There is nothing inherently wrong with offering a buffet-style feast if the situation is appropriate: for example, a gathering of friends in a neighbour's back garden on a sunny Saturday afternoon. But you could not expect a business lunch for successful company executives to forsake formality for familiarity, no matter how well they were acquainted outside of the boardroom. Corporate decorum demands that the high status of the members be complemented in a salute to success by the high-status foods which are themselves rare and expensive. Having money and authority involves the serious pursuit of high standards. Rituals are created for the elite that would make the average person ill at ease with habits that are completely foreign to them – a fish out of water. In fine dining, a water glass is topped up after a sip has been taken. If you feel that you have to drink simply to make the waiter's efforts worthwhile, you will certainly be needing to relieve yourself more than you'd like. Shedding crumbs while indulging in the beautiful sweet-crusted bread will attract waiters who elegantly scrape up the flakes with their sterling silver tools. This pampering is familiar fanfare for corporate heavyweights who can appreciate the luxury their larger-than-life allowance affords them. Selection of food and strict attention to its formal elements as an exclusive dining experience exhibits the status values that are honoured. This social ceremony of eating is not overly simple, nor is it spontaneous or casual; it is wrapped up in the higher economic brackets and upper-class morality of the business world. Nothing really personal, just enough to make it seem so, for the required familiarity of professional relations to be established. Lofty expectations in etiquette are complemented by similarly lofty expectations in business. The friendly rituals are waded through for the sake of a successful financial equation. One's guard cannot be put down. Manners must be upheld. The refined tone of the meal affirms discreet standards for food preparation and presentation that in itself screams success – nothing more, nothing less.

Food porn relates to sensual subtlety and the intuitive quality of putting together tastes and foods. Often the unexpected arrangement of ingredients creates unusual flavour combinations that go beyond the common code of expectations. Chefs are forever experimenting with the unconventional positioning of foods to create refreshingly new flavours that successfully bend and blend in unconventional ways. Eggplant fritters with an arugula cocktail, or sweetbreads and scallops with savoy cabbage and an orange anise sauce are daring escapes from the normal and familiar nature of boiled chicken and rice. Creativity keeps the practice of eating interesting and appealing – eating and sex, the terms here are interchangeable.

Good taste in the kitchen involves the highs offered from stimulating menu items – roasted pheasant breast, stuffed veal cheeks, chanterelles and roasted peaches in double cream and brandy, or just a beautifully grilled, tender T-bone steak with sautéed mushrooms and onions. The list of pleasures, packed with possibilities, takes a person far beyond their wildest imagination to the land of quasi-illicit delights served on a plate. A flat ceramic dish can hold the meal that carries you away in the pleasure of culinary perfection – both in taste and texture. A fine-quality meal can transform a main course into a dream come true. Enjoying food provides a climactic experience of sorts that is all-consuming in the pleasures derived from the physical act of the melding, churning and chewing. It will put a smile on your face as long as you are not against the high fat content that a lot of decadent meals are about.

Unfortunately the typically fat-laden beauty of culinary delights consolidates the sinful nature of their allure. The disgust felt by health food fanatics who are stunned by the popularity of unhealthy cuisine does little to curb appetites for these rich delicacies. For many people, the physical gratification outweighs the benefits of healthy living. Public exposure to the temptations of junk food or 'rich' foods makes it virtually impossible for many to maintain a commitment to eating well. Nutritional health warnings of the deadly risks of habitual overeating are thrown out the door for the sake of a banana split made with Häagen Dazs ice cream, real milk-chocolate sauce and authentic whipped cream. Celebrity gourmet chefs, publishers, media moguls and restaurateurs have all had cause to rejoice. Although there is an increased awareness of the hazards of eating rich foods, it is usually thrown by the wayside on any or many occasions that warrant choosing from a menu of amazing temptation – and we're not talking an apple. Culinary *chefs-d'oeuvre* too often mean real butter, cream and fresh fried delights – the stuff that makes for a health fanatic's worst nightmare. This public obsession with rich foods that taste good has made oodles of money over the last two decades (or more), through lucrative merchandising rights, sweet endorsement deals, unstoppable cookbook sales, packed dining rooms, and exorbitant advertising rates on prime-time cooking shows. There have even been major motion pictures and bestselling literary fiction with plots centring on the cultural fascination with the 'joy of eating'. The book and film, *Chocolat*, is a story about a woman who breezes into a town with her daughter and sets up shop to sell chocolate. Her recipes of piping-hot pepper-spiked hot chocolate, moist cakes, crushed cocoa, truffles and rose creams entice a change in the puritanical sentiments of the townspeople. Through the sensual experience that accompanies indulging in bittersweet delights, they come alive to the physical pleasures of life – laughing, loving, singing and smiling. The sensuality of the palate liberates their pious fear of feeling passion. *Babette's Feast*, like *Chocolat*, is a story of how the forbidden pleasure of food in the end becomes the catalyst for realising the sensual nature of godly creations. In this case a Parisian woman moves to a small reverent Danish community. After winning a lottery, she asks permission to cook one real French meal for the puritanical townspeople. The town's citizens, terrified of falling into hell for the decadence of the experience, are determined not to enjoy the feast – they focus their concentration towards the heavens. Food and heaven quickly converge to form a blissful reality, as the townspeople awaken to the sensual nature of spirituality itself. Liberated and alive, they are better able to cherish the teachings of their beliefs. Similarly, the book *Aphrodite* is about a woman who defines her sexuality in light of experiences to do with eating and food. It addresses the sensual quality of eating using direct metaphors connecting the pleasure of food to the physical experiences of a rumpled bed, caresses and even an orgy. In the film *9½ Weeks*, Kim Basinger and Mickey Rourke use food to stimulate each other under the irradiating glow of an open refrigerator door. Foreplay includes milk showers, fruity kisses and the drizzling of syrupy honey on strategic body parts. There is even a blindfold that gives the action a hint of S&M. In overcoming the fear of forbidden fruit, the characters in all these fictional works discover the liberating power of food to entice. Other books such as *Like Water for Chocolate*, *Big Night* and *The Man Who Ate Everything* similarly have plots highlighting passions that stem from the sensuality of food. The forbidden pleasure of food is unveiled, leaving the viewer and the reader free to enjoy the sensual freedom of the experience.

The fictional vignettes highlight relationships with food that often become larger than life – the synergy of enjoying a luxurious meal frees one of the pious inhibitions that restrict sensuality. In real time, food can often serve as a surrogate for true physical contact. A plausible substitute for intimate relationships, it gives sensual gratification. There is no denying the comfort of a triple-decker ice cream sundae, a braised lamb shank or a chocolate éclair: it is a poor substitute for the date who just stood you up, but a consoling alternative all the same. Foods can reawaken dormant feelings of ecstasy and passion that are not always so easy to come by in the world of social relations. A flash-in-the-pan one-night affair can be quickly forgotten through the pleasures of a plate full of quality chocolates and cheese. Unrequited relationships are declared against as taboos, with pain and depression often accompanying a difficult break up. Ultimately, however, the impulse to enjoy food instead of worrying about whether someone is going to call can lead to unhealthy consequences. When overeating is used to compensate for unrealised relationships, the solution becomes part of the nagging problem – an overeating binge will often bring on the big guns of guilt. A crème brûlée is not going to get up and walk out on you, but it can become part of the problem when a relationship goes sour and an eating binge balloons you out of shape. Consuming a pound of excellent French Brie for a snack between meals may be ecstasy, but it will likely lead to the unpleasant reality of excess weight gain.

The media portray the guy or girl who gets the mate as the thin and beautiful one. It is not often that two overweight and less-than-attractive individuals are cast in the leading roles of a romantic drama. Whoever said that reality shows are what draw the audiences these days? Overindulging in rich foods is not healthy, nor is it attractive in that it suggests little self-regulation and concern about personal health and hygiene. Television offers an escape into worlds where experiences become virtually lived and understood through the examples the 'boob tube' gives us. Sit-coms of beautiful people being exceptionally heroic, funny, talented, intelligent, brave or brilliant are all about excellence and ideals. Any bad person or overweight person is coupled with a good, thin person to balance the equation into an optimism about reality – a yin to complement the unattractive nature of the yang. A show full of beautiful yins, however, does not necessarily have the token unattractive yang there to neutralise the fairytale. The law of casting seems to prefer the bold and the beautiful over the baggy and the bulgy. And although overweight individuals can themselves be extremely heroic, funny, talented, intelligent, brave, sensitive or brilliant, their 'unhealthy' image does not make for what the 'majority' channel into. The image of two large people performing erotic acts hasn't been a story line that screen writers have rushed to adapt. Plato believed that art should depict only the ideal states of humanity – he would have scored highly as a programming director in forecasting public viewing preferences on national broadcasting.

Food Porn

Food, then, although it affords wonderful moments of ecstasy in eating, is good for us only if it is balanced by temperance – quality in moderation. Ideal meals are not about excesses that run amok with a foot on the throttle of pleasure. Eating, 'uncensored', jeopardises quality of health and fitness. This brings us to that puzzling lexical equation, 'food porn'. *Food porn is a lack of self-regulation in the act of eating*, whereas good taste includes an appreciation for the preparation, creativity and presentation of quality dishes as well as an awareness of balancing health with the pleasure of eating. In a similar way, sexual porn in its raw sexual nature is a fragmented package – an incomplete image of the nature of sex. It is concerned strictly with physical pleasure that requires no emotional commitment. Adam and Eve were committed. They had to spend time together, get along, laugh, agree, disagree – agree to disagree – work, play, eat – sometimes even the wrong things. This is a story of a human relationship that was complex intellectually, physically and very likely spiritually. 'Porn' does not aim at reproducing a healthy code of social expectations, rituals and conventions that orient the norms of human relations. 'Food porn' thus suggests an obsession for the sensual, while disregarding the intellectual and emotional qualities of food.

Porn can become so habitual that it replaces the need for a holistic understanding of the phenomenon. The act of sex simply for the physical pleasure of it offers very little other than corporeal stimulation. Eyes wide open or shut, it really doesn't make much difference as long as the anatomy can accommodate the act. A healthier approach to sex is not only about the physical pleasure that it can arouse for the person – although this feature shouldn't be repressed – it should, at best, stem from a fun and meaningful courtship. If not love, then at least attraction is a prerequisite that sex becomes a natural consequence of. Healthy eating is a requirement from which quality living naturally stems. Avoiding nutritious eating habits until a doctor has to point out symptoms from a personal history of dietary malpractice is unfortunate evidence of a diet that is regulated strictly for raw sensual pleasure. An individual who strives to eat healthy meals does not want to enjoy their food any less than the junk food junkie or saturated fat lover. Good taste in eating involves choosing foods that appeal to the senses (smell delicious, taste fantastic and look great!) without forgetting the cardinal purpose of eating – satisfaction in *nutrition*. It is about initiative and self-regulation to accomplish the best of all worlds. An individual who eats healthy food – notwithstanding the occasional treat – understands the difference between right and wrong, good and bad. Their mental health is thus left unscathed by a weakness for eating piles of junk – submitting to the worst of 'food porn'. A person with a secure sense of themselves is aware of the dangers of pursuing habits that are detrimental to the maximum performance potential of the body. There is no value in sacrificing fitness, health and welfare for bad habits in eating. Physical pleasure works from the same principle of weighing satisfaction and fulfilment in relation to our well-being.

A person in a fulfilling relationship does not need to resort to a steady diet of erotic images to satisfy natural sexual drives. Intimacy, as a consequence of picking flowers, making garlands, taking Spanish lessons together, going on long walks and having romantic talks, builds a repertoire of experiences that make companionship meaningful. Viewing images of a sexual nature intrudes on an activity that typically is intended to be private. Too much may instil a sense of inadequacy similar to the feeling of going about enjoying food the wrong way – too much too fast makes for a self-esteem crash.

To illustrate the extremes food porn can take, let's consider the dream meal of an unabridged and uncensored teenager: lunch involves the pleasure of filling an empty stomach with a Kit-Kat, a Snickers bar and a jumbo bag of ketchup crisps – biting off the chocolate coating of the Kit-Kat, one wall of chocolate at a time, and savouring the milky cocoa gently in the mouth until it begins to melt away before swallowing. The wafer layers are then removed piece by piece with precision from the yet untasted parts remaining. The delicate crunch of the cream and wafers are savoured before being consumed. The erotic unfettered enjoyment is repeated in the two courses remaining – the

Snickers bar and the jumbo bag of ketchup crisps. Hunger has been satisfied; the sensuality of the food completely exploited. But what will happen to the individual if he continues to eat in this way every meal, every day? This lack of nutrition is not a normal and healthy alternative to eating. It makes, however, for a good example of food porn at its best – and worst. The teenager has cared only for physical gratification, with no thought to nourishment. Many other stellar examples of toxic lunches compare very capably to the previously described nutritional disaster. A dozen Dunkin' Donuts, a Big Mac 'Real Meal Deal', Cheesies, Coke and a hot dog, etc., etc., etc.: any of these experiences becomes lost in the blind unhealthy sensuality of junk food.

Good taste in food is the ability to recognise quality through understanding the rules that make eating a positive part of our lives. The appeal of the flavour should accompany the real benefits of a healthy approach to food and nutrition. Millions of dollars are spent to synthetically formulate food strains that don't need temperamental mother nature to threaten their availability. A crop of coke bottles will make it to the market whether or not drought and bugs have destroyed the availability and affordability of their 'Sunkist' competitor. Investment in scientific research ensures that the chemical additives used to conjure up and spruce up a desirable taste will win over the taste buds of the average unsuspecting kid. Young minds have no concept of the long-term health effects when it comes to delicious synthetic flavours. A Twinkie that will expire in three years is more desirable than a banana yoghurt that will only just make it to next week. The simple natural compounds of aged milk that are easily digested and broken down to fuel the body's various functions don't have a hope in hell if the youngster is free to choose between them and an Oreo cookie – even if the thickening agents and preservatives of its hydrogenated, chemically infused, fluffy white stuff have more in common with a polyester skirt than nutrition. In the long run the Oreo, Twinkie or any junk food will bog and clog the human machinery if it is not balanced with some real food. Deep-fried fritters, animal fat, creams and butter, even though they come to us from natural sources, exist as infamous 'weapons of mass destruction' when they are not consumed in moderation. Health consciousness and energy are the point and principle of good taste in food – it is about quality. A clear mind and sound body allow an individual the luxury of a quality life that is less likely to deteriorate because of poor eating habits.

The Slag of All Snacks

Let us consider a popular advertising campaign for 'Pot Noodle' that recently appeared in the UK. The commercials were first aired on national television during prime viewing hours, only to be banished to 'late-night' programming, and then completely banned despite their success, if not critical notoriety, among advertising consultants and popular culture commentators. Disgusted viewers complained vociferously to the Independent Television Commission (ITC) – effectively an industry watchdog and censoring body – about the adverts' mature content and sexual overtones. Consequently, the commercials were reviled as tasteless and offensive by the moral shepherds of the UK's media airwaves, and deemed not suitable for transmission at any time!

One commercial is set in what, at first glance, appears to be a 'red light' district somewhere in urban hell. On the surface, the scene has all the familiar markings of a seedy part of any major metropolis where a veritable cornucopia of nubile bodies is always ready for hire and the most unimaginable of carnal pleasures lurk just a payment away. But a closer inspection reveals a difference. Instead of languishing under the fluorescent hum of flashing signs calling attention to peep shows or live sex acts, the boulevard and its patrons are bathed in the neon glow of banners pushing triple-hot 'Hot Dogs', 'Live Food' shows and 'Burgers' to night crawlers seeking exotic forms of culinary satisfaction on the sly. Reeling from a repressed gastronomical desire for a variety of meals, the protagonist, 'Desperate Dan', moves through the truculent shadows of darkness, passing from one squalid drinking hole to the next, in search of anyone who will give him what he craves, 'something filthy, like a kebab but harder', to counteract the boring familiarity of his wife's bland home cooking of white bread sandwiches. That nasty 'something' is Pot Noodle – a gutstripping medley of dehydrated veggies, artificial flavours and chemical preservatives that stew and ferment the hydrogenated soya or enriched wheat contents of a plastic cup. Adding hot water makes this mixture a 'meal'. After speaking on the telephone to an anonymous friend who suggests Pot Noodle, Dan is indeed desperate to take a walk on the wild side. All he gets for his trouble is humiliation and generous helpings of abuse. Finally, after being slapped around a few times at the mere mention of Pot Noodle, Desperate Dan finds a companion of questionable virtue and taste more than willing to do the 'dirty deed'. She meets him 'round the back' where they cavort on a bed, shamelessly savouring a pot of noodles as their muffled pants of mock sexual ecstasy, uncontrollable gyrating and unadulterated moans of pleasure fill the stale air while they chow down. In the afterglow of that illicit moment, when the joy of eating has subsided into a pale reflection of momentary ecstasy, Desperate Dan confesses the contradictory morality of his actions and the full extent of his guilty satisfaction by admitting: 'That felt so wrong and yet it felt so right.' The commercial ends with the trademark slogan of the product: 'Pot Noodle – the slag of all snacks.'

The major thrust of the public outcry over the commercial was that the advertising campaign was guilty of not keeping with the ideals of decency and good taste befitting the genial morality of a civilised society. Most viewers objected to the use of the word 'slag' – meaning a woman of free and easy virtue who expects nothing in return for providing sexual fulfilment. The implication is that a 'slag' is to be used for the guiltless relief of bodily urges and thrown aside without worry like a dirty napkin. The Desperate Dan commercial plays with the cultural legacy of Pot Noodle in the UK as a product that provides an unpretentious form of quick nourishment and satisfaction – the main reason for its cult-like status among workers, students and just about anybody looking for inexpensive and filling eats you can make in a pinch without too much bother. Linking food with porn, the word 'slag' solidifies the reputation of Pot Noodle as a snack that is always ready to be had, is very cheap, and is ultimately most satisfying, even though it isn't necessarily good for you. This is precisely the point the company was trying to make about its product without deception, haughtiness or glossing over the reality of what it is – junk food, which is an obvious form of food porn. In fact, the commercial was more or less forefronting the public perception of Pot Noodle as an edible substance of low nutritional value that is enjoyed primarily by young people who want their appetite assuaged immediately without considering the health consequences.

The morality of eating junk food invades our consciousness every day almost like a sermon preaching fire and brimstone against the sin of self-slaughter. We can't avoid the ingredient warnings on the packets detailing in grams the high price to be paid for weaknesses of the flesh: it seems that heart attacks, blocked arteries, strokes, scurvy, rickets, tapeworm, falling hair, bad gums, bad breath and consti- pation can all be traced back to the stuff we put in our bodies a little at a time. And yet we succumb to the deadly temptation of saturated fats, glucides, complex carbo- hydrates, sugars, cholesterol, nitrates, monosodium gluta- mate, chemical food dyes and 'artificial preservatives'. Still, there is some ethical merit to the quasi-religious fervour of food phobia. It forces the overwhelming question: how healthy is a food that needs to be artificially preserved? For years, there has been an unconfirmed rumour that US army scientists have been working on synthesising a loaf of bread that would stay mould free and 'fresh' for up to 20 years. Even if it were flawlessly preserved, would you eat a mummified loaf of bread after almost a quarter of a century, even if it were still edible? Perhaps we might have to, when the taste buds have irreversibly 'soured' by being deprived of everything natural in a post-agricultural, post-nuclear age of scavenger mutant societies who have forgotten how to mill wheat or even what whole grains are. The Desperate Dan advert takes advantage of the dark side of eating that makes Franken-food fun, simply because we know we shouldn't be eating it if we want to live longer. Put in that way, the generous portions of guilt served up with every bite of a burger, chips or candy bar that we dare to consume on the sly, far away from judgemental eyes, help us get another mouthful closer to the grave. The 'I told you so' will make sense in the end. Now the question becomes: is the taste of 'anti-health' food so tempting that we willingly choose the low road?

Well yes! A raw ruby red Braeburn apple can pale next to the sinful pleasure of a fountain of praline cream. Tasting the 'forbidden fruit' is usually much sweeter, especially if it is sweeter. What is more tempting to eat: a piece of New York cheesecake smothered in sugared sour cherries with brandy sauce, or a celery stalk? Processed or not, most people enjoy the experience of eating rich food or junk food more than a plate of lettuce. The link between good taste and good health is not always made. All caution is thrown to the wind. Health doesn't matter as much as savouring the experience of stepping out of a boring domestic lifestyle to expand our dietary boundaries. Nutrition, as a principle guiding good taste, doesn't cut it when buttered, whipped, creamed and fried foods have to be turned down to get to a bowl of fruit. It is all too easy to go for the fatty or hydrogenated stuff, even if it hurts our health or makes us feel guilty, after the fact. The reward is temporarily fulfilling, the desire to try something intoxicating, satisfied. The underground and twisted nature of this bizarre desire to eat unhealthy food, and enjoy it, is very real.

The allusion to porn culture that is used to promote the self-consciously anti-health image of the Pot Noodle brand was thought by many potential consumers of the product to debase the principles of good taste and morality that television and the information media ought to support. In a survey conducted by the ITC, the BBC, the Advertising Standards Authority and the Broadcasting Standards Commission, 'slag' – the root of the controversy – was judged to be the 16th most offensive word in the English language. The marketing campaign was eventually banned due to negative public opinion. Pot Noodle, however, never sold better.

For some, it would seem ridiculous to take offence at what is essentially a commercial about textured soya. But morality – the sense of right and wrong – has traditionally defined what is taken to be 'pleasing' and 'beautiful' in accordance with what is considered to be 'virtuous' and 'decent'. When brought into the critical light of inspection that constitutes the public eye, the cultural value of any object or action is determined by the extent to which it can be shown to others without inciting feelings of shame or guilt. To say that 'unhealthy eating' in itself is 'immoral' or 'bad' would definitely be an exaggerated characterisation of the practice, even if it is unhealthy by nutritional standards. People have to eat, don't they? Many lack the time, money or savvy to prioritise nutrition. Therefore we go on cultural practice and folklore which the Desperate Dan commercial exploits. Pot Noodle, as the 'slag of all snacks', serves an important purpose for many despite its nutritional short-comings. The taste compares to the flavour of 'real' broth – a virtual grandma's chicken soup – and the product is cheap and filling. The commercial seems to be saying: 'Don't worry if you are eating Pot Noodle. There is no need to feel guilty about the good taste of your actions. Others are doing it too, just behind closed doors.'

The Pot Noodle adverts underscore the unsavouriness of the snack and parody the self-humiliating consequences of eating a junk food. The good taste of any object or repre-sentation comes down to whether or not it can be shown or performed freely without causing general offence and consternation to those who observe or use it. Pot Noodle itself is nutritionally valueless as just another example of pharma-food. Only we human beings can give it meaning and significance with respect to whether or not we use it as a quick-fix replacement for an unsatisfied hunger. The Pot Noodle advertisements objectify the product until it becomes a type of anti-food or junk food. Good taste is not always the result of a common, tacit and unquestioned judgement that is self-evident, if all other choices are or seem to be just plain wrong. Personal mediation is necessary to determine the value of a thing or a social practice. 'Junk food' undoes the traditional notion of good taste in food as it affords exemplary experiences of steaming 'simulated' broths that feel good going down. The physical and psychological consequences of satisfaction without any commitment closely resemble the nature of porn. Quick and superficial, its unrefined nature is void of healthy elements – making it a risk. And yet, some like it just for this reason. Restricting a specific behaviour often creates an inexplicable need to walk on the bad side – to flout taboos forbidding it. To break a taboo is to defy the unspoken rules that prohibit the expression of particular notions and words, as well as certain deeds and actions, for reasons of morality and good taste. Claude Lévi-Strauss refers to taboo as a culturally constructed prohibition against thoughts and activities with the potential for harming human life and dignity. Ideas and practices that threaten to bring about the dissolution of a social and moral order are dangerous. Because a taboo puts into cultural practice a judgement of morality against certain actions, it then encourages association with forbidden elements. An appetite for misadventure is initiated. We could say, as a concept, 'food porn' is morally twisted and consequently in *bad taste*. Which, of course, makes it wildly popular and attractive given that a taboo has to be reckoned with and flouted, and, when deconstructed, perhaps points to a sacred rule ultimately made to be broken just for the hell of it.

Rich Food

Food porn is about exploring the appeal of food by idealising its sensual possibilities to the maximum without consideration of the long-term negative effects. This is not, however, limited strictly to fast food and junk food. The 'food porn' junkie can also be an elitist. This 'higher' form is cut from a different jib than the 'fast food' devotee who revels in the lower forms of unhealthy food by flouting the nutritional taboo against it. The elitist food porn junkie eats only *haute cuisine* or 'rich' food made with pricey ingredients that are laden with buttery solids, triple creams, whipped creams and rich oils drained from exotic fruits. Like the junk-food junkie, the upper-crust junkie's concerns about health and nutrition are set aside in the crusade to achieve ultimate taste pleasures.

The elitist 'food porn' groupie intensifies the sensual experience of eating by enjoying the viewing process before eating is even considered. The acts of cooking and its presentation become as sensual and intoxicating as the act of consuming. The attraction of one texture beside another, the pleasure of one shape over the next, the red colour of the sauce on the tender green of the asparagus, are all elements soaked up with the naked eye. The delight is in the physical beauty of works created by those who specialise in staging the pleasures on a plate. The would-be culinary expert lives primarily by the motto 'I like to watch' rather than 'I like to do', simply because the skill of performance is lacking – not everyone can cook, even while following a recipe laid out very clearly in a cookbook. Voyeurism, however, does not come without a price and the succulent images seem more than worth trying. The psychology of human behaviour is governed by instinctual and emotional attractions rather than controlled and rational decisions.

If you have ever looked at contemporary cookbooks, chock-full of apostrophes to good taste and mouth-watering pleasures that one could never hope to make without divine intervention, you will know what I mean. Instructions for navigating towards the experience of consuming the lovely illustrations, including directions and terms that obviously originate from foreign vocabularies – terms like confit, concasse, deglaze, panko, posole – will serve to completely befuddle any hopeful aspiration of making the dish. The food preparation manuals, however, easily arouse the gastronomic passions of even the most stoic of eaters, making the pulse quicken and the lips wet, arousing cravings for oeufs en cocotte, crusted sea bass with shallots or Ballotine of quail with rhubarb and candied apples. Desires are created through the glossy displays of these gourmet dishes. Turning the pages with fingers sticky from the appetite of anticipation, one cannot help but pause on full-page centrefolds depicting intricately prepared delights of rare and abundant proportions. The colour photographs are exquisitely crafted for the food porn addict and the novice alike. A shock is elicited by the full-frontal exposure of a meal of such exquisitely seductive cooking that it is surely unattainable without years of apprenticeship in Europe's finest kitchens, but most certainly seems within the reach of mere mortals because we can see it and imaginatively taste its complexity. In such elitist cookbooks, the finest ingredients – sunflower sprouts, cane syrup, black truffle and freshwater crayfish – are combined in a manner which is so neatly described in cryptic prose that it makes the process seem 'oh so easy', until you try it and the results are horrific in your eyes because the requisite level of perfection was not achieved. The best recipes promote unprecedented levels of anticipation and heaps of performance anxiety – usually accompanied by words of consolation, after a premature declaration of the cook's proficiency in the kitchen. The disaster of a meal gone terribly wrong is realised too late to order Chinese take-away for dinner guests whose growling stomachs curtail any weak attempts at casual conversation prior to eating. Yes, you 'julienned' the black truffles that were procured from a centuries-old, family-owned pig farm just outside Aix en Provence and flown in to you from Paris on the first flight of the day. And you 'sweated' the fresh-water crayfish that were alive and well when specially couriered to you from parts unknown in a specially constructed, breathable water displacement container with multiple chambers, purity filters and pressure gauges engineered just for the contents of this dish. However, the meal still tasted less than perfect in your eyes. At least, not the same as the picture.

Of course, most of the world cannot afford to cook this way – with rare ingredients purchased at premium rates from speciality stores that are really foodstuff commodities brokers for the rich and famous. Some foods have more social capital than others. 'Sophisticated' upper-class tastes hunt out indulgences simply for the pleasure of finding masterworks to pamper the palate with. At these high elevations, prestige is measured according to whether you've tried the divine black bread from Castelvetrano or the crusted creamy butter of Caciocavallo. At a bed and breakfast in a bay of Lago di Garda the patrons are treated to fresh squeezed orange juice shaken for 30 seconds to be sure that the juice will arrive fresh and foamy to the client's room along with a house-made nectar of pears and figs. A silver tray holds a shining silver coffee decanter with fine bone china, and an exotic fruit salad alongside a beautifully baked croissant and muffin. The small vase of roses completes the treats served at morning bedside. Good taste is driven as much by the pretentiousness of 'conspicuous consumption' as it is by the attention paid to the formal elements of dining and the fine art of extravagant decor. There are frescoes on the ceilings and paintings on the floors, woodwork carved by angels and chandeliers shimmering by their own light. And everything is so beautifully displayed that it offers the patrons sources of conversation to share in formalising the decadence of their own experiences.

Chef du Jour

Food porn – high and low – is about having an excessive and single-minded, obsessive and almost manic interest in everything to do with decadence in food: eating and food preparation or cooking. In fact, the subject of cooking – talk about cooking, exhibitions of cooking – has preoccupied the radio and television airwaves as the food craze continues to work its way into the real and symbolic life of contemporary, post-hunting-and-gathering society. The existence of food networks televising cooking programmes that are re-run 24 hours a day is irrefutable proof of a widespread addiction to food. Ratings and market share demographics analysis in the United States bears out the fact of this phenomenon as house-bound wives no longer make up the largest single viewer group in an audience that now spans a gamut of ages, genders and professions. The most committed prime-time followers are males (37 per cent) and females (63 per cent) aged 18–54, within households with a $75K or higher annual income. These categories are divided into a majority of 'viewers who like to cook' and a minority of 'viewers who do not like to cook', a surprising 10 per cent of the total number. Men account for nearly 40 per cent of the audience, but they also account for 48 per cent of those who do enjoy messing about in the kitchen. College graduates aged 18–24, never-married singles and those aged 55 or over make up the rest of the non-cooking group. According to demographers, the male viewer is said to be attracted more by the aesthetics of the cooking show experience than the 'secret knowledge' to be gained about food preparation for fun and social profit that motivates a female audience. The programme *Barely Cooking* puts stereo-typical observations regarding the marketing of food shows along gender lines in a revealing light, given that the male and female chef co-hosts of the programme are practically nude, wearing nothing but an apron. Frequent shots from behind the kitchen counter expose the tan hue of their well-shaped legs and naked buttocks. The naked chefs work side by side, exchanging gibes and quips, while the conversation often turns to double entendres of 'whipping cream' and 'oiling your machinery'. The sexual tension between the man and the woman lies beneath the surface of the dialogue and eye candy drives the programme. So, a situation that seems a bizarre premise for a television cooking show becomes quite a natural spectacle. The invitation being: 'Why don't you take off your clothes and try this at home?'

Food and sex are often seen as compatible commodities – items to be freely traded by those with social and amorous aspirations. Casanova (who was able to seduce even the most unresponsive of women using aphrodisiacs), the Marquis de Sade and Confucius all knew the power of food and sex and their potential to seduce. As do the celebrity chefs of today, along with their publishers, television producers and marketeers. Cooking shows today offer generous helpings of food porn that parallel the real slap and tickle. Plenty of hand-held camera work, from all angles and positions – over the top, from the sides, around the back, looking up – allows the viewer to see all of the action in real time, non-stop and explicit. It doesn't matter that the final dish everyone in the audience lusts to feast their eyes upon has been cooked earlier that day, numerous times, to make it perfect, by fluff chefs who support 'the Star' as he will strain to achieve a culinary climax. The 'money shot' is worth it. That is: watching Emeril Lagasse sweat, growl and tease spectators in the brazen heat of a studio kitchen, tensing only slightly at the point where he reveals the pudding, so to speak, via a slow and lingering resolution expertly achieved with the precision timing of a Swiss watch; or seeing Nigella Lawson – the unashamed goddess of the kitchen – savour every last drop of the extra-virgin olive oil dripping from bites of prosciutto-wrapped asparagus stalks she has been expertly manipulating for a good while. One might object to the characterisation of cooking programmes as food porn. But any way you slice it, the label fits to a certain degree. Why on earth would a cooking show be called *The Naked Chef*, if it were not to infuse it with a certain sexual appeal and taboo attraction? The fact that the culinary protagonist is a handsome lad with features reminiscent of a young Mick Jagger in the peak years of the Rolling Stones circa 1975 does not hurt television ratings any. Having achieved quasi-rock-star status, Jamie Oliver has the women of the world eating out of his bare naked chef's palm. Tours, book signings and interviews dominate the world of the celebrity chef. Groupies aside, their impact on public opinion outside of cooking and food nutrition has been enormous. Celebrity chefs are more revered in popular culture for their deep insights on how the existential angst of the human condition can be relieved by simply getting busy in the kitchen than the great philoso-phers who have spent their lives patiently thinking through the moral conundrums of life's experience. They are shown more devotion for the psychic healing power of a well-prepared meal using garden-fresh herbs and spices than some of the sacred figures of religious movements whose actions and ideas have inspired the wisdom of ages. These chefs are given more respect for their ability to lay out how ideological differences can easily be solved at the dinner table over orange-glazed pheasant stuffed with foie gras and a cheeky bottle of early vintage Bordeaux than political analysts seasoned by years of engaging in diplomatic relations between warring nations. Has the world gone food mad?

Since time immemorial, humanity has been seduced by the quest for the perfect meal. Today, long after the 'stone age' crusade began with our prehistoric ancestors chewing the bark off a tree, eating a dead enemy or roasting a mutilated pterodactyl, the evolution of contemporary cuisine has moved away from the single main motivation for securing food: survival. Indeed, thanks to the rise of cultivation methods that enabled human beings to settle in agrarian-based colonies we now call villages, towns and cities instead of pursuing a nomadic existence, most of us in the developed world enjoy a relatively stable supply of things to eat without any worries about a shortage of abundance. In developed countries, thoughts of food have gradually turned away from the practical goal of securing sustenance for survival to the more complex desire of experiencing a variety of tastes simply for the pleasure of it. The greater the diversity of staples, flavours and textures, the better the eating. As a result of the basic nutritional needs of the greater population being superseded in most post-industrial nations, more and more attention is now paid to developing the sense of good taste with respect to food rather than agonising over how to get it. The palate has become more sophisticated and the tastes more bizarre. If you have any doubts just ask master chef Anthony Bourdain, the seemingly unflappable and elegantly wasted host of the hit autobiographical documentary *A Cook's Tour*. Chef Bourdain traverses the globe desperately trying to find 'the perfect meal' in the most exotic localities and hidden kitchens. If you can catch him between bites of smelly ripe durian (the sublime 'potty fruit' delicacy that reputedly tastes 'heavenly', stinks like a toilet, and is more addictive than absinthe), or wait nearby for him until he has finished scarfing down the still-beating heart of a freshly sliced live cobra, kindly let me know what he says about what tastes good. Advances in cooking and the availability of different food sources have helped to usher in a new era of culinary excess and tastes, both high and low. We are now living in the golden age of food porn.

CHAPTER FOUR

The Creative Substance

They say that time changes things, but you have to actually change them yourself

Andy Warhol

If nothing ever changed, there would be no butter-flies

Anon.

Within the last hundred years, the world has moved from horse-drawn carriages to supersonic jets, from carrier pigeons to email, from paper to the computer screen, from the photographic image to the television set. Our lives have been profoundly changed by the introduction of technologies and designs that have revolutionised the ways in which we interact with nature and with each other. It is unfathomable just how far human creativity can push towards new horizons of understanding and taste. We can never predict what will be 'the next best thing' to emerge from the imagination at some indiscernible time in the future. And that makes taste very unpredictable! What is 'hot' today may be 'cold' tomorrow.

Music, media, literature and fashion can spawn new creations of exemplary quality, if we are lucky. The best products of human ingenuity often work as examples from the past and the present that can help orient a 'better way' for the future – thus enriching the spirit of invention and pushing the desire for change. 'Better' means better than always having to resort to the same static models of creativity day after day, year after year, decade after decade, century after century. Good taste cannot be entrenched into a single frozen moment, but has to be living – a natural consequence of human evolution. Survival of the fittest means that the fads bearing the mark of 'great styles' and enduring habits are forever revisited in the guise of new twists on old archetypes. If good taste were to be timeless, then creativity would be of little importance.

But not all discoveries and inventions are 'good': the atom bomb, fast food, and cigarettes cannot be classified as creations that are the pride and joy of the human race. The atom bomb – intended as a deterrent to mass destruction and world conflict – left ghostly images of instant death to hundreds of thousands in its wake. During the 70s, the multi-billion-dollar market of fast food eating burgeoned with the prospect of saving busy consumers time and money. The low nutritional value, high calorific content and saturated fat levels of its products, however, have proved it to be as deadly an invention as the A-Bomb itself. Diets rich in blood-thickening processed fats have given heart disease an infamous reputation as one of the top killers of our time. The dried weed commonly known as tobacco – set on fire, inhaled and absorbed directly into the lungs and blood-stream – unabashedly offers up lethal tar stains to soil any hope for smokers of healthy living. Cigarettes have proved to be a leading cause of lung disease, which reached epidemic proportions years ago but today still destroys the quality of life of those who choose cigarettes as their own personal vice and recreational pastime.

Creativity – the source for discovering or manufacturing new options for public and private tastes – does not always produce inventions that are predictable or welcome. It all depends on many factors that influence the bittersweet fruits of change. We have to live for a while with the uncertainty of creativity and suffer through the pain of understanding different values, challenging ideas and provocative behaviours before tastes actually transform and are accepted as something fresh and exciting. New ways of acting and thinking are meaningful in relation to their long-term effects on us. We envision the world and redefine ourselves relative to the role our tastes play out through the experiences that make our reality. The goal is not only to live, but to live well!

The significance of individuality in today's society highlights the importance of creative insight as necessary for good taste. Social competition has given way to a sense of personal accomplishment through consumption. But one can't just buy anything. Why settle for a wooden chair when you can afford a gilded throne? Don't you owe it to yourself? Buying power is the key to expressing an individual sense of quality and taste. There are benchmarks of status and success that give others knowledge of us – a big house with a pool, a BMW, a permanent suntan. Ultimately, the goal is to please yourself, but nevertheless, the social obligation we have to buy beautiful things because they define who we are cannot be ignored. We all have a direct relationship with objects that bring self-realisation in a unique way through other people's judgements on our good taste. Thus, we have to be wise and creative in the consumer choices we make, or at the very least be aware of the images and values we project. Personal objects represent individual taste; although it isn't necessarily good all the time. Socrates may have said that the 'unexamined life' was not worth living, but contemporary consumer society has taken this philosophical statement in a whole new direction. The average consumer is filled with an almost obsessive keenness to understand and adopt new trends. Simply for the pleasure of it! The trick is in making what everyone else is buying your own good taste.

The Human Chameleon

We experience life in relation to the social rituals of taste that are determined by the cultural times we share with others. We observe 'correct' sensibilities, actions and attitudes as the rites of passage to a community. The tastes we encounter may be classic and seemingly timeless, radical and vulnerable, or perhaps detrimental to personal well-being. There is enough variety for everyone. But the choice to accept some and reject others is ultimately ours to make and change at any time. Whatever the style we choose, there is a consistently changing kaleidoscope of taste choices that must be adopted confidently as though they were a second skin. We must be able to change motifs and make the appropriate (quality) choices, comfortably slipping into styles, habits, dialogues and manners that suit any given social situation. Confidence is necessary if we are to engage and develop a cognitive and sensual appreciation for the principles that underlie a new trend. Fads are forever changing. So we must constantly make adjustments to compensate for our natural preferences so as to create an image of good taste and blend our individuality in with others. Like chameleons.

Fashion choices must be appropriate to the demands of different social settings. If necessary, we have to be willing to change our tastes at the drop of a hat or risk not blending into the scenery with others. Consider the wardrobe of a 'jet-setting' female journalist: she is expected to choose outfits and display mannerisms that suit the dynamics of the locals, places and spaces to which she is being sent on assignment. When in Cuba writing a piece on the natural beauty of rural life in a fishing village that is an ocean paradise, it would not be in good taste for her to wear the very same high-heeled black pumps and vintage fitted suits she wore at a venue the week before while covering an *haute couture* exhibition of Parisian designers. How would the local population relate to a foreign woman who is dressed in clothes worth more than the semi-annual earnings of the local families? In the same way, a funky, unbuttoned black cocktail dress and strappy shoes would work well for a writing assignment that involved the journalist covering the mad Manhattan nightlife of New York City. Linens or cottons, coloured in creams and whites and worn with comfortable classic flat sandals, would work better as a professional image for interviewing the fishermen on the coastal waters of Santiago de Cuba. To show good taste, all the journalist's choices have to be seen as attractive, appropriate and comfortable fashion options that are suitable to the social circumstances. Nothing less.

That is why the race for good taste in effect implies never a dull moment. We must be constantly attuned to the challenges of creativity and its 'proper' application. A style that has been around too long becomes tiring and less than desirable. The lack of attention given to it signals the need for innovation in designs that can make selections and choices popular and attractive again.

Tastes, however, are not always about practical new alternatives. When all is said and done, a lot of what has come down to us as a challenge to good taste is just about offering an amusing detour to the status quo of recognisable patterns. Why are all of these fads and trends that are throwbacks to the 70s now in fashion again? Well, their legacy has been so ingrained in the historical consciousness of pop culture that we have paid little or no attention to their resurfacing in fresh ways and innovative forms during this new millennium until it is impossible to avoid noticing. The 70s ended long ago. That much is true. However, the traces of the 70s have never left public memory and have been determining our contemporary sense of good taste for some time now. Without our consent, without our knowledge. I doubt that the Gen Xers of today felt a burning desire in their collective unconscious to wear flared leisure slacks and midi dresses made from indestructible man-made fabrics 'having the names of Greek shepherds' (Polyester, Pilamide, Polymer), as the critic Roland Barthes put it. So, fashion designers – those rich gatekeepers of human aesthetic evolution – all looked into their crystal balls and recreated the vibrant colours of disco prêt-à-porter in a selfless act of benevolence toward the kids of Baby Boomers who expressed a subconscious urge to experience the culture of their parents' generation. Give me a break! That scenario is too neatly constructed to account for insurmountable differences between individual taste preferences. All Gen Xers are not alike. Nor can all people born between 1960 and 1975 be categorised as Gen Xers. Understanding some of the curiosities of style in music, art, fashion and interior decorating that come to be 'in vogue' can initially seem like a ridiculous exercise in blind faith. Who could have predicted the current popularity of 'emotional rock' bands or post-Grunge 'EMO', velour jogging bottoms for women, Celtic tattoos and Art Deco? But it is here. So, we must keep trying hard to appreciate the excitement of 'the new' and balance it with the sentimental feelings of loss that we have for the expiration of 'the old' – or its well-orchestrated return. Only by being open to changes and attempting current trends can we find our way towards creative choices and the satisfaction of desires we did not know existed. New-spun fads replace the present winning, but waning, fashions with stimulating design alternatives. We have to acknowledge the new forms of creativity that innovation sparks because being open to change stimulates and invigorates us to experiment and try things we have not tried before. Not all creative adaptations work well. Yet how would we know without the adventure of attempting something new for the sake of change? We have to take someone else's word for it.

Many fashion trends have certainly merited high honours for creativity. In retrospect, it is difficult to imagine why anyone would ever have wanted to go where good tastes have sometimes gone. During the early 1600s, the dress of the French upper classes was refined and 'beautiful' in its ornate complexity – on a china doll figurine it would certainly look exquisite and ornamental. If you didn't have to actually spend the time, money and energy to put together the excessive regalia of intricate layers and accessories, nowadays it could be said to be very 'fine' and 'fancy', though in a very odd way by contemporary style standards. Today, however, in the age of comfortable and threadbare wear, it would quickly be evident that a daily fashion diet of restricting corsets, powdered wigs, gartered leggings, inflexible bodices and yards of stiff fabrics could easily wear one down and take years off one's life. Meeting friends for a morning coffee in the 17th century, just as many do today, would have meant hiring a servant, or possibly a few, simply to help you be properly ready and adorned before being too late even for afternoon tea. Men wore makeup, trendy white-frilled shirts made of cotton or silk, taffeta blazers, pointy-heeled shoes, breeches (perhaps with a 'cod-piece') and knee-high hose, and were adorned with curly, shoulder-length platinum wigs. They dressed, in all serious-ness, to be admired and envied by all. If a man decked out in the foppish style of the post-Renaissance French nobility appeared in public today – whistling happily on a barstool, codpiece and all – he might get much more than the muffled laughter, filthy jibes and toothy sneers from tipsy patrons he bargained for. Without too much trouble, our dimwitted courtier could perhaps find himself deflecting the unwanted attention of forceful police officers and leery psychologists called to the watering hole to investigate the scene of a disturbance. The outfit would be so far out of taste that the only way he could probably be excused for wearing it would be by concocting a cock and bull story about being on his way to deliver a singing telegram. And then – here comes the hard part – trying to get others to believe it. But then again, who is to say what is tasteful and appropriate? The 'Homeboys' of Hip Hop who wear their oversized 'baggy ass' jeans magically suspended below the areas they are meant to cover and protect have not managed to surpass the 17th-century French fop in defining a sensible and com-fortable fashion solution that is acceptable to everyone. And yet, we have to ask ourselves: is it worth taking the chance to try on a pair, just for a little fun? To see what the fuss is about. Yo!

Throughout history, many fashions we could call 'novel-ties' have proudly adorned the bodies of minds willing to define good taste. Some of the most unexpected designs and creations have become the signature pieces for the fashion sense of a cultural period. The Etruscan toga and laurel wreath worn by Caesar while governing the lands surround-ing the Tiber and beyond are synonymous with the ancient Roman Empire during its imperialist glory. The bowler hat has dubious origins. Some say it takes its name from William Bowler, who perfected a pre-existing version of the hat in 1860; others claim it was invented by John and George Lock for the Great Exhibition of the Works of Industry of All Nations that was convened in Hyde Park during the same year. But whatever its origins, the bowler became the prototypical English export of culture throughout the world from 1860 to 1960. Popularised by the vast colonial empire of the United Kingdom and the growth of the middle classes, it was known as a hat of unusual sturdiness and durability. During the Greek war of independence that started in 1821, the freedom fighters called 'Evzonia' wore the equivalent of a pleated, thigh-high white skirt, a crimson sash, a cutlass, a white leotard, a black fez with tassel, a dark vest embroidered in gold trim, and pointy turned up red shoes with blue and white 'pom-poms' on the end. Since Greece was under the rule of the Ottoman Empire for over 500 years, the costume has a Turkish feel, and its purpose was to inspire fear in the oppressor. How prevalent are any of these styles today? The toga has vanished, along with the laurel wreath. The bowler is virtually non-existent outside of rusty pockets in the British Isles. The Evzonia outfit is worn only by military personnel who guard the tomb of the Unknown Soldier at Syntagma Square in Athens, where it entertains tourists instead of causing panic in the enemy. The language of clothes is not universal. Fashions are rooted in cultural history. Styles are created and acknowledged within a definitive time and space and often for specific reasons. Ultimately, fashions are supported by those who wear the garments proudly. Any style of clothing survives under the desirable label of being in 'good taste' only for a short while. Eventually, a fashion falls into the pit of stale and expired samples of bygone days and fads that take their respective places as pieces of history in costume museums. Then, we describe it as 'antiquated' or 'traditional'. Sometimes clothing trends are dusted off and make small comebacks as designers look to the past and other cultures for inspiration on creative new 're-intro' possibilities to influence stale markets and tastes. But fashion is essentially timely. And therefore clothing is not eternal – despite appearances. No matter how pleasant or attractive a style may seem, with time it needs to fall to the sidelines to make way for fresh and exciting new possibilities.

There can be no monotony when tedious repetition is stripped of its value as an option. Although hard on the wallet, the short shelf life of a style does guarantee that trends change before there is time to tire of them, always giving way to youthful and invigorating successors. We are easily bored of the same fashions. *Homo stylisticus* has a short attention span and a natural inclination to quickly tire of redundant stimuli. So a lot of what is beautiful now has only a certain life expectancy. Variety sustains pleasure. Trends in clothing change with the seasons of withering taste, surviving for only fleeting periods as 'must-haves'. You must be careful to keep up with the game, because fashion manias will inevitably eventually become *faux pas*, as fashions fall out of style and you are left wearing anachronisms of taste. Mistakes will be made, but if we are to learn from them, the annual misdemeanours of good taste in clothing style that we make require careful attention. You have to ask yourself difficult questions to get to the truth of good taste: Why didn't I think twice before picking that skinny leather 'New Wave' tie to wear to little Joey's Bar Mitzvah?; How could I not have noticed that purple and green don't go together?; Who else will be in wide pin-stripe lapels?; Are narrow 'drainpipe' trousers really a leading cause of impotence in men over 40? We must pay attention as the fashion alarm goes off in our heads, signalling the end of one dress code and the beginning of a new line of attractive players and designs.

When a style has served its sentence, it sours into a category that the 'fashion police' of unforgiving critics in the media will describe as ridiculous, hideous, nauseating and outright dated. There is no second chance at redemption for the glitterati who commit a style crime. The comedienne Joan Rivers – the self-proclaimed judge and jury of good taste and fashion sense on prime-time TV in North America at 'Oscar' time – can condemn famous young Hollywood beauties to a lifetime of self-conscious insecurity and designer oblivion when making their wardrobe choices. The Academy Awards are the ultimate showcase of star-studded style, a fashion cornucopia of flesh and fantasy. They are the celebrity runway where some of the biggest name designers get to show off stunningly styled outfits composed for anxious stars trying to create images that radiate good taste. As publicists know, fame is about the 'the buzz' and how you control it. Many starlets have chosen to pay huge consulting fees for 'image counselling' rather than risk committing a style crime. Anything to avoid the likes of Joan Rivers tarring and feathering them with the stigma of bad taste for all the world to see: too much of a chubby thigh gets put down; a gown that is made of a swan gets the starlet called flighty; see-through bustlines are criticised as exhibitionist; a dress that plunges too low into the backside causes deeply retentive consternation; eye-popping, cup-spilleth-over cleavage is tacky; too tall tottery heels show instability; a plaid bow tie is old; wearing no tux is disrespectful; ratty tails are unwieldy. Actresses like Jennifer Lopez, Halle Berry, Sarah Jessica Parker and Sandra Bullock pay enormous amounts to image consultants, but in so doing hope to avoid the ridicule of making a style mistake of global proportions. The post-red-carpet rag trade waits on the judgements of the 'fashion police' then crazily scrambles to create reproductions of outfits and accessories catering to all wallets that will guarantee star-like quality in the design. The 2003 Academy Awards celebrated a 'Diamond Anniversary'. So chandelier-like earrings with dangling baubles the size of ripe pomegranates were the accessory of choice for many of the starlets. But these vintage diamond pieces would have to be borrowed from Madison Avenue or Beverly Hills jewellers wanting to flaunt their stately treasures. No self-respecting star would consider paying for the privilege of advertising a product, no matter how rare or exquisite. It just isn't done.

A new twist resulted from the Oscar precious gems trade show – coloured diamonds. Many celebrities were wearing new forms of rare and expensive rocks that can be bought in pink, blue and orange. Barbra Streisand reportedly just bought a pair in red – costly, but impressive. With diamonds being the jewel of good taste for the 'sparkling entertainers' of the year, the rare gem quickly threatened to become a popular accessory because of the high-profile Oscar night attention. Diamonds may be a girl's best friend, but money talks. The market was soon flooded with look-alike designs in brilliant colours – quartz and glass sufficing as an inexpensive alternative. After all, who would know?

Fashion enthusiasts differentiate themselves as often as they can from those who don't care a fig about style by keeping an eyeball on the latest fads and trends saturating the public sphere. Good taste never sleeps – it always changes. Keeping up with the light speed of fashion time means having the power to understand and assimilate what is current, desirable and suitable. Fashion changes – there is no escaping it. So why resist? Learn to adapt gracefully. Try to blend in naturally. Like a chameleon. Become part of the scenery. And fill in the ever-changing landscape of your own good taste.

Eating Out: Did You Say Two or Three Stars?

In a perfect world, having the ability to 'case out' attractive new design options means homing in on arrangements that are refreshingly different from the usual tastes around us. Twists of change and creativity offer an appropriate challenge to the status quo. But, from manners to dressing, decorating to eating, the choices we make have to feel like a second skin, and not like we are wearing a mounted moose on our back simply for the sake of conjuring up a creative bend on personal style. An original idea that is not at all hip and happening is a poor taste statement for any scene.

The exercise of 'choosing well' – kept alive and interesting by the need to judge between alternatives for new options – helps us to understand the psychology of our aesthetic predispositions. We need to consciously reflect upon our reasons for making the taste decisions we do: What looks and feels good? Why? What makes it work? What is the message conveyed to others? Does the incoming style or practice fit in with the tastes that are already 'IT' for the social groups that form our comfortable niche? How and why? Thinking about the way we make choices about new alternatives is a deliberate attempt to stay in touch with the forms that taste represents through us as the creative personality of an era. Attention to aesthetic detail gives 'character' and 'style' to a dress, a table, a shoe. Designers can transform these – like fairy godmothers, waving their magic pencils to miraculously change any old plain pumpkin into a very trendy golden carriage. Maybe even complete with mini-bar! The carriage has only till midnight to transform from gold to pewter, bamboo or solid blond maple, depending on the fabrics and fads that are enchanting in the era of Cinderella-choices. Objects without style have functionality, but no lasting social currency for good taste, no magic, no spark to delight, wonder and cause envy. Staying on top of fads, trends and fashions means following the latest accounts of attractive designs and understanding how they affect our experience. Tastes typically dodge any strict long-term uniformity and frustrate the possibility of keeping permanent ideals. What is good and beautiful is subject to many revisions as choices cut across society. Communities of taste are created around a freedom of choice and chance. Designers are at liberty to romance the public by offering tempting ideas that can be appealingly slipped into today's trends. Chance exists in the haphazard nature of creative inspirations come up with to initiate changes in tastes. Jewellery – beaded, tiered chokers, thick leather bracelets and dangling earrings – suddenly becomes an accessory of choice that appeals to the real expectations of a style conscious of its social place and setting. From long hair to layered hair, to softly spiked and streaked hair, identity evolves from moment to moment, year to year, by being synchronised with a group psychology. Personal choices don't always merit unending buckets of admiration. But a trend is well appreciated when a cultural following can signal that it is in good taste. There can be many different solutions to finding an appealing order to food, clothing, interior design, art and music to share with others. In the end the formula is a highly unstable blueprint that continually moves in new directions.

Nowhere is this more evident than in the act of choosing a restaurant. In the competitive field of culinary arts and fine dining, the desire for innovation has given rise to new, interesting and intriguing 'tastes' that reveal creative menu options and stimulating restaurant decor to enrich the sensual experience of eating. The contemporary mania for gastronomic quality and style has produced an incessant search for new dishes and fresh decor. If the medium *is* the message, as high priest of pop culture Marshall McLuhan said, the pressure to find a better meal is definitely being reflected on prime-time television, with food shows cashing in on the viewing and eating public's rising interest in cooking. Unwittingly, consumers are being educated in what to look for when considering a fine dining experience. Celebrity heavyweights like the influential and ageless Graham Kerr and the masterful 'Iron Chefs' are feeding the mania for finding new ways to savour culinary delights. Restaurateurs are sensitive to the influence of food shows and the lofty standards for innovation that are being set for the industry. The frenzy to create novel, aesthetically pleasing experiences for the palate has resulted in high-budget cooking competitions across continents and cultures taking place on the airwaves. The adversarial spirit of good taste in food preparation is clearly displayed by *The Iron Chef*. The Japanese cooking programme – complete with hilarious out-of-sync voiceovers for English audiences – is a kind of culinary olympics. The contest awards the winner the coveted title of 'Iron Chef' – an acclaimed talent in cuisine arts! Instead of using raw physical strength, coordination and flexibility, the competitors use raw ingredients and draw on their abilities to prepare, combine, heat, chill and serve in order to create innovative mouth-watering delicacies. The kitchen athletes – practising chefs with international reputations – are limited to a single main ingredient to be featured as a full-course meal, although anything can be added to it, and it can be cooked in any style. In one such case the appetiser, salad, *entrée* and even the dessert were all being derived from a sardine base. The chefs turned water into wine. The feat could have inspired poor souls watching at home to take out a can of sardines that had been lying dormant in the kitchen pantry for over a year and proceed to tempt fate, having borrowed some cooking tricks from the televised masters. No doubt, a painful realisation would soon become clear: creating mouth-watering masterpieces from bits of smelly sardines truly is an art to be attempted only by the masters of gastronomy. With its single thematic source, *The Iron Chef* gives us a glimpse into the imaginative process of designing tasty dishes as they go from pan to plate and then to your table. But could you recommend to friends a restaurant specialising in one ingredient? Signature dishes aside, probably not. 'Pass the tripe cookies, please.'

The gastronomic enterprise, like fashion, art, science and technology, takes pride in identifying the new, the latest and the avant-garde of cooking and style possibilities. Culinary taste at its best offers possibilities that go beyond common experience, thus extending the range of the palate for the better. But it never denies the value of the classic dishes that are passed on and enjoyed because they are respected as a culture's culinary representation of itself: pastas and pizza exemplify the Italians; hamburgers and apple pie define what it means to be American; souvlaki and baklava remind us of the Greeks; shepherd's pie and trifle are England's claim to classic culinary fame. Modern day cuisine has come to blend these traditions with an enticing unusual quality of food preparation and presentation.

If you are looking for a new dining experience, many restaurants now offer a fusion of ingredients and tastes that makes up a dining genre known as *nouvelle cuisine*. Innovation in cooking has long been respected by the French as forming a repertoire of new and exciting examples in fine eats. The best chefs have long been considered to be the most imaginative. It is appropriate, then, that the creative cross-culinary and multicultural experimentation of *nouvelle cuisine* is authenticated with a French title in the world of fine dining. Creative mixing, searing, reducing, whipping and basting of fresh seasonal ingredients satisfies the expectation of novelty in food preparation that makes or breaks a restaurant. More and more eating establishments are providing the client with menu choices where innovation and unusual combinations are tastefully served. This sort of gastronomic exercise demands a great deal of skill and knowledge. High-end restaurants that specialise in this kind of food arrangement attract attention by hiring or partnering with a well-known chef to plan the menu and provide input on the decor. Indeed, regular newspaper and magazine reviews and a system of guidebook ratings (*GaultMillau, Michelin Red Guide*) ensure that quality has to be proved before a high-end eatery can achieve fame, fortune and popularity. Should the chefs not be up to the challenge, the restaurant quickly goes out of vogue. Or it fades away into one-star oblivion. Chefs' professional freedom and reputation are acquired through years of studies in gastronomy – the culinary arts – and apprenticeship in 'the world's finest kitchens'. But still they must practise, practise and practise some more, to create spectacular new flavour combinations that entice their intended clientele with high-priced menu items. By mixing and preparing food staples in new uncharted ways, these kitchen stars become popular for their ability to create 'beauty' in a gastronomic sensation. Just as other performance artists are rated by their own professional academies, chefs can achieve cult-like celebrity status by demonstrating superior intuition and skill in combining and designing the elements of their art to create dishes that reconfigure standards of good taste.

To parallel this quest for novelty in menu items, the best restaurants also offer compatible musical interludes and interior design. From the complimentary valet service to the intricate embroidery barely visible on the waiter's vest, such attention to details establishes a distinct style that goes along with the food and makes eating pleasant, but does not distract from the serious business of fine dining. The musical selection is especially important in providing an acoustic backdrop that will encourage good digestion and plenty of conversation. In a restaurant that can charge more than a few days' wages for an *entrée* and a bottle of wine, you would be more likely to find medleys of Deep House Jass by the Street House Originals playing than 'Can You Smell That Smell?' by Lynyrd Skynyrd. The 'serious' dining establishment dedicated to prising open your wallet wants patrons to experience a subtle mixing of musical influences and tastes to go with the style in food preparation, but nothing too depressing or with an oppressive beat or moral tone that would dampen the desire to let loose your Gold card. There has to be no guilt or negativity associated with spending money to raise your cholesterol levels and shorten your retirement fund. The social ambience and promise of a good time draws people as much as the unforgettable brilliance of the cooking.

Likewise, in architecture and interior decor, many trendy restaurants are fusing designs, depending on the location and the client base they want to appeal to. Situated in a garment warehouse district, a downtown establishment wanting to attract '20- and 30-something' professionals working nearby – mostly single types, with plenty of disposable income – will make the environment appealing for meeting people and doing business. Being at the centre of an economic hub means that you have to associate having fun with making money. There are only so many hours during the day in which to socialise and get rich too. You can expect to see a long bar with lots of seating room. Adjacent to it, there will be a sunken dining room area situated a step or two below the main floor. To encourage human interactions, conversation and natural background noise, no televisions will be found – suspended just above eye level as in sports bars – to distract customers from looking around the restaurant. You could negotiate a deal as well as make a date at the bar. Young professionals are used to tight deadlines and multi-tasking. Stunning bartenders of both sexes mix drinks and chat up customers incessantly, while Motown horns punctuate any awkward silences with an infectious groove that makes you forget the missed opportunities of the day. A lounge area with deep sofas and *chaises* scattered around over-sized glass coffee tables enables more intimate conversation and a place to sign contracts or exchange furtive glances, business cards and phone numbers. The colour scheme would reflect a light-hearted seriousness to underlie the puritanical work ethic pervading the atmosphere, but also not detract from the most important visual aspect of the restaurant: the people. You could expect silver and black tones applied on smooth, shiny surfaces using clean geometrical lines composed of glass, granite and soft metals that suggest rare materials, an environmental calm and sophisticated 'coolness'. Exposed brick walls would make the space feel warmer and give it a sense of agelessness. Even though the restaurant is housed in a Victorian sweatshop, as evidenced by the hydraulic pumps and thick pipes that snake across the ceiling, the ghosts of industrialisation have been swept aside by the technological revolution. There is no guilt here. Such an interior design provides the visual dimension and feeling of 'upscale fun' in the physical plan that reflects the mindset and social culture of the young business professional living in an urban fishbowl. The style has to be economical and futuristic without barriers to seeing others at work and play. Competitive advantage is everything. From brunch to dinner, the food would cater to a bistro-style menu, for fast and slow eating, with speciality items of fish and pasta punctuating the protein-based cuisine of 'the Zone' diet. Too many carbohydrates make you fat. Eating has to facilitate both business and pleasure, but not one at the expense of the other. You could even buy the original art that is sold off the walls, if it makes you happy or you can use the investment to get a date.

Contemporary restaurants strive for novelty in cuisine, pleasing soundscapes and luxurious decor that represent a postmodern mixing of styles, historical periods and cultural influences. A variety of aesthetic openings means everyone can feel at home, and makes the fine dining experience welcoming to all, not just to particular communities of taste. And yet, individual preferences and choices are dependent on the moment and situation. Despite restaurateurs' best attempts to make their restaurants welcoming to all, the specifics of individual preferences mean that we will not always like what they offer. Taste is eclectic. It changes. If taste were static, the world of culinary treats that emerge in so many assorted forms would be bound to a shelf piled high with tired-out food trends going nowhere. We would all eat the same dishes, prepared in the same way, at the same restaurants, furnished with the same decor. Although good taste would be much less of a pricey affair, in the end, it would do little to keep things interesting. New styles of cooking, presenting meals and developing innovative aesthetic ideals for achieving gastronomic pleasures in the dining experience would be unnecessary if the standards of taste were set in cement. We are free to judge between what we feel is good and bad. Yet it is important to keep an open mind and willing palate. Tastes uninclined to budge beyond accepted routines would cause the demise of any creative initiatives to uncover buried treasures that have not yet seen the light of day.

Archie Bunker and Captain America

Sometimes we are tempted to take the easy road; the path well travelled. But always choosing the familiar route leads to a lifetime of unwavering tastes and, most likely, the boredom of stale ideas. 'No risks' equals 'no variety'. Individuality becomes lost in a stagnant battle to defend the choices that we have frozen ourselves into for the sake of aligning and validating our tastes with others. Safety has its own easy rewards. Rejecting current sources of influence outside the self that challenge the status quo keeps decision making shamefully uncomplicated. We just do what others do, think what others think. We can justify this attitude by saying: 'I know what I like. See, others like the same things too! So it must be good.' However, ideals, values and tastes that are locked into the style of a specific class, community or generation are closed to new ideas and innovative designs. They lack an adventurous, playful and creatively 'pleasure-seeking' side of experience that promotes growth by trying new things. As a result, a deficit of imagination culminates in depressing personal struggles: emotional instability, insecurity and unfulfilment. Alienation is spawned by the lack of desire to authenticate, question, re-evaluate and make sense of our likes and dislikes. A closed mind unwilling to open up to scrutiny and make novel choices in order to break with tradition cannot escape the meagre horizons and petty frustrations of such an existence. Such a person's idea of living a 'good life' is never challenging a tedious and insular sameness relative to popular opinions and familiar surroundings. This is because not enough thought is given to maturing as a person by breaking through mental, physical and emotional boundaries – taking risks. This myopic attitude of suspicion towards new ideas, fashions and tastes leads to a malaise and hostility towards creativity. Any and every aspect of change is rejected. Individuals who crystallise their ideas, tastes and aesthetic sensibilities quickly find a false sense of security in thinking that they can apply the same judgements and practices to all sorts of situations and always come out 'on top', no matter what the cause or context. They choose to ignore the fact that good taste is not an object to be stored in a box indefinitely and tightly guarded, a precious gift taken out and displayed unchanged and untouched across oceans of time. They forget: Pandora had a box too!

What can we say about the creative potential of someone who has no time for anyone or anything that does not agree with a personal agenda of limited and unchanging preferences about every aspect of society, culture, politics and human relationships? This character type – exemplified by the jingoistic boor Archie Bunker in the 70s American sitcom *All in the Family* – maintains a hyper-judgemental attitude and an all-round negative view of contemporary life. An inwardly focused nostalgia for 'the good old days' discriminates against anyone and everything that is not in sync with the highly idiosyncratic ideals, values and tastes of a bygone time. For Archie Bunker, freedom of choice and liberalism are the causes of what is wrong with modern American society. Too many tastes and values are eroding the moral fabric of society. Defending against a plurality of alternative lifestyles and revolutionary ideologies that put into question the ideals of the status quo, Archie Bunker exhibits a bitter resentment of 'foreign' ideas and cultures that borders on paranoia and delusion. But the negativity is in fact just the psychological expression of nationalistic pride gone mad and turned into a fear of change. This narrow-minded and surly prejudice parallels the rabid conservatism pervading the culture of conspiracy and suspicion in the United States that took root during the 50s. Through the post-war propaganda of Senator Joseph McCarthy, the seeds of anti-communism were planted deep in the American psyche. Archie Bunker is a reactionary mouthpiece for the conservative fear of change that defies scepticism. A detestable yet adorable buffoon who is always getting himself into trouble because of the moral absolutism he preaches ad nauseam to anyone and everyone, Archie Bunker has a great deal in common with Homer Simpson. Both are 'punch-in, punch-out' working-class anti-heroes, who like beer and TV, hate their neighbours, and are oblivious to the world outside their little domain. A doughnut could captivate their attention for hours.

Like his 50s comic-book namesake 'Archie', Bunker is a larger-than-life cartoonish caricature, a cultural image of naivete. Not an all-American teenager full of hope, adventure and optimism, but a bitter and loud-mouthed older man who cannot stand what has happened to the youth of today. He hates the jeans they wear, despises the 'rock and roll' music they listen to, dislikes their long hair, satirises what they read, ridicules who they vote for, condemns what they smoke. Not to mention the fact that they are not all staunch nationalists. Archie Bunker mourns the heyday of childhood innocence and the spirit of American idealism that are gone. There are no silly adventures to be had with Archie, Jughead and Moose in the lotus land of California sunshine. Rather, Archie Bunker reminds us that there can eventually come a time for the all-American boy to grow up and begin making sense of life as it is – not as it was. A time to take into account how and why the world has changed. Archie Bunker was driven to find the meaning and value of being an American in the cultural pluralism and urban decay of Queens, New York, during the Cold War. The problem was, he could not think beyond the rose-coloured memories of a past era.

The invention of the television and its proliferation at the end of the 50s enabled Americans to visualise a sense of self and develop a fierce national pride and cultural history. Both advertisers and politicians offered plenty of soap-box propaganda for those ready to soak up the bubble-gum-chewing essence of a Yankee-doodle identity. But before that, comic books were a major source of pop-culture character education that helped to develop aesthetic and moral ideals of taste and patriotism in young and not so young readers. Superman, Spiderman, the X-Men and Batman depict superheroes in violent conflicts that are motivated by ideological difference, not purely by violence. Moral messages about core human values, institutions and tastes form the subject matter. The stories are about love, revenge, justice, respect, dedication, citizenship, race, gender, sexuality, education, progress, work ethic, the state, war, friendship, loyalty, community and so on. Comic books are morality plays where you think you are allowed to choose sides. The problem is, there is only one *right* choice. Who do you identify with while the battle of good and evil rages on, Batman or the Joker? Today, the comic book genre is being transferred to the big screen because the stories are compelling entertainment and the themes contain didactic depth that can move an audience. The best film adaptations are not just an excuse to use special effects to amplify the abilities of the superhero. Because then it would be just as easy to glamorise the supervillain. They are successful because a cult of personality has formed around the superhero because of the human need to believe in 'The Great Equaliser', someone who will seek justice in a world that is often not fair to ordinary people. This moral sentiment that we see in the comic book genre is exemplified by Captain America. A superhero with a decidedly national-istic agenda, Captain America is first and foremost a symbol of the patriotism that preceded the entry of the United States into the Second World War during the Golden Age of comic book superheroes.

Designed by Joe Simon and Jack Kirby for Marvel, Captain America has been around since 1941. The story line is straightforward. Captain America is Steve Rogers, a sickly young man who wanted desperately to fight for his country in the Second World War, but did not qualify for the army after medical testing. With no other military options available, Rogers meets different criteria and is selected to be part of 'Operation Rebirth'. He undergoes a top-secret experimental procedure by taking a serum that turns him into a 'Super Soldier'. Juiced and bulked up, Steve Rogers becomes Captain America – a killing machine who battles German spies and saboteurs while waging the fight of good against evil. Captain America rode the wave of fervent nationalism and public spirit that followed the Japanese bombing of Pearl Harbor. His red, white and blue costume – complete with winged ears and bull's-eye shield – was decorated by the stars and stripes of the flag, 'Old Glory'. The symbolism was clear and direct. The common man turned superhero foreshadows the grassroots triumph of those 'good, old-fashioned values' of the United States over the 'axis of evil' that endangered life, liberty and democracy. Every conflict Captain America endured was a test of faith in the American way of life. Yet he always won! Just as America was victorious – before Korea and Vietnam. That is why the war-torn 40s have been called the Golden Age of the United States. During this tumultuous period, America effectively became a military policeman of the new world order.

Archie Bunker is definitely not a superhero. But, like Captain America, he is a cultural relic harking back to a less complicated era, a time when patriotism meant unquestioned loyalty to one nation indivisible. Archie Bunker is an anachronism whose ideologies and tastes build barricades around the American dream to protect it from invasion. His bigotry and conservatism support an ethos of nostalgia for the Golden Age of the United States before the fall from grace. Supporting the idea of a 'common decency' and the call for a return to traditional WASP values, Archie Bunker reflects the attitudes of a right-wing moral majority that considers any different perspectives to be subversive and un-American. The comfortable stronghold of a closed system of personal tastes and preferences that are static and uncreative safeguards against any threat to the ego of the citizen or the security of the state from the real world. Through Archie Bunker, we see how xenophobia and conspiracy theories rise up to offer psychological protection against an invisible enemy that is contrary to the American way of life. Gays, Blacks, Jews, leftists, women, the younger generation and college students are just a few of the groups he blames for what is wrong with society. In an age when the United States was growing prosperous, air travel and the construction of highways, tunnels and bridges connected parts of the country that were not previously accessible. It soon became obvious to the middle classes that not all citizens of the United States looked the same way and spoke one language. The battle over recognising difference among individuals and communities rages on today. The security of single-mindedly holding on to an ideological framework supported by a blind nationalism makes forming an opinion of what is good and what is bad simple – since every other choice can only be just 'plain wrong'. Archie Bunker represents the Cold War generation of self-centred, God-fearing, communist-hating Americans, not immigrants, who desperately want to hold on to the nostalgic image of the United States as the land of opportunity. A country where people have equal rights, where men are men and women are women, so long as they are straight, white, non-denominational patriots who fought in the war, voted for Richard Nixon and love the bomb. Those were the days.

Home Sweet Home

'Your home', it has been said, 'is your castle.' A humbling abode where you can be yourself and keep the world at bay. How we choose to decorate the space we call 'home' – the place we are exposed to more than any other – affects the psychology of our existence. Carefully assembling a pleasant environment that accents current design principles and features the latest domestic gadgets goes a long way in demonstrating the personal development of our good taste to others. It can also be an inspiring learning experience through which we get to know more about ourselves and the reasons we make the choices we do. A person who loses sight of the potential for emotional and spiritual growth that can be achieved by making changes to their habits of taste gets trapped within a maze of redundant stimuli that sustain a banal, uneventful and even cruel existence. Design choices influence lifestyle and reflect attitudes towards living.

Stepping into the living room of an old house that served as a striking example of good taste in its time is like entering a museum. Immediately, it becomes evident that extra-ordinary care has been taken in the selection and arrange-ment of every detail and object within the interior design. But a setting in which nothing has been moved or altered for four decades can be a little unnerving in its strange detach-ment from the contemporary world. The yellowing tinge of age seems to infiltrate every piece of furniture in the room. Hand-sewn lampshades, geometrical ashtrays, blowfish-shaped vases and ancient copies of *Reader's Digest* magazines exude the stale, musty odour of permanence, although they are quite clean. Even the billowing purple, blue and red crystal vases, once imported with care from Czechoslovakia, reflect a jaundiced, filmy yellow tinge from years of being stuck in the same spot, rendered immobile on the same tawny coffee table with sculpted legs, in front of the same forest-green synthetic, square-armed couch bearing an old water stain that has symbolised the spoiling contents of the room for what seems like an eternity. Once upon a time, this room was the very picture of good taste: from the tear-shaped crystals hanging off the light fixtures to the now mustardy, plastic-coated dining room chair cushions and the fraying cloth grille of the RCA short-wave radio/record player console occupying the corner. Basking brightly in the glow of all its painstakingly deliberate faux textures and intricate deco designs, the decoration was proudly displayed. Once this picture of good taste had been carefully painted, the image was left alone, as if it were Michelangelo's Sistine Chapel, beautiful for eternity – a classic masterpiece.

To the owner, the room that taste forgot must have seemed so to be a work of art. Generally, functional items that are used and abused every day are not considered creatively unique or aesthetically rare enough to be referred to as 'art'. Commonplace objects like hats and watches are usually called 'cultural artefacts' when they are no longer available. Unless, of course, the symbolic value of a design is so innovative and stylistically important that it can be displayed as an artistic creation of historical importance. When an object is simply an uninspired and functional replica of a mass-produced model, many of us think it is no longer in the running for 'greatness'. Most artisans, designers and collectors know better than to follow this line of thinking. After all, entire museums and galleries showcase the beauty of the functional arts as well as the decorative arts. Antique furniture, vintage automobiles and designer clothes are obvious examples of 'useful' objects that have residual cultural value as historical artefacts of style and taste. Everything from motorcycles to toasters can be collected and displayed for pleasure. But the archiving of objects always happens within the social context of taste judged by others. There are unique museums and collections that feature unexpected products and obsessions many of us would find strange, petty or perhaps downright offensive: the 'International Museum of Toilets', the 'Museum of Questionable Medical Devices', 'Crushed Pennies Collections', the 'New Orleans Voodoo Museum', 'Vintage Telephone Equipment Museum', 'The Gallery of Monster Toys', 'World Famous Asphalt', the 'Burlingham Museum of Pez', 'Vintage Vacuum Cleaners Virtual Museum', the 'Sherlock Holmes Museum', the 'Museum of Dirt', and the 'Museum of Menstruation and Feminine Hygiene Products'. Beauty and taste are in the eye of the beholder. After Andy Warhol, should we be surprised that someone thinks of the items in these museums – or a beer can or Band-Aid container – as works of art? No. But that does not mean they are. And nor is interior design. Works of art are timeless; interior design is not.

Updating a living and functional decor with an eye towards contemporary design trends helps to sustain the feeling of currency and gives a spry appeal to a tired setting. A style inevitably becomes aesthetically benign if it continually offers up a well-worn set of stimuli. Given that the creative possibilities and choices available to us are growing and many, something 'new' can always be interjected into something 'old' to embellish a sense of design and make it uniquely eclectic and refreshing. A sustained or repetitive noise begins to grate on the nerves and irritate the emotions because of the continual similarity of tone and cadence. In the same way, our visual field needs relief from redundancy – of shapes, textures and colours. The constant sameness of a pasty beige splashed on the walls of a room without the relief of complementary hues tinting the upholstery and floor coverings frustrates our natural desire to draw stimulation from a setting that has the potential to energise us. We travel to exotic holiday destinations and explore far-away lands for a broader cultural experience that will leave us feeling mentally refreshed and spiritually content. Change is equally appealing in fashion, if clothes titillate the mind, free the body and please the passions by serving more than their obvious function. A new toy is exciting and fun for a child to play with until familiarity diminishes its ability to excite. Then, much to the disappointment of the parents, the child plays with a discarded cardboard box. Something that is 'brand spanking new' indeed attracts our attention, for a while. Until the psyche gets saturated with the content of the experience. Bored, we then move on in search of objects and activities that can renew the sense of happiness, meaning and positive energy we crave. And yet, we need the structure of routine and the comfort of identifiable actions and objects to feel at home in the world.

Repetition of elements is not a totally unattractive principle in design and in real life unless it becomes an obsessive compulsion. Human nature feeds off familiarity, in moderation of course. Since we need to feel 'at home' in the world, when we encounter an object or situation, we relate to it by searching through a mental encyclopaedia of shapes, symbols, relationships and schemas for relevant frames of reference. Repetition is necessary to a degree within any design for it to be understood and received as 'good' – basically, because it activates the mental archive of shapes, forms and colours we already know and identify with. It creates a comforting rhythm through the familiarity of certain beats. Repetition helps us to be at ease in settings we are experiencing for the first time when there are signs and symbols we can relate to from our own history. The familiar elements we notice and take in allow us to interpret and accommodate the feeling of newness without anxiety. Repetition prepares and acclimatises human perspectives toward what is new by blending the differences of innovation with what is already familiar and identifiable. Creativity builds layers of new experiences over the ones that have come before, like the ripple of waves that spread when a stone is thrown into a calm pool. Circle upon circle, a wave is created from the current of a previous wave, which influences the start of yet another wave. Good taste in design can never be completely original but is touched by the tastes that surround it. Similarly, any attempt at exact repetition cannot yield identical results. There is always a difference between the original and the copy; although it may sometimes be difficult to determine which is which. The antiques road shows that have been popular for some time now on global television make a point of situating the artefact to a historical period through an analysis of style and design. In this way, the experts can identify copies, fakes and forgeries. What they are looking for are repeated features and unique markings that authenticate the piece without a doubt. Only then is a Tiffany lamp or Le Corbusier 'Pony Chaise' valued, but in relation to the products designed and manufactured by artisans and their peers at the time. The more distinct and original the piece, the greater the cultural and artistic value, if well preserved. A fake or replica has limited worth, because it does not have a history that authenticates its value as the original does. If there were an identical copy of an original Picasso it would still have value, but much less than the original that was painted at a specific point in time and has accrued a genuine cultural value. This realisation should be of no surprise. Cathedrals have an architectural structure that is related to matters of faith and the science of engineering. It is easy to identify the style and appreciate its historical and spiritual value based on elements of design and religious symbols (e.g., a bell tower, crosses, arched doorways, parapets, a nave, narthex, gallery, stone vaulting, iconography, vestibule, altar), but Notre Dame is not the same as Lourdes and Chartres.

In relation to interior design, paying attention to the principles of coherence and unity is critical to establishing a balanced image: a room that is made busy with too many unrelated variables and styles does not succeed in creating the comfortable impression of an ordered design. Unless, of course, disorder is the intended theme that serves as the 'unifying element' or 'common thread'. In this case the intentionality of the arrangement effectively ties all diversity together, like a surrealist painting by Salvador Dalí, where clocks appear to be melting off trees and unusual juxtapositions and proportions seem to defy the laws of physics, and yet the scene makes perfect sense in its consistent disharmony of images. Interestingly enough, a style that uses disarray in colour, shapes or textures to instil a creative look and rhythm through a repeating motif of discord can serve to unify a decorative arrangement. Chairs sporting symmetrical checks and crisp stripes can be mixed with deeply embossed pillows, the borders trimmed with fringes and glass baubles. Sleek lamps, sculptured neon vases and flea-market side tables with peeling paint complement the focal centrepiece of a glass dining room table containing a wooden trough planted with a patch of bluegrass when the emphasis is on creating unexpected and whimsical motifs. The interplay of opposing colours and the pairing of disparate patterns or textures infuses a decor with the dissonant appeal of contrasting tastes. The approach creates a stimulating and aesthetically fecund setting based on a planned expression of chaos. Interior decorating that excels at combining seemingly disparate elements and styles reflects a postmodern aesthetic. The sense experience is primary here, fed by the need to create something new that surprises or shocks, challenges and pleases a heterogeneity of tastes out of existing designs. Playfulness and irony come to be valued more than seriousness and tradition. Function is a secondary consideration in postmodern design as meaning and integration of styles are privileged. Still, an interior designer must labour through a guiding vision to create a *pastiche* of styles that work together by using a wider perspective to enhance proportion, balance, rhythm, symmetry and the scale of furnishings. If not, the confusing array of seemingly unrelated artefacts, odds and ends, serves only to agitate emotions rather than please taste. A complete lack of repetition in design results in a lack of unity and cohesion – a sense of chaos that leaves you with a sickly feeling of unease in the pit of your stomach.

A common design element – a colour, a pattern, a texture, a shape, whatever it may be – instils a consistent and meaningful creative order uniting unique components. Establishing thematic threads or stylistic echoes builds visual continuity and aesthetic equilibrium. Attractive design possibilities that heighten interest and pique the senses are stimulating and attractive when unity is achieved through the repetition of some element – colour, texture or pattern – and the parts begin to work as a whole. The different and singular elements become integrated into one. A lot of repetition, however, leads to boredom. The dullness of a never-ending and unchanging experience denies the possibility of pleasure. Routine is boredom incarnate. The apathy it produces makes us slaves to habit. There is little if any likelihood that the adjectives 'exciting', 'stimulating', 'enjoyable' and 'intriguing' would be used to describe a design whose guiding theme was routine. The mother of necessity would not have been invention.

In the world of art, the transforming nature of taste is as obvious as it is in design and interior decorating, fashion and the culinary arts. Often the political and social circumstances of a culture influence the themes and images that begin to surface on gallery walls and in artistic works. Art movements have repeatedly proved to be linked to the changing cultural dynamics and interests of a society.

Impressionism came into being at the end of the 19th century, a time when the magic of a photographic image was new enough that artists were intrigued by the question of how painting could be compared to these perfect copies of vision. Impressionism sought to understand the scientific nature of vision and then render it onto canvas. The style focused on depicting the atmospheric effects of the external world by emulating light entering the retina by way of hundreds of rays that bounce off objects to tell us what colour the object is. Without light there is no colour. Illuminating sunlight using specks or dabs of painted colours offers a visual experience similar to the scientific realities of colour theory. The exciting phenomenon of light and colour was revealed. It allowed for an explanation of why colours from nature are always so much more vibrant than colours from the palette. Every colour we see – red, blue, yellow, orange and violet – reaches our senses with hints of alternative rays of colour infiltrating the purity of the predominant hue. The external world and the radiance and brightness of colour in nature were revealed in atmospheres of impressionist colour application.

Expressionism, a movement that displaced impressionism, challenged the art world's preoccupation with merely displaying the external effects of light as it illuminates the atmosphere. The external world of light and colour had been beautifully validated through impressionism, establishing the grounds to search out alternative visions to assert through the arts. The First World War was about to begin. The psychological unrest and disbelief of the barbarian acts war brings with it established the stage for a change. The political drama left no time to lament about colours displaced by sunlight. Serving to establish the new style, war-torn Europe offered a setting perfect for the expressionist art of the early 1900s. Clashing and twisted colours, lines, textures, shapes and forms all symbolised the violent and desperate ugliness of war. The style contrasted harshly with the innocence of the people and families afflicted during war. On expressionist canvases, intense colours like blood reds dominated by stark blacks and whites replaced the delicate serenity and pastels of the impressionists. Calming sunlit forms were taken over by nightmarish apparitions engrossed in shadows and jagged angular lines that writhed with agitation. The style was a reaction to the social circumstances that legitimated the value and personality of the expressionist. It lasted until a period when the social mood was again to change, in need of relief from the constant reminder of what horrors people are predisposed to.

Creativity is playing with ideas – discovering how to make something that did not exist before come alive, out of the energy expended through the imagination. Innovation is the result of learning to put together new and familiar ideas in different ways. Creativity can be a fundamental quality of good taste. It may not be economically sound or psychologically healthy to be altering the interior of one's house every year, but the fact remains that inspirations for change stimulate and excite the mind's eye through transformation of scenery. A perfectly attractive and functional Kimbel & Cabus chair is replaced because the cushions and wood-work convey the interests of last year's modern gothic style cycle. Let's say Japanese traditionalism resurfaces with the vengeance of a butterfly wing silk screen, for no obvious reason. Out goes the Kimbel & Cabus chair into storage. As do the colonial revivalist cherrywood hutch created by the Potthast Brothers around the late 1800s and the Ettore Sottsass geometrical, polymer laminate, multicoloured pyramid desk. Only to be replaced by a small Scholar's desk with side drawers, a simple bench and a honey-stained Kaidan Densu or an oak cabinet with staircase shape from the Meiji Period. The furniture reflects a reverence for economising on space. The multiple drawers and compart-ments of the desk and chest promise 'a place for everything and everything in its place'. The Japanese style of furniture building advocates the natural beauty of simple materials, design, balance and formal unity over a flashier, lacquered, geometric complexity. Putting creativity aside for the time being to address material concerns, change is sometimes arbitrary. It is dependent on whim or timeline more than logic or need. The current styles will lose their market attraction too, when furniture trends are again redefined in the sketchbooks of the top designer portfolios next season.

Manufacturing Good Taste: The Creative Process

Yes, the desire for change promotes creative growth. But the latest design is almost always preferred over the previous model simply on the precarious assumption that 'newer is better'. Styles have to keep changing in order to be desirable and attract attention. But this regular cleaning-out of dated wares and decorating practices provides opportunity for designers to retool their skills. The unrelenting process of the 'new season' presents a creative challenge to make over our sense of good taste. But the transformation doesn't happen overnight. Before any design makes its way into your living space, it has passed an appreciable amount of time as an idea in a designer's mind, a sketch or a prototype that may or may not work as a final product. A style becomes fashionable only when consumers buy it and welcome it into their lives.

One year, for no good reason, the change of designer focus can mean revisiting classical ornamentation – dark, lush, grained veneers and stains, elaborate embroidery, triple-tier mouldings, patterning, textures and tassels. But even the most valued craftsmanship that we see in the Chippendale or Hepplewhite 'art furniture' of the 18th century or an *escritoire* from the reign of Louis XVI has an aesthetic shelf-life, despite the astronomical cost. Feeling emotionally drained and aesthetically fatigued from endless exposure to Neoclassical, Colonial, Baroque, Rococo or 'too much' of whatever the theme of the day has been, a designer suddenly comes up with a 'new vision'. They throw it all out, intricate curves, textures, head-spinning patterns, for something less that will offer more in innovation. A few designers will notice and feel the need for a change in their own creative focus. Not to be undone or left behind, more and more follow the trend and produce momentum for the new vision to gain force.

This clearing-out allows the newest organisation of space to be showcased. An area wiped clean of anything that has unnecessary curves, embroideries, tassels or trinkets manages a look that is minimal, at best, a break from ornamentation on overdrive. Open spaces and simplicity replace sensual complexity as decorating journals cultivate a lack of interest in the dated and expiring images of overworked frills found on every surface. Fads change and the new styles work their way to the hearts of those who feel the interest and financial ability to redecorate through the visions set up for them by world-class designers. Reference guides for decorating illustrate interiors with the latest popular fads as they are reconfigured in thousands of successful ways. But this daring new intruder to the world of 'how to beautify your interiors' must first be accepted by the 'pros' who study the phenomenon of interior design. Designers applaud a concept that they then make popular through the appealing choices they set out in order to display their own take on the fad. Competition feeds the fire to exemplify strikingly hot new alternatives to decorate by. Modernist designs are gradually pushed to the forefront once again as exemplars of good taste. Retro fever suddenly swells. Tastes arrive in waves of relatively uniform definitions and dimensions to adorn an era. The young and hip prodigies of the design frontier begin to offer advice and directions to the consumer public on the decorating paradigm shift. Everything you wanted to know about 'what is hot' and 'what is not' begins to proliferate in the sources of popular culture we encounter around the city. New fads serve as refreshing changes to the tired modes of the past by way of their uniqueness. Scaled down ergonomic sofas with or without arms, industrial chic stainless steel toilets and neo-geometrical form-fitting chairs multiply in home furnishing stores. Modernist decorating takes simplification of form to the max as it multiplies and spreads. The general public – who must usually wait for the production of affordable replicas of designer furniture – participate in a gradual appreciation of the trends made popular by example. Copies are mass-produced. The 'high culture' artefacts of designer furniture are sooner or later consumed in a lower-cost, ready-made form by the everyday shopper who reads newspapers, listens to the radio, gazes into display windows and notices billboards. Having been introduced to the new wave of good taste by way of media outlets in the form of printed and televised images, we want to see more and more of it to better understand how to arrange a similar trendy decor for ourselves. To our relief, the latest methods of interior decorating in 'Modernist Style' find their way to be shown in the eight-by-ten and full spreads of trade magazines. *House and Garden, Better Living, Architectural Digest, Dwell, Your Source* and *Architecture Now!* soon feature the preferred style in the homes of celebrities, ordinary people and architects. The power of innovation and creative quality established through example is often enough to persuade us, the consumers, to throw out items that in previous times were our favourite daring new conquests of taste. As the new ideas are filtered to the general population, they are sold through the media by examples set out by the rich and famous who have the means to keep up with the changing styles. *Famous Homes and Hideaways, Homes With Style, Rock the House, MTV Cribs* and *World By Design* are decorating programmes that are more singularly focused on consumer voyeurism and curiosity about the way the glitterati live. Spacious rooms from Beverly Hills to Manhattan are seen wiped clean of anything that has unnecessary complexity, embroideries, tassels or trinkets that might disrupt the flow of positive energy through a space. Makeovers are recommended, initiated and featured on *Changing Rooms, Trading Spaces, Designing for the Sexes* and *While You Were Out*, where 'Before' and 'After' shots show renovation-bound singles and couples working at transforming the living quarters of strangers, friends and relatives in the good taste style of the day. The television designer hosts illustrate the latest popular fads and give advice on how to reconfigure light and furniture in thousands of successful ways to achieve the flavour of the day.

Most of us need 'gurus' to show and tell us what merits attention when creating a brave new look that exemplifies contemporary styling, thus demystifying our path to good taste. New styles that intrude into the world of 'how to beautify your interiors' must first be explored by design professionals who demonstrate the successful use of tangerine or lime as a primary wall colour – the decorating neophytes are inspired. We consumers of taste are informed of new styles through literature and media that illuminate what the professional designers showcase as the prototype for their latest ideas. Motifs are passed on to millions to apply in their decorating with flair and confidence. The emergence of high-profile designers sustains the 'buzz' created by a wide distribution of stylistic guides and models. The media scrutiny signals the shift of creative standards on a large scale. Public taste preferences follow suit. A homogeneity of style results.

Good taste is further cemented by the limited menu of choices imposed on consumers by manufacturers who synchronise their product inventory with the current trends. The availability of a Phillippe Starck 'Eros' chair to the buying public depends on the market demand forecasted for the product. If designs are not produced, they cannot be acquired, so if you happen to feel a creative twinge and want to find a brown and mustard sofa with orange piping, you are out of luck unless the designers and manufacturers happened to experience that very same twinge. Market availability and affordability determine the tastes that will nourish and flourish as furniture on your living room floor. Projected consumer demand and the cost of manufacturing and marketing all affect whether an egg-shaped see-through plastic receptacle supported by a polished aluminium rotating base is a viable design for a chair. Can the retailers envision the public gaping at, sitting in and wanting to purchase the contemporary look? If the promo pictures in the magazines pedestalled by top designers do not promote the image of the chair as 'sexy' and 'popular', there is a good chance that the design will be one of many that never make it to production. The more exposure a design is given, the more familiar and attractive it becomes, and the more likely it is that it will be in great demand by those who crave creative, up-to-date possibilities in their immediate surroundings. Strong media presence and marketing create physiological desires and emotional cravings that make a particular design seem as attractive as a cold glass of water on a hot summer day. Megastore furniture showrooms such as Elte, Pottery Barn or Ethan Allen display stylish interiors that are so appealingly arranged that they inspire the shopper to buy the whole kit and caboodle. No questions asked. Boutiques or smaller dealers showcase designers and decorators in the same way as art is showcased in a gallery. It is after all about a visual experience that we must make a qualitative judgement on. Experimental pieces are placed side by side with traditional favourites, allowing independent-minded customers to mix and match forms and styles according to taste. The new design can be acquired without having to prematurely oust a particular favourite held over from a previous trend. Fads come and go, but when they are at their peak of popularity – still with a future ahead – they offer a satisfaction that quenches an innate desire for change. When a style becomes a common practice of the general population, its widespread acceptance signals that the time is probably near for tastes to find a new style of legs to stand on that will be able to support the next exciting phase of designer-inspired templates to decorate by.

Feng Shui

Taste is above all a phenomenon of culture and time – past, present and future. Classic styles from the past will always be needed in the present. Human beings need sources of stability to complement transitions. Contemporary designs often turn to look at the manifestations of interior decorating styles throughout history. And classic styles will always prevail when the imagination is uninspired. But taste is not static, and these classic styles are often eclipsed by the creative and ever-changing ideas of the present. Fads and trends change, sometimes without much notice. It seems as if new styles work their way into homes across a country without mercy, swallowing up what signs of good taste are already there. The desire to be 'up to date' consumes the hearts and minds of those who feel the social pressure to 'keep up with the Joneses' and have the financial ability to redecorate their worlds with a blank cheque. Brand new styles surface as taste alternatives to the 'same old, same old'. Now, everyone wanting the good taste of contemporary trends in design has had to acknowledge the influence of Feng Shui.

The Feng Shui look is purgative. It is a break from the elaborate, neoclassical interiors, the eccentrically detailed, unaffordable and impractical forms of good taste that have in the past characterised the 'stately home', as an ostentatious demonstration of extreme craftsmanship, rather than a place to live. Open spaces and simplicity replace frilly excess and material complexity. Feng Shui exhibits a cultivated and studied lack of interest in the otherwise appealing images of exasperated designers juggling intricate shapes and busy textures. All of which are now *passé*, so yesterday. The practice of Feng Shui (pronounced 'fung shway'), currently popular among professional designers and hobbyist decorators, is the ancient Chinese art of object placement. Translated, the phrase means 'wind and water'. In Feng Shui style, spaces remain uncluttered and materials are 'stripped down' to reflect a sense of connectedness to the organic building blocks of creation. No plastics are allowed. The basic elements of nature that are required to harness or encourage the flow of energy currents, or *chi*, are used in decorating a dwelling. These substances are earth, wood, fire, metal and water. Feng Shui works by the unifying principle of balancing comfort with style to bring good luck, well-being and prosperity into a building. The idea is consistent with the Western supernatural tradition of 'geomancy' – reading and manipulating the influence of natural structures on human lives and fate. Feng Shui may seem like supernatural mumbo-jumbo to some, or the hallucinatory aftermath of a granola-eating fever to others, given that it is connected with homeopathic cures and New Age philosophy in the Western consciousness. But is it really a coincidence that the great sea-faring explorers Marco Polo, Christopher Columbus and Sir Francis Drake were born in landmasses located on major bodies of water? Or that beach-front property is the most sought-after real estate? The sea induces a vision of exploration and also has a calming effect. In the years before air travel, the sea-faring nations produced the world's first explorers.

At any rate, the origins of Feng Shui can be found in ancient astronomy and Chinese folk wisdom, Daoist cosmology and philosophy, as well as the *I Ching*, or *Book of Changes*. The point is to apply the healing power of *chi* to the design or arrangement of objects and possessions within a living or working space to counteract the flow of negative energy (*Sha chi*). A simple illustration of why Feng Shui is important is the parable of the crooked man:

> There was a crooked man, and he walked a crooked mile,
> He found a crooked sixpence against a crooked stile:
> He bought a crooked cat, which caught a crooked mouse,
> And they all lived together in a little crooked house.

Existing in a 'crooked house' has filled the man's life with 'crooked things'. Before you can straighten things out, however, you must know something about what has made the man crooked. The areas of interest that are applied in home design and link Feng Shui to human life are *Yijing* divination (from the *I Ching*) and astrology. So you must analyse and evaluate the crooked man's complementary and antagonistic relationships with the world surrounding him by looking at how he lives. This can be done by identifying the areas in the crooked man's life that need to be brought in proportion because the energising *chi* has been blocked: social relationships, family ties, work satisfaction, career worries, financial obligations, love life, creativity, health and so on. All problems can relate to a lack of balance between heaven, earth and humanity reflected by the material arrangements of the crooked house the crooked man lives in. Feng Shui will work to improve deficiencies by counteracting the yin of negative energy with the yang of positive energy and defeat a destructive cycle with a creative cycle. Depending on his year of birth, oriental astrological sign and psychic orientations with nature, the crooked man could benefit from changes to his living conditions, short of moving out of his crooked house.

There are many schools of Feng Shui. The most authentic versions are over 4,000 years old and are based on the compass or arrangement method, astronomy and mathematics. Some are more historically rooted in millennia of theory and practice, and therefore more credible, than others. The pop psychology forms of Feng Shui that concentrate on raising your belief are severely frowned upon in Asia by today's practising masters as a mockery of the true teachings. The 'new age' form offers you 'cures' and the promise of creating purifying and 'lucky' places in your home such as 'relationship corners' and 'wealth spots' teeming with red money packets to encourage the flow of cash. These hybrid simplifications represent the Western mindset gone awry. You can recognise its ingenuous symptoms by the generous use of *Ba-Gua* mirrors representing the yin and yang cycles, wind chimes and bamboo flutes. Among the more authentic schools, the advice may vary, but the ancient system is based on the Yin and Yang, the Five Elements and the *I Ching*. Classical Feng Shui is referred to as 'Compass, Form, Eight Mansions and Flying Stars'. One of the tools a *Ba-Gua* and Five Element Feng Shui practitioner will use is a compass (*Luopan*) that represents eight cardinal directions. Each point is marked with a trigram consisting of 'Yin and Yang' combinations and associated with the natural phenomena (fire, earth, lake, heaven, water, mountain, thunder, wind), the five elements (earth, wood, water, fire, metal), human attributes and a beneficiary (ranging from youth to old age and covering family relationships such as son, daughter, mother, father). Numbers and colours are also defined by direction. The way these factors relate to one another reveals what is happening at an invisible level of energy flows.

Let us take the south, for example. It is considered to be the best compass bearing because it promotes fame, fortune and festivity. Selecting a house that has a north-facing entrance is not preferable given that the coldness, bleakness and blackness of winter is suggested by the direction, as is death. The Chinese place so much importance on the south that they navigate from it and put it at the top of maps. It is the direction of summer, containing the element of fire, the colour red, the number nine and the animal spirit of the bird. Still, one can offset the negative energy of the north by using the element that characterises its positive *chi*, water, to initiate a creative cycle, not a destructive one. In Feng Shui, balance is everything. So, placing running water, in the form of a fountain or tap, close to the entrance of a house counteracts the negative *chi*. It begins a creative cycle: water nourishes plants and trees, thereby creating wood; wood feeds fire and produces earth from its ashes; the earth gives up its ore to make metal; metal brings forth condensation to create water. And thus we are back once again to the beginning of the creative cycle of elements, a cycle that is always to be repeated. Water also symbolises wealth and the flowing of money and so works well with a north-facing house because it feeds this compass point's orientations toward career and business.

Likewise, with a knowledge of the importance of directions, their characteristics and spheres of influence, it is possible to create good Feng Shui or make a positive adjustment to remedy an unfavourable situation by making changes to the spatial arrangements of objects in a room. All you might see in a lavender room with honey-stained wood grain floors is a plain oak bed, a glass-topped desk with metal supporting legs, a cloth-woven chair and a wardrobe. Not artefacts that say, 'Look at me, but don't use me.' You would not think any out of the ordinary care had been taken in the selection and placement of the objects. But if the room was situated in the southernmost corner of the house, the lavender colour would symbolise wealth and prosperity. As would the number four, taking into account the pieces of furniture – if they belonged to a 43-year-old man born in the year of the Rat (1960).

The arrangement of the furniture would also be purposeful. The foot of the bed would not be in line with the entrance to the room, as this is the traditional death position in Chinese culture. Nor would it be located under a window, a sloped ceiling or roof beams. Heavy paintings, shelves and cupboards above the bed are to be avoided, as is furniture with sharp corners. The body should not be left exposed to injury during sleep. The position of the bed would also depend on what was on the other side of the wall. It would not be placed near a wall that had a toilet or kitchen stove on the other side. Nor would it be placed facing stairs. A more favourable location allows the person in bed to see the door, in order to avoid surprises during sleep, and a mirror can help to reflect around the room the positive energy taken from the sunlight – assuming there is a window. But the mirror must not reflect the sleeping body and has to be positioned so as to allow the person in bed to see the door, if it is not visible otherwise. The desk should be facing the door head-on or from the side, to have clear knowledge of who is entering the room, and it should not be directly facing the sun. It would be impossible to read or write while blinded by ultraviolet light rays. The wardrobe would be placed opposite the bed, on a wall adjacent to the desk. Mirrors, live plants, chimes, candles, water fountains and crystals are used as talismans to enhance the positive *chi* circulating around a home to maximise the ability to achieve a harmonious alliance with the environment (Earth) and the cosmic spirit (Heaven) via a creative cycle. Feng Shui is a very involved philosophy that largely extends the examples given. It requires a thorough knowledge of the whole house, its inhabitants and their relationships, the contents and floor plan, and what is done in each room, as well as the interior and exterior structures affecting the building, both natural and artificial. It is no easy undertaking!

Understanding a design theory and decorating trends, so that you can effectively put into practice a vision of good taste, signals a mastery of the concepts at work and play. Depending on the quality of the finished product, the exercise shows to others your ability to assimilate the new information into a successful work of art, desire and culture. Fads and trends do not typically arrive on our doorstep in the form of a style that will decorate an era, solidify a movement and promote a universally-agreed-upon philosophy of beauty in action. Design choices are modelled by those who have defined taste towards a discrete system of aesthetic options for reasons that are both general and particular. But it takes time to establish a cultural tradition of decorative and life aesthetics like Feng Shui. Trying to reinvent the wheel could prove to create a problem – maybe even a square wheel – a very ineffective solution to living expectations. That is why we must understand the history and utility of a style, always respecting its conceptual underpinnings, if we want it to serve as a suitable alternative to models of taste familiar to us. You cannot accept what you do not know. Designs confirm their staying power when the suitability between form and function is recognised and imitated widely as an acceptable practice of good taste. When we do not understand the dynamics of a system, the solutions may fall short of accomplishing the intended objectives, for example, exacerbating the presence of already bad *chi*. There are many who call themselves Feng Shui practitioners by appealing to an 'intuitive' application of its design concepts and arrangements. Nothing could be worse than passing off a lack of genuine knowledge as 'expertise'.

Tastes are always expressed in entirely different ways as time passes, always borrowing and growing from past knowledge and trends. Objects, places and practices become dated and devalued, thereby creating a need for new possibilities that offer novel experiences. The differing dimensions of taste make the challenge of finding pleasure and satisfaction in the world around us a real and important problem, since the psychological effects are both lasting and meaningful. Thus, a bigger picture of community and the question of where we belong within it is always at the forefront of any consideration of taste. Tradition creates clusters of similar likes and dislikes. Free choice alters the patterns of our understanding and the aesthetics of the world through the immense potential for novelty. Were group attitudes on taste always to stay the same and be unified, there would be no effort to reconsider the precedents of good taste. Our aesthetic preferences and desires would be uniform. Good taste presupposes a systematic understanding of features that have an established groundwork in what sort of choices are suitable and functional for a community and its way of life – but always in relation to our own needs and beliefs. A fad gone stale – for whatever reason – means any new choice must take its cue from workable alternatives that reveal valuable and useful design options to replace the styles the critics and public are tiring of. Good taste has a history and its future must evolve from past forms to indicate an appreciation of what changes can be meaningful and beneficial to us and to others. Hot trends and flashy designs can sometimes prove to be ill-suited to the ways of a community at large. That is, if its members do not show a sincere belief in the lasting value, proper application and usefulness of the style. Overindulging in any 'new thing', simply for the sake of change, soon creates a satiation of desires and appetites and leaves plenty of room for innovation and experimentation, good and bad. In the worst case, gimmicks and unsound ideas take over. Then, good taste is lost in a missed opportunity for creative growth. Originality flourishes because we as human beings have short attention spans that feed an inspiration to produce something 'new' out of something 'old', all the while trying to remember which is which. There is a misconception that good taste is timeless, never in need of re-evaluation. On the contrary, the desire for change enables new understandings of the aesthetics of the world to take place through the immense potential of novelty to stimulate, shock and please. Creativity and originality refresh and redefine the past habits of design, and decorating necessitates recognising new visions of good taste that provide daring alternatives to the usual players. Feng Shui most certainly challenges the ways and reasoning behind how we in the West have taken to making the aesthetic choices we do.

Walking Like an Egyptian

The grandeur of imperial Egyptian decorating was about preference for colossal statues in basalt and granite, statuettes, scarabs and papyrus paintings that inevitably told stories representing the realities and beliefs of the civilisation. These were the items of a symbolic and religious life that inspired the royal interior decorators and architects to invest thousands of working hours in modelling precious metals, woods, stones and paints. In Ancient Egypt, wall decorating was as much a focal point for interiors as a sofa designed by Paolo Piva would be in the modernist style of simple upon simple. The point was to demonstrate the luxurious and prescribed tastes of the culture as an ideal reality. Walls were not decorated by applying a coat of Ralph Lauren paint in the latest popular shade, and then hanging paintings of a pleasing figure, a boat or flower, on the wall. Rather, there were scenes depicting real life, but also related to cultural mythology, the lives of gods and pharaohs and historical events. The Ancient Egyptians prioritised the decorating of walls with painting and writing to beautify as well as to educate and reinforce public memory and beliefs through interior designs. The practice was an important expression of cultural fervour, popular history and spiritual inspiration, as is highlighted in the interiors of ancient buildings, palaces and tombs. Walls became an art form in themselves as scribes carefully followed the ritualised patterns for depicting stories of gods, kings, nature and the slave classes. Standardised and stylised representations of human and animal forms paired up with hieroglyphics, columns and large statues to decorate the rooms. The cultural and religious fervour of the times promoted the visual beauty of highly prescriptive and decorative choices for wall design. A narrow band of allowable techniques formed the stylistic templates for the art. The complete uniformity of form demonstrates the era's clear and definitive take on good taste in interior design. The rhythmical repetition of only prescribed and specific motifs was fashionable and evocative. The walls represented a powerful combination of artistic renderings for aesthetic pleasure. Through painted images and hieroglyphic columns, decorated rooms radiated the beauty of intricately patterned motifs that created a place for the rhythmical movement and identification of the self in space and time. When the eye looked to the surface forms for diversion and entertainment, it also found instruction about what it meant to be an Egyptian. The systematic beauty of the stylised designs and hieroglyphics created a bond between the visual structures of a painting and delicate signs of the writing that is incredible to behold – especially now, given that the artistry and craftsmanship cannot be reproduced exactly and do not have the same religious significance or cultural motivation. Among the Ancient Egyptian royalty and ruling classes, painting and interior designs retained, for thousands of years, a style that has little resemblance to what decorators are doing today.

Archaeological excavations have revealed huge rooms and passageways containing large stone statues all sitting stiffly, hands on knees, with elongated head-dress and squared tunic, in the expected style of royalty. On the walls, men and women stand stiffly caught in motion, heads turned forward in two-dimensional profile, while a single wide eye looks out at you intently. Seemingly, it follows you around the room. The torsos are somehow twisted unnaturally into frontal view, strategically adorning the profile. Shoulders are in full perspective, arms and legs in side view – positions only Harry Houdini could have considered. The stylised perspective was the Ancient Egyptian prescription for tasteful depictions of the human form. It allowed the spirits of the afterlife to take an inventory of the physical features that the pharaohs possessed while living, so as to duplicate them exactly following the death of the body. The accompanying hieroglyphs formed a textual commentary on the significance of the scene, but it was a history told in pictures that represented concepts and ideas in a way similar to the Cyrillic alphabet and the Chinese ideogram combined. For a long time, the markings were indecipherable. When the code of the hieroglyphs was eventually cracked, in the 19th century, it opened new paths into the mysteries of Ancient Egyptian civilisation, avenues toward understanding the history and social practices of a once powerful, dynamic and influential culture that are still being explored today.

The decoration of walls today in public buildings and private homes is fairly banal in comparison to how the Ancient Egyptians embellished the blank slates of their plastered stone enclosures. We think we are being very daring if we paint with a colour that is anything more intense than the grainy, neutral tones of the Sahara desert sand dunes. Egyptian wall decorating was an elaborate mix of text and image that has never re-established itself as a measure of what is tasteful in decorating. Even though there is archaeological evidence of the practice in other ancient cultures, it would look decidedly strange if you had a mural on your living room walls that depicted the history of your family through feast and famine. Gone are the hand-crafted visual swags, the overabundance of gold leaf trim around the edges of full-blown scenes of heroic struggles and epic battles. The only parallels we know of today in Western society that reflect a symbolic pleasure for telling stories by writing and painting on wall surfaces exist in the form of street and toilet graffiti – hardly the traditional symbols of good taste in decorative motifs. The literary and pictorial commentary of graffiti art is typically created in protest against social injustices or just for humour and comic relief. Pictures and writing on home walls could possibly make an appropriate interior backdrop for a goth, a skinhead, a satanist or another anti-establishment identity seeking the comfort of self-defining symbols at a glance, like a kind of personalised hand-stamped wallpaper. But only if the balance with the other elements in the room was not too sickly or overwhelming. The aesthetic beauty of graffiti normally relates to the opportunity it offers for contro-versial issues to be displayed publicly in an open space, for all to see and respond to. The forum is ideological and political as much as it is social and artistic. Some of the most breathtaking and imaginative street graffiti and murals happen in the urban core on pavements, in school playgrounds, and on the sides of buildings. The creative expression is inflected by the need for disenfranchised individuals and communities to make their voices heard, to tell their stories without judgement or social retribution. Other more forgettable forms of lexical and pictorial graffiti can be found rather easily in the toilet cubicles of any downtown drinking establishment. Just don't call the telephone numbers!

The Ancient Egyptian love of decorating walls with images and script that take up events current and past is now quite dead, relative to good taste. The living and breathing stories decorating the walls of the most influential of patrons to the arts – the pharaohs – made up the complex signals and codes of the era's greatest dynasties that lie buried in the sand. We now have the television, advertising and publishing industries to perform the media function of preserving cultural memory for us on a grand scale – therefore leaving the clean slate of our walls flickering with the iridescent shadows of the airwaves. Tastes peak according to what we believe and value about life and living. And it isn't likely that interior designers will reintroduce the Ancient Egyptian practice of filling our walls with complex and intricate schemes, a Moebius Strip of images and lettering, meticulously defining the histories of our families and paying tribute to the cultural struggles of our times. But ancient traditions and design fetishes are seen as unappealing and even ridiculous only in the light of our own contemporary expectations of good taste. During the height of their popularity, the wall frescoes of Ancient Egypt were the envy of all for a culture that conceived of life as a predestined journey before the possibility of an afterlife.

The styles of a period are essentially up to the creative imagination of the artisans to discover. The arts and crafts industries are responsible for transforming raw materials of wood, clay, cloth, stone, glass, plastic and metal into objects fit to orient an interior or art space around, through the prescribed principles of good taste. And in every era they give birth to 'classic' designs that represent the aesthetic and creative sensibilities of the period in the best possible light and stand the test of time – until the next new thing comes along to shock taste. Aesthetic and creative sensibilities change, so that despite being fascinating historical artefacts, it is unlikely that it will be appropriate to revive the old classic designs in a new period. We are at home in the modern world. Stepping back so as to revive the decorating trends of the pharaohs seems an unlikely direction for the upcoming decorators to take in order to manufacture their own new and symbolic twist on good taste. However, more bizarre things have happened.

The New Babylon: Taste After 9/11

Changes of taste are often a reaction to the social and political realities of a time. The disturbing events of September 11, 2001 offered ample reason for a re-evaluation of personal priorities and cultural dynamics in Western and Eastern societies alike. When the two shining towers of the World Trade Center were brought down, the course of global politics abruptly turned towards a new agenda that took us back to the sentiments of Cold War times. Once again we live in a time when suspicion and distrust prevail, and the CIA trusts no one as it searches for intruders and terrorists within one's own nation – the Cold War revisited. '9/11' began the psychological unrest and disbelief that the threat of war and terrorism brings along with it, leaving

American politicians to interpret and act upon the angry sentiments of an otherwise stunned population with a muted optimism for the future.

At first, observers and analysts in the United States could not believe the unlikely images of two jet liners crashing into the twin towers of the World Trade Center that filled the television airwaves. Were the pictures 'real' or just a Hollywood publicity stunt gone horribly wrong? Perhaps a movie studio was using the latest special effects technologies to promote a flick on terrorism. The spectacle of 9/11 recalled Orson Welles's fictional radio play, *The War of the Worlds*, that was taken all too seriously as it sent American audiences fleeing from their cities in fear of 'Martian' attacks. The scenes of terrified crowds running from the collapsing buildings, trying to stay ahead of the impending destruction amidst clouds of trailing smoke and noxious debris, looked more like a scene from the Hollywood science fiction blockbuster *Independence Day* than a news broadcast on CNN. Remember, New York has been attacked by Godzilla, King Kong and even the 'Stay Puff' marshmallow man in *Ghostbusters*. The psyche of the typical American movie-goer would have been prepared for anything but the truth. As the details of another hijacked passenger jet hitting the Pentagon surfaced and a failed suicide mission on the White House came to light, the severity of the situation began to sink in. The headlines read: 'America Under Siege'. For days and weeks after the horrific events of 9/11, the United States was consumed by disbelief and shock, anger and mourning. The intensity of emotions among its citizens and policy makers ran the gamut while heroes gradually emerged, victims were identified and revenge was sworn against enemies. September 11, 2001 was a day of reckoning that shifted the course of many perspectives, attitudes and priorities in the United States away from the crass pursuit of individual happiness towards national interests.

With regard to media and taste, American public opinion polls determined that after this staggering event, the viewing habits of the general public had temporarily shifted. Moving away from a pop culture preoccupation with the themes of sex and violence shortly after 9/11, television audiences tuned in to programmes about 'family values' and sit-coms that featured familiar faces. The opening episode of the new *Friends* season had the highest ratings in its seven-year run, with more than 30 million viewers in the United States. Realising that the grieving public would need time to work through the stress and recovery phases of the traumatic experience, television stations ran 24-hour news reports without commercials instead of regularly scheduled shows immediately after the attacks. Thousands of news stories were left to document the sadness of severed relationships – last-minute phone calls from the burning towers, babies to be born without parents, people never to be seen again, potential left unrealised and worlds destroyed in the wake of the billowing smoke from 'Ground Zero'. Producers had to adjust programming to accommodate viewers' altered preferences. Writers were asked to rework scripts that dealt with the sensitive topic of terrorism and public safety. A scene from a *Friends* episode that contained a joke about passing through airport security was cut for fear it would offend. The new Ellen DeGeneres show deleted a reference to collapsing buildings. Advertisers followed suit and edited or cancelled commercials that were likely to cause negative responses among television viewers. Prior to 9/11, Coca Cola had aired ads running with the slogan 'Life Tastes Good', but pulled the campaign in favour of ads glorifying a baseball hero bidding farewell to the game that is called 'America's national pastime'. Airlines – who had the most difficult marketing task of all – focused on rebuilding a tarnished reputation with combative slogans. 'Fly without being taken', 'We're all in this together', and 'If there's going to be a war, we'll fight it on our own turf' were the tag lines of some commercials that featured images of employees instead of planes. The theme of patriotism had replaced the need for edgier ideas and catchy twists that advertisers had come to rely on for mass-market appeal.

'Made for family' reruns were in great demand. Programming reflected a sympathy and awareness of the importance of community safety and family bonds. The classic American television programmes *I Love Lucy*, *The Brady Bunch*, *The Mary Tyler Moore Show* and *Love Boat* were getting high ratings once again, drawing more viewers in syndication than prime-time 'giggle shows' featuring Pamela Anderson in an undersized bikini. Disenchanted with the bleak outlook of terrorism after 9/11, the public needed a taste of nostalgia that allowed them to get back to the good old days, to a time before mass murders and virtual violence were a common denominator for entertainment and real life. Movies geared towards raising American spirits and positive sentiments with the reassurance that goodwill could triumph over evil were huge successes. Fantasy, comedy and action films with no reference to terrorism were the strongest performers. *Harry Potter and the Sorcerer's Stone*, *Monsters Inc.*, *Shrek*, *Rush Hour 2*, *The Mummy Returns* and *Lord of the Rings: The Fellowship of the Ring* led the way at the box office. The gratuitous violence that typically saturates a large part of what is available on screen proved too real for many to stomach post-9/11. Movies that served to graphically remind the public of human suffering at the hands of terrorists and criminals were edited, postponed or scrapped altogether. The debut of *Collateral Damage* with Arnold Schwarzenegger was moved from October 2001 to February 2002 because its plot contained a vendetta by a Los Angeles firefighter against terrorists who killed his brother. The original tag line for the movie, 'The war hits home' was dropped. *Nose Bleed* would have starred Jackie Chan as a World Trade Center window cleaner who uncovers a conspiracy to blow up the buildings, but its production was halted given the bizarre similarity between the film premise and the subsequent attack. *Spider-man*, *Serendipity* and *Zoolander* digitally modified shots of New York City, erasing the twin towers from the Lower Manhattan skyline. The remake of *The Time Machine* deleted footage of meteors showering down on the 'Big Apple'. The ending to *Men in Black II* was supposed to feature Tommy Lee Jones and Will Smith blasting away aliens at the World Trade Center, but the climax was hastily rewritten for a change of venue. How would an American audience react to seeing a national landmark that was no longer there? Studio executives decided images of the World Trade Center still intact or under siege would have been too painful for many.

Viewers slowly recovered from the solace of sentimentality raging after the distressing events of 9/11 – but only to trade the spiritual comforts of rediscovering a sense of community and nostalgia for images of heroic retaliation – killing in the name of goodness. Violence was suddenly back in with a vengeance, but only when it provided the means for achieving a moral victory of good over evil at any cost. The change in taste paved the way for a cinematic retaliation on crime in the form of heroes that were larger than life. Hollywood feasted on the opportunity. *Spiderman* was soon brought to the forefront of American consciousness. Pitted against unpatriotic bad apples like Green Goblin, the web-slinging *alter ego* of Peter Parker becomes the unlikely saviour of a cultural morality and a communal way of life. Why else would he describe himself as 'your friendly, neighbourhood Spiderman'? Armed and ready with every necessary 'state of the art' technology in high-fidelity combat wear, James Bond was ready to *Die Another Day* so as to fulfil the all-too-tempting prospect of employing the war toys 'M' had constructed to foil schemes for global domination and tyranny. 007 is played as a global hero always ready to fight for world security against a 'menace without a country' and Peter Parker is the embodiment of American humility. Vin Diesel becomes XXX, triple X, the hell raiser with an environmentalist conscience forced to turn secret agent by the CIA rather than spend time rotting in jail. It is an intriguing scenario with surprising plot twists. The Hollywood point of this movie as a piece of entertainment was to blow up and incinerate a lot of cars while Vin Diesel flexed his muscles for scantily clad women. Sex and violence fill cinemas. Let's not fool ourselves. But *XXX* also depicted how and why the underdog, the ordinary citizen, should be willing to participate in saving the world from nuclear peril if asked to do so – even at the wrong end of a gun. The message is echoed in *Black Hawk Down* and *Behind Enemy Lines* – movies that displayed images of American soldiers stranded in foreign battle grounds, willing to die for their country and fighting back to rid the world of a faceless nemesis, all in the name of violence for peace. The targets of the US military we see in these films did not have to have any direct link with 9/11. And yet, the reason for the violence is vengeance. The enemies have chosen the wrong side as long as there were sides there for the choosing – any hint of prosperity after the battle helped to rally the cry for victory against an evil force. After September 11, 2001, political leaders in the United States provided an ethical grounding to the whole of human affairs, but asked the world to choose sides. Tastes changed, signalled by a blind patriotism that was ready and eager to fight back against terror. Producers sensed the box office draw and came up with a series of movies about war and American nationalism. The fragile state of a population post-disaster leaves a people vulnerable to the intelligence of those who have the power to provide easy solutions. Charisma and the gift of the gab, borrowed from the astute minds of great political speechwriters, can persuade the people to blindly believe in political actions that seemingly will help heal their wounds. Changing political climates affect the tastes individuals are drawn to. A national disaster permits a re-evaluation of values and leads to a search for easy solutions. It is comforting to believe that we are always the good guys. Hence the popularity of war games, movies, and programming – it's clean patriotic stuff – easier to digest than the real McCoy.

CHAPTER FIVE

The Media Machine

The ideals of good taste portrayed in the media affect our personal choices and decisions every minute of each waking hour. Life in the new millennium means consuming an enormous daily diet of advertising. Every day the average person is actively and passively exposed to thousands of images that show and tell the standards, dimensions and limits of good taste. Its characteristics are pictured on the glamorised covers of popular magazines, plastered on billboards, hyper-sensationalised on the front pages of tabloids in supermarket checkout lines, and commercialised on television, film and radio by celebrities and sports personalities as sound bytes, jingles and video clips. They are also embedded in the clipstream of web page banner ads, chiselled on coffee mugs, stapled on ads covering telephone poles, tacked up on bulletin boards, delivered through flyers, product catalogues, labels, logos and coupons, and find their way around the world online in the form of virtual news groups and mega-viral 'SPAM' marketing email campaigns. As the forces of the media and the proliferation of new technologies rapidly shrink the world, the spaces of public and private life are invaded by images of what we should want. Good taste has become a marketing industry based on showing us what is 'it', why we should or need to have 'it', and, of course, how to get 'it'. The media present consumers with views of the world we should want and could have. Our capacity to realise an ideal of having good taste depends on our accepting a vision of reality already processed through the commercial media and their marketing machine. This is of course reflected in our actions and what we own or subscribe to in the living of our everyday lives. But, more often than not, the sources of influence upon our personal and social behaviours – including the realisation of our dreams and desires – go unquestioned.

The standards of good taste and its sensibilities drive the global economy through the media marketing machine. *Marketing creates needs and desires in us where there previously were none.* These desires are cultivated as passions by us as people and acted upon by us as consumers. There is not a facet of human life that is not concerned with finding satisfaction and pleasure in our existence among the world of things and each other. And good taste is the social measure of what we value around us. From the drudgery of work to the leisure of games, sports and entertainment, from the glamour of fashion to the lure of television, music and film, the cultivation of passion and pleasure is what drives the course of human endeavours. Good taste is always at stake, no matter what we think, do or say, because it produces culture, and consumers of culture, by defining what our choices should be in relation to the products and services that are available to us for consumption. This in turn has social implications, as people of converging and divergent tastes relate to each other in support of one taste or another. Good taste thus turns into the passion that defines and begins the personal quest of finding satisfaction, pleasure and happiness – what we call 'life'.

We generally accept the values and norms of good taste

represented in the media without question, for what they are: 'paid for' advertisements. We then move on to what in marketing messages is meaningful for us at the personal level by asking, 'Will this product or service increase my happiness?' The answer determines our tastes and consumer habits. The value of a product or practice, an object or an action we may choose to buy is subjective and not as universal as advertisers and marketers would like us to believe. Good taste does not exist 'out there' in the stratosphere, an ideal independent from any particular points of view or life situations, just waiting to be found. It is bound to social contexts and personal beliefs. There are as many tastes as there are people and communities – a fact we often choose to forget. At some point or other in our consumer lives, we have all asked ourselves the question, 'Do I really *need* this?' It is the job of marketers to make you think you *want* it! The standards of judgement in good taste that loosen the purse strings are always with us because of the examples to be emulated and desired that lurk in the back of our minds, thanks to the imaginary rendering of life, history, society and culture by the media marketing machine. The media apparatus of advertising is at work when the meaning of good taste needs to be fixed publicly. That is, when a particular version of reality must be made to seem objective and uncontrived for the sake of making it believable to a mass audience who will take it personally – make it their own. The media resist the fragmentation and plurality of cultural memory by allowing us to take for granted the contradictions between all of the mixed messages happening around us in everyday life, asking us instead to buy into an idealised reality – not what life is, but what life could be! In marketing, life is made easy and 'demystified' for painless consumption – all in the name of selling an image of taste designed to give us pleasure and make us happy.

Skin Deep

Cosmetics products are marketed like alchemy: with a promise to bestow endless loveliness and to enact upon a woman a magical physical transformation that could never have been imagined before advertising. A simple face cream by Shiseido offers tempting results – to *make you a vision of heavenly beauty* with its 'Advance Luminous Technology'. Dior introduces Capture R60/80 through a campaign that promotes the creamy concoction as the next best thing to the fountain of youth; the formula is suggested to have the power to reduce wrinkles by up to 60 per cent in just one hour – the caption flaunting 'Triumph over time'. Neutrogena's ad campaign headlines pledge *'firmer skin from a makeup'* and the ROC line promises to *'Defend your youth'*. CoverGirl sells a miraculously 'Multiplying Mascara' that can make lashes longer, fuller and *'twice as nice'*. Estée Lauder pitches the miracle of anti-aging by offering to break Newton's first law of physics through the incorporation of *anti-gravity* ingredients into its lotions and creams. Aveeno promotes a moisturiser by asking, 'What if you could capture radiance in a bottle?' Would you buy it? If not for yourself, then what a great gift idea!

Traditionally, women have been forced by social and cultural mores to care about their appearance. Rightly or wrongly, enhancing the ideal of feminine beauty has preoccupied the sexes since time immemorial. In antiquity, wars were waged over beautiful women by men seeking to possess an image of female perfection at all costs: Mark Antony gave his life for Cleopatra and Agamemnon sacrificed whole armies for Helen of Troy. This is the stuff of legend. But it sets the standards of femininity impossibly high and has created an industry dedicated to a cultural obsession with helping women 'measure up'. In contemporary society, with the proliferation of print and televisual media, it is quite easy for a woman to feel inadequate. We are inundated with marketing images of female beauty that are unrealistic. After the Second World War, cosmetics companies re-entered the retail market of dreams on the premise of having the ability to correct 'imperfections' in a woman's appearance. The marketing implication was that every woman is subject to flaws, and little 'touch-ups' are welcome for every part of the body. From head to toe, if you need refining, there is a lotion, cream or tonic that can 'fix' and 'enhance' to restore youthful beauty. Surely, everyone wants to look their best. Cosmetics marketing sells us on this idea. Why depend on a natural beauty that is imperfect and flawed? Why not become the standard of female perfection?

Today more than ever, cosmetics advertising relies on the idea of 'defect' in the male and female consumer to create a demand for 'beauty' products. Maintaining and caring for the face and body has become the existential dilemma. Everywhere you look on billboards, magazine covers, even in cyberspace, getting in shape and looking young has become the moral imperative of the new millennium. The media-driven desire to be and look good has led to fitness clubs, 'zone' diets, aromatherapy, Pilates, yoga, Zen and spa retreats – all to make us look and feel better than even Aphrodite, the goddess of beauty, or Hercules, the ideal male, could ever have imagined. Cosmetics advertising supports a preoccupation with fit bodies and looking young by featuring slim, red-lipped fifteen to 'early twenty something' teens and women with smooth skin, no pores, no wrinkles. The dieting industry prospers as the media create 'supermodel' concerns about image and shape for the average Joe and Jane. A study of university-age men and women revealed that personal dissatisfaction about body size and form increases after simply viewing slides of fit, slim women and in-shape, muscular men. Diet programmes thrive as the media give the impression that most of the general population is overweight. The public pressure to be thin, toned and fit has resulted in eating disorders – it is anticipated that anorexia and bulimia will strike more than a million women in the USA this year. Weight loss supplements and remedies provide health warnings and disclaimers that are overlooked by unwary customers because of the supposed effectiveness of the product. Good food management in the form of a pill warrants the health risks of consuming the chemical contents on the label. Diet books sell millions of copies each and every year to men and women hoping to find the Holy Grail of thinness.

Despite the seemingly 'perfect' image of female beauty that cosmetics models portray, it is still not good enough. Why be a woman when you can be a goddess? Gillette wants to *reveal the goddess in you* with a 'get back your femininity' marketing approach to selling a Passion Pink Venus razor with more feline curves and swerves than are found on the average female form. The notion that pink appeal is feminine is played upon to enhance the obvious theme of feminine beauty, agency and strength. One advertisement reveals a vintage pink convertible hosting four pretty pink princesses perked up, sassy and having fun, cruising to nowhere, sporting their shapely swimming-suited and shaved feminine forms. A lifestyle ethic is introduced into the mental picture of 'the goddess' that the advertisers have managed to paint as everywoman – and if the ad is successful the portrait always looks like 'you'. Simply erase the love handles, blemishes and wrinkles from your mind. A successful campaign draws viewers into the object of the fantasy – making it possible for them to embrace it as a conceivable extension of themselves. In fact, the goddess motif has been adopted and exploited by other high-profile brands, designers and pop culture figures. The trend has filtered into the consumer mainstream. Nike has opened a chain of 'Goddess Stores' for women in the United States. Estée Lauder has produced 'Bronze Goddess' tanning lotions to give the skin a celestial hue. Holt Renfrew contends that the modern woman sees herself as a goddess, and it feeds the fire of fantasy with a line of 'curve-emphasising' dresses and faux diamond jewellery to adorn the 'divine figure'. The singer Cher even endorses a 'Goddess Diet'. Nigella Lawson has penned a cookbook entitled *How to Be a Domestic Goddess*. In a culture obsessed with beauty, tanning, cosmetic enhancement, youth and fitness, there is always room for improvement and for narcissism. So why not be a goddess – or at least call yourself one – despite the usual imperfections?

Almost all beauty and health industry advertisements are airbrushed to increase the perfection quotient. If the goal is unreachable, then the demand for the products will always remain. Creating an idyllic image of male and female perfection is the key to marketing cosmetics because it links appearance and image to self-esteem, thus luring buyers into the perpetual fountain of youth and beauty that is symbolised by the products. Recent photos of Demi Moore were altered to reduce portions of her hips and waist, while a picture of Cindy Crawford had to be airbrushed more than 30 times before it was acceptable. The regeneration of aging models and celebrities is fast and easy with the use of cutting-edge digital technology. This airbrush editing of photos is part of the process, no matter how fit and stunning, handsome or beautiful the 'model' is. Images are 'raised up a notch' to enhance the overall quality of the icon by using lighting, hair and make-up professionals, padding, pinning, flattering camera angles and digital technology to retouch perfection. Surveys are conducted to establish what features the artistic designers should be striving for. A recent study of female facial characteristics among mixed gender groups found that the most desirable features are a high forehead, full lips, a shortish jaw line and a thin chin. For men, the results were quite the opposite. A strong, long, sweeping jaw, a squarish, pronounced chin, thinner lips and a low hairline were the desirable characteristics. Most men who were surveyed about the 'sex appeal' factor of the female body preferred a waist to hip ratio of 67 per cent or two-thirds – forming the coveted hour-glass shape reminiscent of the Hollywood starlet of the 40s and 50s à la Rita Hayworth, Marilyn Monroe and Jayne Mansfield. In men, women preferred a muscular but not overly developed 'V-shape' physique, with a minimum of hairiness. What if a man or woman does not possess those characteristics? Is he or she still 'attractive'? Not by these standards.

But in this inspirational age of 'yes, I can do it and nothing will stand in my way to be the best I can be' pop psychology, men and women take it upon themselves to diet, exercise and shape their bodies. Instead of recognising the negative feelings of inadequacy and guilt it may provoke, the beauty and health industry markets its motivational upside as empowerment. Once hooked to the image, if a man or woman wants to look good and feel good about themselves, the only option other than cosmetics is resorting to plastic surgery and dermatological 'weapons of mass destruction'. Chemicals in the form of toxins that paralyse the muscles and surrounding tissue are injected into the face and body to reduce wrinkles or cellulite. In an age when looks count but few have the time, the disposable income or the inclination to endure rounds of Botox shots, laser resurfacing, chemical peels, collagen treatments, silicone implants, tummy tucks, face lifts and liposuction, it is infinitely less painful to buy into the dream of eternal youth and regeneration that cosmetics companies sell. Even if it doesn't work, you still feel like you are doing something to be a little closer to the perfect you.

For years, tanning salons have banked on the health appeal of energising spas that consumers of cosmetic products and beauty services crave. But the feeling of well-being that comes with a few moments of exposure to the rejuvenating warmth of shimmering ultra-violet lights now pales before the knowledge that what you do to your body today can lead to a troubled future of medical demons. Dream creams developed by cosmetics companies are promoted as a 'safe' alternative for getting the psychological benefits of sporting a 'healthy' tan. Bronzing rays are packaged as a way to good taste emulsified in the form of rich lotions that stain your body with the illusion of sun-filled hours spent on the beach. It is obviously not a hard sell, given the rise in cancer rates and the social capital a good tan has to place you in that upper echelon of affluent consumers who fly to Bermuda for the winter months. Health-wise shopping is a viable market demographic that cosmetics manufacturers have been quick to address. Right out of a tube and onto your skin, the artificial pigments give the impression of having had 'fun in the sun' with very little personal loss in cost and time. And with reduced health and social risks comes the best marketing ploy of the *faux* sun glow creams. The product has improved in quality over the years, so it is more difficult to achieve orange blotchy stains on arms, legs and palms that were never meant to be there. By carefully following the directions you can avoid the tell-tale signs of pseudo 'tanning' that in the past gave away the fact that you did not go to Cabo San Lucas over the winter break – and, of course, caught you out publicly in a little white lie. What better bandwagon of beauty to journey on than the one that creates envy and comes with a bonus ticket to protecting health and wellness? Today, deep, rich, naturally sun-soaked skin is about as appealing as inhaling on a stick of nicotine. It is medical and social dynamite. Conscientious people do not smoke or go out into the rapidly depleting ozone layer without a hat, sunglasses, long shirt and trousers, while covering all exposed skin in 30+ UV sun block. Cosmetics advertisers bank on this and offer the *faux glow* of self tans for the illusion of a love for outdoor living. Clarins Paris' new line, New Radiance Plus, promotes 'Moisture with year round healthy glow'. Neutrogena gives a 'perfect sunless tan instantly' and the brand name Origins coos that 'Bronze have more fun' with added 'protection against premature aging'. Who would not want to stay young? This is tanning that offers *a healthier way to have fun in the sun* – but is it really so? Do the long-term effects of tinting agents on the skin provide completely inert chemicals to replace the perils of ultra-violet rays? Only time will tell. Stained legs, faces, arms and even palms are everywhere to be seen, proving that the retailing and advertising initiative has been a successful one. Who can argue with a marketing campaign for tanning products that will help keep you out of the GP's office, waiting on the results of a mole biopsy? For the time being at least, tanning oils and creams suggest a benign and safe way to keep those lily-white limbs appealing once the sun melts the last snows away.

Under the marketing spell of the Nike philosophy 'Just do it!', we run, we bike, we jog, we lift weights, we try to eat right, hoping all the while to reach a ripe old age healthy, wealthy and wise. But what matters most to us, more than anything else – after the media have impressed upon us the power of image for success – seems to be appearances.

The Disney Effect

Disney is a part of a culture industry of corporations that offer entertainment choices. From cartoons to sports teams, its media products have immeasurable influence on minds young and not so young. As the educational critic Henry Giroux tells us in *The Mouse That Roared*, it would be too easy – unfair and unethical – to concoct conspiracy theories portraying Disney as 'part of an evil empire [of marketing] incapable of providing joy and pleasure to the millions of kids and adults who visit its theme parks, watch its videos and movies, and buy products from its toy stores'. But advertising does not discriminate between innocent and street-wise shoppers in the global age of fast capitalism where instant gratification is the order of the day. Disney has to turn a profit and please its shareholders by selling childhood dreams and playing on adult fantasies of what life could be like in a town like Celebration where time stops and the world is transformed into a vision that we can control to please ourselves. For the culture industries, marketing is a means of focusing consumer desires and creating obsessions. Self-fulfilment today means buying the products we want to have and 'amusing ourselves to death'.

Disney is a fantasy machine. It endlessly reworks themes of escapism and utopia that glorify adventure and the joys of play. Disney seems to make possible unrealised child-hood hopes, wishes and dreams in the name of fun and purity. Who can argue with the pursuit of innocence, fun and purity as the way to find happiness in life?

The 'dreamscape' is the cultural site of Disney's appeal. It is the source of its emotive power and value. Toys come to life, divorced parents get back together again, we find long-forgotten loves and we experience the wonder of being children again. Disney takes advantage of the image of a childhood utopia that has been lost in the urban jungle – the idea of a time when reality could be read like an open book through the eyes of a child. The 'nostalgia machine' of Mickey Mouse and his pals, sometimes goofy, but sometimes heroic, counteracts the debilitating effects of the pessimism that permeates society today. It replaces adult negativity with the hope of a better world, a better place. Disney creates the physical and emotional preconditions of a 'wish-landscape', locating the desires of adults and children in provocative settings and different worlds where powerful themes such as survival, separation, love, death and loss are experienced. *Holes*, *Atlantis*, *Inspector Gadget* and *Spy Kids* are examples of situations where human strength is tested and good overcomes evil in funny ways. The 'Disney effect' is thoroughly escapist. It causes excitement because it is spontaneous and unexpected. Fantasy distracts us, enchants us, makes the moment of living meaningful and truthful again as a new experience. The Disney effect is a heightening of experience that suspends disbelief. The intellect knows that there will be a 'swindle of fulfilment', because the world of Disney is only an illusion, but we are nevertheless willing to play the game for the sake of distraction and the reward of feeling good at the end.

The 'play therapy' of Disney is available to those who choose to take up its offer. But its movies, toys and theme parks are neither innocently conceived nor haphazardly constructed. And we would be naïve to think so. Disney culture is fully invested in the concept of innocence. It repackages and sells childhood dreams. On the surface, there is nothing wrong with giving people access to enjoyment and happiness. Walt Disney realised the value of cultivating an image of purity that is centred and grounded in the notion of security and the romance of the past – a future where anything is possible and happiness is just around the corner. *Angels in the Infield* and *Aladdin* are stories about how a teenager defies destiny to regain a sense of belief in love and the worth of human relationships. A concern with such themes makes Disney a media corporation synonymous with the notion of childhood innocence and family values. Only a child could ask an angel to help bring his estranged father back home, and every one of us has dreamed of being more than we are. But in these movies, you have to accept the premises uncritically, learning lessons about life along the way.

Because of its film and television companies, its involvement in the radio and music industry, and the reach of its publishing empire, Disney cannot be anything but a 'teaching machine' that exerts tremendous influence on the shaping of cultures worldwide. Its undeniable commercial success reminds us of the power of entertainment to mediate and influence almost every aspect of our lives. After major sporting events in the United States like the World Series and the Super Bowl, when baseball or American football players are interviewed by the media, one of the first responses to the question, 'What are you going to do now?' is: 'I'm going to take my family to Disneyland.' This might be a strange coincidence. Or not. To adults, Disneyland represents a life without worries and celebrates the nuclear family unit as the seed of childhood innocence. To kids, it's just a theme park with wicked rides, cool stuff and tons of junk food. The appeal to innocence and the nostalgic quest to find the 'inner child' masks the motivations of the corporate agenda. The Michael Jordan films were littered with product placements; the *Mighty Ducks* films eventually became a cartoon and then a real-life hockey team in Anaheim, California that plays at 'The Pond' where its fans cheer 'quack, quack, quack'. Disney is more or less turning the world into a toy store or an entertainment channel. How can we not find this commercialisation of ethics and values problematic?

Disney establishes a marketing strategy with effective yet disturbing results. It joins entertainment with education in a unique way through its products, for commercial interests. In short, the teaching machinery of Disney is its retail outlets, movies and toys. By equating learning with entertainment and the innocence of childhood and play, the corporate agenda is infused into its educational goals – in the end helping to make it a media giant. This correlation of entertainment and education banks on the image of teaching and learning as a dull cerebral activity. For Disney, forms of education without the distraction of entertainment are overly serious, monotonous, and cannot be made to be 'fun'. So the danger is that kids will develop a market-based notion of identity and be passive consumers of taste as defined by Mickey Mouse.

Disney is hard to resist. We have known that since we were children. Sometimes, Disney has shown us a representation of the world as we have experienced it both realistically and allegorically. At other times, it has revealed a vision of the world as we would like it to be, a place of innocence and enchantment where all is well that ends well.

Wrestling With Ourselves: The Good, the Bad and the Ugly

Recent cultural figures from Walt Disney to Homer Simpson have analysed, commented on, put into practice, resisted and exemplified the dimensions of good taste. Popular culture filters the interests and obsessions of an audience yearning for an ethics of fun into easily digestible forms of entertainment not always morally sanguine. This is easy to see if we take a look at the spectacle of professional wrestling. Let us put aside for the time being the intellectual and ethical questions of why anyone would want to watch professional wrestling in the first place. You might object: 'Yeah, I know it's fake. So what? I like to watch professional wrestling anyway!' Its remarkable popularity worldwide as a form of entertainment and bad taste is indisputable. But there are also those who dismiss professional wrestling as the cultural epitome of bad taste. An event that exploits the strongest of human emotions – love and hatred – for profit, not for the edification of the spectator. It is easy to reject professional wrestling on aesthetic or moral grounds. Shapely female courtesans with ample lung capacity buttress the roseola of their weighty cleavage with the tiniest of sticking plasters while groping the slippery thighs of an equally stunning opponent for a firm hold during a corn oil match to the death. Long-haired body builders in spandex tights strike venal poses for the frenetic females (and males!) in the audience as they recount with surgical precision the anatomical details of last night's slaughter of a fellow wrestler as he was 'taken apart, piece by piece'. Tales of betrayal, adultery, greed, jealousy and even theft abound.

Yet there is more to professional wrestling than meets the eye. Understanding its appeal is like trying to explain why stopping your vehicle to gawk at the morbid aftermath of a car accident is construed as a natural human response. We thrive on spectacles. Sometimes we don't know why. Spectacles that display the struggle between luck and destiny makes us feel alive, as we witness the tragedy of someone else we neither know nor will likely ever see again. So we stop to look at the traffic accident in order to unconsciously reaffirm our sense of safety and well being – we are alive while somebody else is suffering. In professional wrestling, the sense of survival is conveyed through the spectacle we know is fake. There is no point in watching a match we know is fixed, other than to release our anxiety in a scapegoat, the bad person who suffers for our sins.

The myth of 'good taste' versus 'bad taste' naturalises the idiosyncratic nature of the cultural values we find represented in the world of professional wrestling. The big sweaty men in tights we love to hate, yet might secretly admire, are more than their muscle-bound, greased and hairy selves. They are cultural icons of meaning – moral archetypes, muscularly overdeveloped signs – that we engage and interpret as we would competing ideas and values. Arbitrary notions of 'what is good' and 'what is bad' are symbolised through the dress, speech and actions of characters who are combatants in the ring. For this reason, professional wrestling cannot be classified as a sport, that is, a true competition among equals. Like a play, professional wrestling is scripted. The outcome is determined in advance of actual matches. Sport depends on competition fuelled by the technical mastery of participants. Its entertainment value derives from the fact that the contest is always up for grabs, the destiny of the players nebulous. Sport is drama. Anything can happen. Uncertainty fuels the drama and sustains the desire to watch until the outcome is apparent. Some would say that sport is 'honest'. But unlike wrestling, sport is 'lifeless'.

That is not to say that in sport the participants and spectators are without emotion, don't take sides, cause riots or take up arms against each other in the name of loyal allegiances to individual players and teams. But contests of skill are not allegories of sport itself, as a game of abilities with fixed rules depends upon the outcome and not on the spectacle itself. Reactions determined by the conventions of sports do not directly relate to the great struggles experienced in life. Rather, they relate to the performance of sport played as a game. It is an artificial contest – not real life. No moral judgement is required of the player to participate in the game of football or of the spectator to watch it. One cannot go outside the rules of competition to interpret the meaning of the action on the field. For example, it would be absurd to say, 'Averri scored a goal to punish research scientists supporting the opposing team because he doesn't believe in using live animals to test cosmetics.' Social morality isn't on display through every action the players perform for the sake of sporting competition. It would be as absurd and meaningless to say that the spectators began to bludgeon each other with fists because they disagreed about the validity of Averri's ethical stances regardless of the goal. Life does not intervene in the playing of sports. Every time a fan makes an aesthetic or ethical judgement about a sport or its players it is in relation to the rules of the game and its code of morality construed by the dictates of skilful performance. Otherwise the basis for the opinion would be ridiculous.

The enjoyment of professional wrestling, however, flourishes and increases primarily through witnessing the raw spectacle of life's great stories acted out in the ring as a play of moralities. Not to mention the ethical diatribes, free psychoanalysis, pop philosophy and generous smatterings of sexual counselling that constitute the narrative thread of each and every match and entangle the stories of the wrestlers with our own lives. Wrestling consumes life. Nothing more, nothing less. It swallows life whole and spits it back at the audience as an ersatz form of experience. It is an allegory of human existence that begs a response. Spectator emotion is driven by moral judgements that go outside the rules of the 'contest' itself. The outcome becomes secondary because the power of wrestling lies in the ability of the wrestlers to stage the event, the struggle, which is a real product of conflicts in human affairs outside the ring. Who wins does not really matter. What is of concern to an audience is the extent to which judgements about professional wrestlers and wrestling matches can be made by drawing on a knowledge of life experience itself. Spectators use aesthetic and moral principles that they have learned in their everyday lives to form allegiances and antipathies – a sense of ethics. Life intervenes. Wrestling makes plain the struggle of good and bad and universalises it for the viewer by establishing moral archetypes to which the spectator responds regardless of whether they want to or not. The spectacle is predicated on the play of ethical and social norms of behaviour that we experience in our everyday lives and take for granted. We cannot but respond.

In the squared circle, the stylistic and rhetorical flourishes of the wrestlers as performers, not simply athletes, support moral values. The spectator is forced to take sides according to the moral codes and cultural values of a society. For example, 'good' characters are referred to as 'technically accomplished athletes'. They are well-spoken defenders of dominant but arbitrary ideologies and cultural institutions like 'the family', 'the American way', 'civil rights', 'justice' and 'democracy'. Professional wrestling in the United States during the Second World War depicted clean-cut 'good old boys' of unimpeachable character taking on monocled Nazi caricatures with bad German accents. The nationalistic spirit of the times made it possible to exploit the situation of real violence that was being experienced on the battlefield for the purpose of entertainment and patriotic moralising. American wrestling heroes exacting symbolic revenge on the representative of an enemy nation was indeed a cathartic experience. The good guy always won! Consequently, there was hope that evil would not triumph in the real world.

'Bad' characters use 'dirty tricks' to subvert what the 'good' characters stand for, in order to bring about a 'New World Order' – which incidentally was also the name of a wrestling cohort of evil doers and misfits. This group of characters walk on the dark side of the fine edge between good and evil. They punctuate their talk with profanity, a distinctly pejorative masculine bravado replete with homophobic and misogynistic references. That is, if they speak at all. Sometimes menacing grimaces, guttural growls, the pumping of fists and the gnashing of teeth are enough to make a point. These less than savoury characters might include a Satanic High Priest, a porn star or even a raving lunatic who, having escaped from an unidentified asylum, wears a mask to conceal his identity. Whether it be raising the dead, seducing a wrestler's companion, or talking to a sock puppet, their actions are exaggerations of real life intended to make visible the inner state of their troubled souls. Nothing is left to the imagination. We see and hear everything except the depth of their capacity for evil.

Good taste and bad taste are tied to the moral standards that guide the interpretation of human behaviour which generalises the experience of viewing in the wrestling spectacle. The wrestling tries to bring about a consensus of how we perceive reality, encounter the human condition and act in respect to the difference of others as a community. There is always a 'good' character and a 'bad' character. Morally upright figures never fight each other. Never! Even though we know the world of wrestling is a stage-managed sport, its excessive spectacles of human experience – its exhibitions of pain, suffering, betrayal, guilt, treachery, cruelty, desire and elation – allow the viewer a 'purer' or less ambivalent identification with the actors. Some of the wrestlers' symbolic names also facilitate stock responses: for example, 'the Rock', 'Stone Cold', 'the Undertaker', 'The

Phenom', 'Mankind', 'The Patriot', 'Sergeant Slaughter', 'Kane' (the man whose face no one has ever seen!), 'Vader'. The whole point is to have raw-nerved, unadulterated emotion take over the intellectual response. It is an exposed and untempered sentiment but not without an ideological bent that is coloured by a moral sense of taste. The audience quickly has to take sides for the spectacle of wrestling to be effective. They are separated into communities of 'the good' versus 'the bad'. In wrestling matches, as in mythology, imaginary sagas of life and death struggles pitting good against evil are played out before an audience ready to identify within such a play of morality the primordial ethical situations of the human condition. Wrestling exploits the mythological archetypes that preoccupy a consciousness of taste and judgement. A darkly masked figure, a face of evil, squares off against a crowd favourite who displays and defends all that is good in a culture.

The mythical spectacle of wrestling relies on viewers' unconscious desire to work out the psychic and ethical tensions within the ideology of culture. It feeds on the audience's sense of right and wrong. One side or the other is supported on the basis of taste standards and aesthetic and moral judgements. But ultimately, the ethical, social and political boundaries of society and culture frame the way we perceive the mythic struggles among the wrestlers in the ring. Spectators are publicly judged – praised or mocked – according to a display of sympathies and choices of taste. Any rejection or show of support reveals a sense of taste that is morally categorised as 'good' or 'bad'. Let us not forget the system of fashion made up of saleable commodities that accompanies professional wrestling – T-shirts, belts, flags, hats, pins, pens, belt buckles, stickers, water-bottles, coffee mugs, bikinis, etc. – as it brands the sport and markets it for public consumption. By having such items we provide others with a quick and easy way to interpret the meaning of the life-world we inhabit with a view to explaining our present through the archetypes of the past. In other words, your fan gear and paraphernalia represent the 'world order' you support and consider yourself to be a part of, the ideological orientations you embrace and the narratives you spin, with respect to the schematic of life and living provided by the professional wrestling scene.

This symbolic element of taste as either 'good' or 'bad', that demands the viewer's attention and simplifies aesthetic and moral responses, accounts for the tremendous popularity of wrestling. It plays on bias and prejudice. It reduces the excesses of meaning that are present in everyday life. There is no need for interpretation, because differences are made audibly and visibly obvious. Good taste therefore becomes ideological, a mythical rendering of experience. It is 'what-goes-without-saying'. What is good is good and what is bad is bad. There is no in-between. Professional wrestling suspends the need for a critical questioning of cultural representations and the stories we tell ourselves about reality. It reinforces in a most crude way the aesthetic and ethical stereotypes of taste as either good or bad, simply through the wrestlers bringing to life and making graphic the moral consequences of human beliefs and choices. The myth of good taste as the product of virtue and beauty naturalises the distortion of reality that wrestling performs in order to arouse the sentiments of an audience and create fan allegiances. It allows us to gloss over the unsavoury elements of violence and verbal abuse that form the seedy underbelly of each match by forcing us to search for a higher meaning that can be taken on as a ready-made truth about existence. The reward of finding the goodness of truth in such an unlikely place would redeem us of our bad taste and the guilt we feel at enjoying watching the sordid spectacle of professional wrestling. Morality becomes the emotional and psychological after-effect of an uneasy viewing.

Kinderculture

The power of marketing for children gives new meaning to the phrase 'shock and awe' – since everyone who is old enough to watch 'advertising campaigns' is fair game. Only during the last ten years have marketers realised what toy manufacturers have known for a long time: from babies to teenagers, children are important consumers. But kids don't have money? No, usually they don't; however, they exert tremendous influence on those who do – PARENTS. Children have needs, wants and desires that have to be fulfilled because, let us not forget, they are people too. Just because a child cannot walk or talk yet doesn't mean that 'it' doesn't participate in the economic gravy train of consumer culture. There are nappies to be 'pooped', rattles to be rattled, and play pens to be played in. Kids have real buying power and a huge market presence from birth onward. Parents just buy things for them until they are ready to do it for themselves.

Starting from relatively humble beginnings – the simple idea that children need to be entertained – toys have become products of unimaginable power and influence. In *Homo ludens*, the historian Johan Huizinga characterises all of human life as a form of play. We can see the role of contests and games at work in the fields of law, economics, politics, epistemology and the arts that define the social and ethical foundations of culture and civilisation. Play can be marketed to adults by relating it to real trends and needs, physical or psychological. Entrepreneurs need to identify projects that have sure-fire potential to make profits because they make sense for the times. Marketing feeds on ideas that draw on current interests. In this way consumers can show off the latest current affairs that gimmicks or games markets are supplying. Christopher Ruddy, founder of NewsMax.com, and his staff homed in on the playing card gimmick that had been adopted by the Bush administration to label and expose the faces of Iraq's 'Most Wanted' to the occupying US and British forces. Saddam Hussein was the Ace of Spades, and on it went down the list. The faces of Iraqi cabinet members and generals were substituted with the faces of Hollywood celebrities who had not supported the Bush administration war initiatives. By putting the right 'heads' – those media icons that draw huge box office sales – on the cards, along with a short quote regarding their stance on the war, directly from the mouth of the celeb, the trendy product proved to be a wise investment. After three weeks, the decks, selling at $14.95 each, had generated a tidy profit in the United States. By playing their cards right, so to speak, the company proved to be astute to the marketing possibilities of exploiting American nationalism and created a timely statement for a politically involved society to bring out on poker night. Whatever the ethical issues, this is successful marketing: creating a craving for a product that never was, but now is, and riding the wave of contemporary fads.

In *kinderculture* – the culture of children – play is a type of challenge that validates existence and teaches you how to relate to rules and to others. It is not a matter of ironic political commentary or ideological exclusion. A recent toy craze has had kids around the globe downright battling each other within the walls of table-top 'stadiums'. The Beyblade, a spinning top by Hasbro, has competing manufacturers scrambling to create facsimiles that might hitch a ride on the marketing bandwagon of this commercial success. The allure of the toy is the opportunity it provides to be destructive and creative, to destroy and rebuild, without hurting anyone, then to start over again. You have to put together the Beyblade from component parts and launch it with a rip cord. The parts are interchangeable between models. You battle an opponent with another spinning top and the last one left standing wins. Parents and kids alike have felt the impact of an effective marketing campaign by the Hasbro advertising elite. Make no exemptions on our account. At the vulnerable age of four, our son displays an obsessive taste for Beyblades. He revels in reciting all the names of the various versions of this new series of battling tops: Dragoon Phantom, Draciel, Triger, Driger, Dranzer, Amphilion, Grifolion, Bakushin-Oh. He is egged on by the toy's motto, 'Let 'em rip!' The names of the Beyblades we as adults have trouble getting our tongues and minds around he seems to remember more easily than the simple words 'mom' and 'dad'. Playing games of hide and seek or going to the sprinkler park are no longer of much interest since the mind-moulding appeal of this toy effectively infiltrated our child's materialistic side. Not a day goes by that we're not informed of the attack and defence power ratings of other yet unpurchased Beyblades, which he sincerely believes 'he needs'. He reminisces on this consumer emergency at least a dozen times a day – usually after a particularly exhilarating spinning top battle. Beating your brother is good; doing it with a Beyblade he doesn't have is even better! But even if it were his birthday or he had been chosen as the top student in his kindergarten class for the week and we wanted to offer our son a surprise, it would be very unlikely that we could easily find this most desirable of rewards in the shops. The new battling top, at least for the time being, is hard to come by. The buying frenzy created by advertising, media coverage and an animated series featuring Beyblades has made them about as rare and basically extinct to the market as dinosaurs to the earth. The popular animated series has helped generate immense interest in the toy. It depicts vagabond kids travelling around the world in search of opponents to challenge, tournaments to win and glory to be gained. The music is loud and catchy and the plots are based around simple morality plays of good versus evil. The characters are easy to identify with and live through vicariously, because they have the same concerns as all kids – finding friends and having a good time. Everyone wants to be a hero, at least in a secret life of make believe. The cartoon animations give children a context for living out their fantasy lives while making them want more Beyblades too! Pokémon, the phenomenon which most closely parallels the marketing prowess of Beyblades, says it best through its theme song: 'Gotta Catch 'em All.' Get your VISA ready.

As far as good taste in toys goes, the Beyblade is the toy to buy! For this month at least. The toy will impress and make friends. If you walk into a room full of kids with any model of Beyblade in your hands, you are sure to draw an exuberant crowd of interested Beyblade hobbyists keen to discuss the power ratings and defensive capabilities of your combating top. Even parents are inclined to take note of the commercials and listen in on the complex, quasi-religious language of 'Beybladism', so that they are not left behind when their youngsters use the cult-like jargon native to their favourite pastime. But, like adults, kids are teased with the appeal of scorching hot new choices that often move in on the consumer radar so quickly that there is little time to realise what has hit the fan. The commercial media pump out a continuous stream of gimmicks and clever sales initiatives to entice the unsuspecting pool of young and adult shoppers out there to buy toys, cereals and lunch boxes. Clever advertising gives the items a magical persona, tying the fantasy to the product. Each child dreams of having a piece of make believe in their hot little hands. To believe that children's tastes are not affected by advertising is an escapist view of marketing. The power of the media images kids see cannot be denied, as consumerism promises to bring the virtual to life. The young and naive are often hit the hardest because they have not yet developed the defensive auto-immune strategies adults use to fight off at least some of the clone market appeal of every single item they are hit with by advertising. For that very reason, the effect of mass advertising and commercialism becomes a major influence on children's taste and material preferences. Why? Because children are consumers.

Kids from the ages of eight to fourteen spent a staggering 300 billion US dollars worldwide during 2002 on appearances, entertainment and food. In the book *BRANDchild*, marketing consultants Martin Lindstrom and Patricia Seybold call this group the 'Tween' generation – no longer tykes but not teens either. These kids are described as 'smart consumers', based on the fact that they learn to identify brands at an early age, and in the process have become sophisticated consumers of culture, keenly attuned to the marketing strategies aimed directly at their disposable income. 'Tweens' are also described as avid users of technology, including Playstation 2, XBox, mobile phones, DVDs and music downloaded from the internet. This skill is supposed to situate them well as consumers in a global marketplace. 'Tweens', we are told, also often suffer from social and cultural dislocation as members of broken homes or neglectful parents. Otherwise, how would these kids watch the 22,000 commercials that marketers claim they do each year? There are some other judgements about 'Tweens' beside the fact that they are 'brand slaves' without individuality: they love rewards, like secrets, have a mind of their own, are moody, competitive and exemplify the transition between the comfortable and familiar and the new and exciting. Sounds a lot like Harry Potter. Even the consumer habits of the young wizard and his friends fall in line, if we consider that some brands of magical broomsticks are better than others.

Could the fact that Harry Potter resembles a 'Tween' account for the popularity of the novels among children aged eight to fourteen? Can it also explain their phenomenal marketability?

Books are cultural commodities – pieces of history that are bought and sold. Books are also works of artistic flair we call 'literature' that comment on society and reflect cultural preoccupations and concerns. The *Harry Potter* series has sold in excess of 200 million books around the world and is being furiously translated into every major and minor language on the planet. Children's novels are not supposed to do that! The sales of the book are rivalled only by some of the largest grossing bestsellers and the greatest literary works in the English language. J.K. Rowling, like Stephen King or David Mamet, is not Shakespeare. But then again, no other writer dead or alive can compete with the literary clout of 'the Bard'. The American literary critic Harold Bloom believes that the way we define our cultural selves is by reading and studying stories of the human condition. Bestseller lists don't lie, however. If popularity is any indication of public taste and value, then the tales of Harry Potter's childhood adventures are to be considered masterpieces of literary genius that touch the human soul.

Children love the books because they see themselves in the otherwise ordinary protagonist. Harry Potter is a power-less child who is an orphan, lives with an unloving surrogate family, looks like a nerd, but discovers he has the heart of a lion. Oh, and to his delight, he also turns out to be a wizard. Harry Potter is an underdog who has fears and insecurities like all children, but he faces them head on and gives young readers a fantasy hero to identify with and live through. When the underdog becomes a hero, it is empowering. The popularity of the novels is great, owing to the fact that schools and critics have urged kids and adults alike to buy and read the books. *Harry Potter* has become a modern day vehicle for promoting literacy across cultures. Reading books helps develop lexical decoding skills no matter what the age and language. We hear amazing accounts of primary-school kids reading Rowling's 600-page book in two sittings. Stories abound of parents desperately trying to wrestle the novels out of the hands of their enchanted children at bedtime. These well-known urban legends are no doubt substantiated by 'grown-up' examples who are seen clutching copies of *Harry Potter*. Holding the book out in front of them, as if in prayer, they are unable to let go of the force of the fictional dream – to be children again. By all accounts, it would seem these novels are the cultural elixir of educational tools for creating a literate society, something that educational systems have had a hard time doing. But there is another side to the books: spin-off products and marketing.

Having achieved cult-like levels of popularity usually reserved only for rock stars and tele-evangelists, J.K. Rowling fills football stadiums for book readings. Literary admirers, young and old, dressed in the traditional wizardry garb of long flowing capes, tall pointy hats and magic wands, hang breathlessly on every syllable of the writer-prophet's words. Demand for the books is so great that facilities where the manuscripts are printed, bound and stored are patrolled round the clock by armed security guards to prevent a copy being stolen and a paragraph or two being leaked before its time to hungry readers. But at the same time the dramatisation rights to the novels have been sold to movie studios, and the spin-off product licensing deals to manufacturers have resulted in everything from Harry Potter glasses to Every Flavour Beans, Harry Potter frogs to board games, not to mention action figures, phone covers, clocks, mugs, T-shirts, shoes, play clothes, birthday supplies, etc. The list goes on and on and on. The spin-off deals have generated more profits than the *Harry Potter* books themselves. An estimated 2 billion US dollars of projected box-office and product 'tie-in' deals was generated from the first movie for AOL Time Warner, who also marketed the film in its magazines (e.g. *Time* and *People*). *Harry Potter* mania has created its own self-sustaining universe of fans of the novels, but at the same time admirers and critics have been repelled by the extent of the commercialisation. One can only hope in the name of good taste that the 'Tween' generation develops the media-savvy discretion to recognise the over-saturation of a theme. Otherwise, sighting a whole crowd of eleven year olds in Harry Potter designer glasses, wearing Ron Weasly T-shirts, drinking 'Live the Magic' Coca Cola and carrying Albus Dumbledore backpacks might not be so far-fetched.

As one would expect, *BRANDchild* is more or less a manual for marketers on how to advertise to kids who, in addition to their own spending, generate another 350 billion US dollars, spent by their parents, essentially by nagging. There could be something to it. The 'Tweens' seem to exist as just another gimmick to be sold to advertising executives who are looking for a phantom demographic group to hang a hat on when making a pitch. After all, we do have the 'Boomers', the 'Busters', the 'Echoes', and of course, 'Generation X'. As Martin Lindstrom says, 'Kids want something to believe in. If you can't believe in families, you can believe in brands.'

Brand Identity?

We spend a lifetime faithfully serving and rejecting brands. There is no public or private space of taste that has not been branded with a logo. There can be no 'product recognition' without a name. The lack of a brand can be a powerful logo too, used to market the quality of simple packaging as a selling point for cheaper goods and services. Advertising dominates the cultural landscape of our modern information society. Unless, of course, we move to the outback and are willing to shepherd a vulnerable and almost unimaginable existence away from the industrial web of the consumer market in a life without factory manufactured products and the relentless 'good taste machine' that is the media. As difficult as it may seem to comprehend today, a pastoral existence of perennial self-sufficiency was the norm for many hundreds of generations that preceded the age of technological achievement and rampant consumerism we now enjoy. There really was a time before mobile phones and Personal Digital Assistants – machines full of 'pop-up' advertising potential for the digital shopper on the wireless go.

The inconvenience of technology tied to a wall and cord inspired a wave of cordless gismos and gadgets. Cordless telephones, computers and the latest craze of Palm Pilots and BlackBerries now offer mobile access to all the consumer amenities. Hand-held access to data banks, messaging services, word processing and email conferencing is conveniently able to sit in your pocket waiting for the touch of a hand to engage this movable technology. Marketing executives dream of being the first to harness an original idea or to appropriate it for a new market that still lies waiting in uncharted copyright territory – having the foresight of Microsoft's Bill Gates, the god of Silicon Valley, who licenses the Microsoft operating system to all personal computer manufacturers on the planet, excluding Apple. Now that text messaging is going commercial, mobile phones will soon be electronic billboards on which advertisers can reach you anywhere, any time, transmitting commercials, offering sales promotions and asking you to enter contests for prizes to be won simply by dialling a free-phone number and typing in the correct answer on your keypad. Brands and stores will be brought to your pocket. Thus the personal 'ad-free' space we have at our disposal will be further reduced. There will be no place to hide from the long arm of marketing.

Along with progress and the quick satisfaction of all our consumer needs and desires come well-earned disappointments and sacrifices. We perhaps do not even notice the loss of freedom, the impingement on our thoughts and personal expression, that marketing enacts upon us in order to sell products reflecting good taste. In the contemporary consumer society of the 21st century, the right to make choices is hindered by the rhetoric of persuasion and the power of branding. For the shopping centre majority that occupies the urban landscape, marketing is here to stay. It saturates our lives with images of good taste that are continually coming at us with blinding speed and high intensity via newspapers, magazines, flyers, television, movies, radio and the internet. No matter what form the content and the messages take through memorable images and clever sales pitches, marketing is more and more disguised as 'important information' required by consumers to educate themselves before making purchases. The advertising media count on the 'good faith' of shoppers with undiscriminating attitudes about how products and services are promoted. Marketing often relies on stirring the emotions of consumers rather than awakening the rational and critical side of our capitalistic consciousness that wants to acquire everything. Advertising cannot be called a public service announcement. It wants your shopping behaviours and choices to be influenced by the marketing twist on *information* – especially when the form and content of the message is being paid for by companies hoping to separate you from your money. Advertising helps you to become an informed consumer who recognises brands and sales pitches – that is a good thing. But marketing campaigns ask you to buy into illusions and dreams as much as merchandise and services. Women will not fall at your feet when you wear a particular brand of aftershave lotion, deodorant or cologne unless it contains traces of chloroform. Men will not follow you around the world because you use a specific herbal shampoo, shiny lip gloss or nail polish.

Consumer psychology is captivated by the charisma of slogans and jingles pushing 'nostalgia', 'cutting edge', 'fantasy', 'classy culture', 'cool culture', 'action culture', 'beauty culture', 'smart culture', 'comic culture' and just about anything that can be sold – as long as it has a hook that is memorable. Advertising used to be based on the premise of quality, quality and more quality. With the intention of achieving recognition as the founders of a new product with *fad fatal* image appeal, marketing powerhouses help make or break specific trends. The red carpet of good taste is laid out for new and exciting products that exist as the prodigies of an advertising executive's latest dream campaign. Advertisers are forever scrambling to come up with successful promotion packages with the power to sway swarms of shoppers their way. Marketing is what consumer dreams are made of. The silver lining may change daily or weekly, however, as newer equally impressive options take hold through persuasive advertising. Whether it is the latest air technology in toilet tissues or running shoes, the newest design in TAG Heuer watches or the current styles of Tommy Hilfiger ties, a brand of life insurance or a flavour of cereal, successful advertising creates products and services we all *must have*. The media keep us up to date and on target relative to what is current and popular from flip flops to Hummers; yet inversely, it lets us know just how out of touch we really are with the popular passions of an era and its tastes.

Sound marketing can make a mountain out of a molehill. Ultimately, the incentive for corporations is to make millions, or even billions, if they can persuade consumers to believe in the 'taste' value of a new idea or image, product, technology or fad. Marketing leads personal tastes down the path of opportunity as a product takes on an image and aura of its own. For consumers, selection is made easier if there is an attractive and familiar brand name to pick from. The process of choosing a toothpaste can be daunting when faced with a retail shelf that holds a dozen or more brands, all containing very similar ingredients. Recognising a label can be like seeing an old friend in a crowd of strangers. You gravitate to the comfort of something or someone familiar. It proves a simple and comforting solution when there are just too many possibilities to choose from.

The clever packaging of the 'Ban' anti-perspirant stick, with its aerodynamic dispenser, makes the product stand out as a tasteful choice for consumers – simply because of the familiarity of its outer trappings. The design of the logo determines its artistic appeal in its own right. The metallic silvers and blues support a meticulously designed label. If it were to be peeled off, removed and enlarged, it could even serve as an attractive graphic design illustration reminiscent of Andy Warhol's pop culture prints, framed and ready for hanging in the modern decor of a study. Its razor-sharp design with dynamic and yet soothing metallic slashes of blues and greys gives the impression of a rally racing image gone commercial. The up-tempo, glitzy and refined cool packaging of the 'Ban' anti-perspirant dispenser would outshine the dated rectangular, yellow 'no name' container with bland, basic black lettering. The confidence of a manufacturer who backs the quality of its product through enormous investments in marketing campaigns and special packaging conveys an assurance to the consumer that the product must be worth paying more for. Discrepancies in price often fail to deter consumers who may pay even up to a third more for a product that has the very same ingredients strictly on the basis of its good looks and competent marketing campaign. But, if two products contain the same basic ingredients, why not buy the cheaper one?

Because of unlimited exposure to a dizzying variety of goods and services available to individuals in our techno-media saturated existence, it is easy to be swept along in irrelevant consumerism – a consumerism driven by the naivete of the viewer who unknowingly is moulded by the marketing finesse of the advertiser. Needs and desires are created where there previously were none. Many of us live with the mistaken belief that we are unaffected by marketing agendas and that all choices are our own. The 'Bud Light' beer we have just decided to try has no relation, or so we think, to the commercial we viewed seven times during the first 90 minutes of show time television it was aired on during the Super Bowl, the 'Granddaddy' of all marketing bonanzas, for a cost of $2 million per 30 seconds. While standing in line at the snack bar during a sporting event, waiting to acquire an adult beverage and wondering what label to try, the catchy jingle and comic relief of the advertisement comes to mind, reminding us that it 'tastes great' but has 'less calories'. In scanning the selection of brand names placed confidently on the walls behind the servers, we recall the images of laughing faces and good times that fill the beer commercials. Or the beautiful people in the great outdoors enjoying a cold and refreshing drink. The appealing examples that have pervaded our consciousness make Bud Light a choice good enough to consider.

Successful advertising for alcoholic beverages offers consumers images and jingles that become signposts of an individual's history. The 'I am Canadian' campaign reintroduced a young generation of beer drinkers to an old brand of beer, 'Molson Canadian'. It worked. Brand visibility and sales increased. The first ads played on the stereotypical image of Canadians as a people with no national pride or unique identity – a long-standing complaint and a source for humour. The commercials featured a young man standing in front of a projection screen displaying a waving, red maple leaf while engaging in a rousing diatribe on what it means to be Canadian. Viewers were treated to a catalogue of well-known, stock images that included igloos, hockey players, great expanses of nature and hikers with a flag patch sewn on a tattered knapsack. Unwittingly, the final phrase of the commercials – 'I am Canadian' – became a rallying cry for renewing a sense of nationalism and pride in the idea of Mondo Canuck, the beer-swilling pacifist world traveller who wears a toque and lives on the frozen Great Lakes. The cultural signposts that had become a painful source of global embarrassment and self-deprecating jokes had provided a source of national glory. Canadians were forced to celebrate and renew their sense of identity, all because of an advertising campaign for a brand of beer that was perceived not cool enough to drink. It is both a fitting and ironic tribute to marketing. Only in Canada you say? Pity.

Advertisements offer a consumer the promise of sheer pleasure through stylish packaging and the pretty prompting of mega-realities that echo the possibilities of a life of virtual happiness always within our grasp yet so far away. If only we would buy 'Brand X' instead of 'Brand Y', then everything would be perfect. The messages of advertising act at the subliminal level of self-consciousness where our deepest and most profound desires are situated and can be influenced by emotional appeals. The strongest sensibilities, fear, love, hate and envy or greed, are the main targets of marketers. Advertisements are designed to intensify the desire for products and services by creating a need where none had existed before. Consumers have always been subject to clever promotional gimmicks and hard sell pitches as the goods prowl the media catwalks of culture. But to be where the marketing giants intend them to be, to soar where Superman goes, up, up and away to the top of the sales charts, products and services have to have the status of a brand. That is, a recognisable image and identity whose 'core meaning' has real and residual cultural value. Coca Cola is 'The Real Thing'; Audi will lead but 'Never Follow'; and, as if we didn't know, 'There's a little bit of McDonalds in everyone.' The brand is the philosophy of a corporation. It is the spirit behind the novel names and knick-knacks that symbolise the well-marketed fruits of labour produced by a post-industrial, media-saturated generation. The brand is the living will of a corporation – its heart and soul. It is an ideological testament that induces big audience appeal and trades for big bucks because it has the power to frame the popular tastes of a nation. Products have become marketing tools. Quality is no longer a major selling point because of stiffer competition. The charisma of a marketing campaign evolves through the characterisation of a product or service by way of a brand identity.

Credit card companies sell imaginary products by creating images of wealth and luxury designed to press subscribers into years of loyal patronage and a fiscal existence that can be measured out in exorbitant debt service ratios at high rates of interest. The competition between brands for those last bits of reserve cash we have at our disposal has been heating up as the bears have taken over the bull markets of the late 90s. Except that money has become so hard to find these days. Consumer debt has risen to alarming levels. Many merchants no longer accept some denominations of currency because of counterfeits, and debit cards are more common than cash. Consequently, credit cards have become the poor man's cash reserve: the preferred form of legal tender with which to buy now and pay later. 'American Express' was a brand once thought to be 'untouchable'. It was associated with money and exclusivity thanks to advertising spots that invited you to partake in the consumer advantages of its famous client base. The 'Don't leave home without it', 'Membership has its privileges' and 'Do you know me?' campaigns featured the likes of Tom Hanks, John Cleese, Pelé, Monica Seles and Elvis Presley in order to bring celebrity shopping habits up close and personal to consumers like you and me. Now, with much more competition from upstart lending outfits with low introductory interest rates and attractive loyalty perks, American Express has been promoting a futuristic makeover for the trademark green plastic so as to make it stand out again at the front of the cashier line. One version of the credit card has undergone a major face-lift that renders it a sublime techno-translucent and cool neon blue card. The marketing caption is 'As if its looks weren't rewarding enough.' The line could refer to the new credit card or appeal to the user's ego – remember only the beautiful people like you carry 'American Express', so why not flash your plastic in true style? The message is subtle and ambiguous – and yet obvious to those who fancy themselves to be more than they are given credit for: *to complement your good looks, you have to have the new and more attractive American Express card.*

Just to make sure the message hits home, American Express

also offer tangible rewards as membership incentives. From the loyalty programme you can get home electronics, airline tickets, sporting goods and *other stuff you've always wanted*, at no cost. Just think of it. Free stuff! Like other lines of credit, the promise of bonus merchandise, entertainment and travel frames the advertising campaign to promote the appealing possibilities of using the American Express card. But one has to ask exactly how much money you have to spend before you are rewarded with that 'free' toaster. If you can afford to squander your credit limit many times over, then you can most probably manage the tiny appliance without having to buy a High Definition plasma screen TV that costs thousands to get it. And yet, there are countless people who are persuaded to routinely spend a small fortune for cheap rewards and continue to remain fervently loyal to a brand. They will cut out hundreds of box tops and 'proof of purchase' labels and post them to product manufacturers in order to get their hands on that precious cache of 'free stuff' – no matter what it is. There is nothing wrong with brand loyalty, but usually there is a huge discrepancy between the cash outlay of the consumer and the value of the reward: purchase a new house and get a free barbecue; buy a car and receive a DVD player; mortgage your property and enjoy six months of free internet access. Some goods and services are given to companies free of charge as promotional items, while the cost of others amounts to a mere pittance when bought in bulk. Either way, for companies the rewards of incentive programmes far outweigh the expenditures: consumers are kept contented and coming back to the same brand, time and time again. 'American Express' still depends on the lure of exclusivity, fame and fortune associated with the brand. Even though the 'Gold' and 'Platinum' are more accessible, few have ever seen the legendary 'Black' card that is rumoured to exist in the wallets of oil magnates, heads of state, and dot com billionaires who use it to buy Lear jets, yachts the size of small islands and palatial mansions. Nevertheless, the American Express brand now has added value for the common consumer as the brand continues to proliferate among those cash poor without the budget for the unexpected perks of membership. It makes one wonder: just how many toasters could you get for buying Aristotle Onassis's island of Scorpios?

Marketers maintain that branding is about ensuring customers are happy dealing with a company, and loyalty is a by-product of buyer satisfaction. You still need an 'unbeatable product' to urge consumers to spend money on your gadget or service – no one will buy something that does not keep its advertised promises. But consumers are creatures of habit, always gravitating to safe and familiar buying territory. All shrewd marketers know that reinforcing perceptions about a brand is easier than changing them if a product offers real value.

A company has to stand by its advertising claims and offer tons of customer service and support to back up its claims. They need to keep customers not only happy, but loyal. Especially since it costs six times more to attract new customers than to keep existing ones. Eighty per cent of sales usually come from the top 20 per cent of a company's clientele. The average business in the United States loses half of its customers every five years. If to achieve a yearly growth of one per cent a company needs a fourteen per cent increase in sales annually, then the effect of 'disloyal consumers' is devastating for the profit margins companies forecast. Thus, behavioural and emotional loyalty to a brand are the main targets of marketers. Companies make income and dividend projections based on consumer demographics that segment the population into groups with specific characteristics relating to income, age, personal habits and possessions, marital status, profession, hobbies and interests, group affiliations, education, gender, sexuality, ethnicity and so on. The point is to 'know your customer', so that advertisements can make value propositions about products and services aimed at well-defined target markets who could want them. Surveys and focus groups are conducted to create a 'living snapshot' of the consumer's world. Market research is straightforward in theory: it will allow a company to better understand how its customers think and feel, why they behave the way they do, as well as explaining the perceptions and attitudes governing their behaviour. Branding depends on understanding how to stimulate the feelings of loyalty and commitment that nurture habitual actions and responses in consumers by turning wants into needs. Advertising has relied on the principles of behavioural modification that B.F. Skinner used to train pigeons to fly in circles during the 1950s. Armed with all of this customer research and rudimentary psychology, companies can then create marketing campaigns that match specific messages to appropriate media for a particular consumer and use the desired emotional stimuli to get the right behavioural response. Why? The financial formula is simple: BRANDING + LOYALTY = PROFITS. The key to a company's success is a high level of customer commitment. As loyalty to a brand increases, consumers are less sensitive to price changes and competitive marketing campaigns. Less advertising is required to maintain sales and the costs of product information and media distribution are decreased.

I'm in Love With My Car

Have you ever asked yourself: 'What car brands do I notice on the road and why?' Cars are metallic constructions of taste that incorporate sophisticated principles of creativity and design in the name of speed. They are ideas in action to save time getting from point 'A' to point 'B'. Yet we barely pay attention to car brands and designs when driving or walking, unless an exceptional case comes along – perhaps a Lotus Turbo Esprit, a Ferrari Testarossa, a Porsche Turbo Carrera, or a Rolls Royce Silver Shadow. The fact is that many cars for the average consumer have common design features that blend together and are not vividly memorable. Close your eyes. Now think: how does the look of a Toyota Corolla differ radically from that of a Honda Civic? Micro branding makes a difference at this level, as it distinguishes between manufacturers more than cars. A dealer trying to close a deal may describe one of these top-selling cars as having the 'mushy feel' and 'slow acceleration' of 'an old man's car', while portraying the other as 'quick' and 'responsive', making driving 'fun' at any speed. But that kind of qualitative judgement about car performance relies not so much on reference to real differences, as on appealing to the consumer's ego and creating pleasing or repellent identifications. The marketing ploy is: 'Do you want to be "young and fast" or "old and slow"?' In reality, cars are put into categories that are defined by engine size, wheel base, weight and seating capacity, thus making them more similar than different in overall performance and dimensions. Design specifications sometimes make one car look and stand out over another. Car performance is affected by engine capacity, body mass and chassis styling. Computer modelling, wind-tunnel analysis and track testing are used to make a vehicle more aerodynamic, and thus able to achieve higher speeds and hold the road instead of becoming airborne. The designs of most domestic and imported cars are not *totally* indistinguishable from each other, but are unremarkable enough that you won't register their uniqueness when you drive by them on the road unless you look at the logo. Yet, it would not be fair to compare a Ford Focus to a Mercedes S500. A great deal of money and technology separates the cars. Ford advertises its cars as 'built to last' with the penny counting masses in mind, while Mercedes emphasises luxury styling for the connoisseur who can afford it as 'smart' money.

A petrol station attendant who is supporting two children, a wife, a cat, two gerbils and his arthritic mother-in-law who lives in the basement needs to consider carefully how he spends what he makes. If a quasi-miracle happens and a 'scratch and win' lottery ticket provides him with a cash windfall, he would have to carefully consider how to budget it wisely. If he bought a BMW instead of fixing the leak in the roof, tiling the kitchen, repairing the broken windows and buying his mother-in-law the wheelchair she requires, he could be demonstrating bad taste in ethics and financial matters. He wouldn't be doing the greatest good for the greatest number. This guy is obviously not alone. To ignore the basic needs of those around him – not putting food on the table, not providing a safe shelter for the kids and not keeping his mother-in-law in a healthy state – for the sake of getting a really hot car does not paint a picture of a rational individual. The desire to buy the BMW becomes superficial, artificial and difficult to maintain. Fixing the house, taking care of his mother-in-law, difficult as she may be, and buying a much cheaper Hyundai would display funda-mental insight in ways of sound money management. His wife would be grateful that the renovations were out of the way. The mother-in-law would thank him for ever and he would still have a new warranty and car to carry him through the next decade or so. For a wealthier person, buying a BMW would be a more justifiable selection. To the less financially endowed, it offers the stigma of being a status seeker. Excessive spending at the cost of not satisfying basic needs makes for an unfortunate situation. Living within financial abilities rather than imitating those who are less monetarily challenged shows good judgement and consequently good taste. A realistic distribution of resources creates a life situation that is not jeopardised by illusions. There is a direct effect between personal cost and economic means. Setting financial goals that have to be achieved before the BMW is bought is not a bad thing. So why not consider a smaller car?

The Austin Mini Cooper is an example of a car brand that has gone inconspicuously about its business since its first taste of popularity in the 60s, but is now redefining itself to gain more market share. Due to a virulent advertising campaign, 'the Mini' has enjoyed a resurgence in demand among single, 'young-ish' professionals, despite its 'boxy' frame and cramped interior. Thanks to the rise of retro chic, the psychedelic tastes of the 60s are back again, popularised by 'Austin Powers' movies, shark-fin suits and remakes of hit songs like 'I'm a Believer'. The 'mojo' of the Mini has been updated to fit quite nicely within the 21st century in 'look-at-me', 'shagadelic' shades of sparkling purple and passion flower red. The car demands the attention of divorced Boomers and Gen Xers alike. Sex isn't a carefree handshake like it was during the 60s, but the free spirit of the Mini Cooper brand is still marketed with the same libidinal force of nostalgia today as it ever was, to people looking for a person to fill the passenger seat. A commercial in North America depicts a sweaty young man and woman rising from the front seats, doing up their clothes, after what we may assume was a pretty strenuous session of impromptu physical exchanges. They say 'Wow' and comment on the surprising roominess of the Mini Cooper. Just then, a third person, a woman, emerges from the back seat – hair tussled, doing up her clothes – and says 'Yeah!' If 'practical' and 'economical' really have to be unattractive adjectives for cars, then why not sell dreams instead of wheels? Car makers do.

With performance cars, designs are more radical and refined in terms of styling and speed, in order to distinguish the expensive tastes and fulfil the special desires of the owner. Branding is more obviously related to a niche market of well-to-do drivers and not a general population just looking for reliable wheels. We do not see much mainstream advertising for such cars – simply because they are unaffordable for 95 per cent of the population. A Lamborghini Diablo has a wide, sleek shape and is only inches off the ground – because it has to be. Before it could reach a top speed of 209.3 mph, a car with the tortoise-shell design of a Volkswagen Beetle would quickly disintegrate. That is, if it had not already flown off the motorway. The design of the Lamborghini Diablo will surely turn heads as it blasts by regular traffic on the German Autobahn or stops at a red light. In fifth gear, about the only thing that you will distinguish is the tail wing designed to apply downward G-force to the 3,366 lb (1,530 kg) bull of a frame. At six feet wide, with variable timing side air intake vents, and massive 20-odd-inch rear tyres, the Lamborghini Diablo resembles an F1 racing car more than it does a 'roadworthy' vehicle used for shuttling across town. The trademark 'butterfly doors' pivot upwards instead of outwards to facilitate driver and passenger getting in and out of the tight seating quarters. You have to first sit down in the bucket seat and then swing your legs into the car because space is at a premium no matter what adjustments are made. Going from 0 to 60 mph in 3.85 seconds means that the driver is more or less at the mercy of the 5,707cc, V12 engine – the beast puts out 530 horsepower at 7,500 rpm with a torque of 446.5 lb/ft and makes the hairs on the back of your neck stand on end during the three phases of ignition. The Lamborghini Diablo is the first 'road car' to break the 200 mph barrier. The Diablo (meaning 'the Devil') costs in excess of $400,000 and changes hands at amounts appreciably higher than the manufacturer's Recommended Retail Price. The most valuable Lamborghinis have driven 1,000 miles or less for every year after production. It is not unusual to find a ten-year-old car with 10,000 clicks on the milometer selling at nearly a million dollars. The performance car is not only a means of transportation: its design holds a dream and a promise of potency that only you could achieve and command. This might explain why middle-aged men make up the majority of sports car buyers. The idea is to show anyone who cares that the machinery under the hood is not only in good working order, but can still perform at high levels of endurance and deliver the goods. Nothing spells success better than excess.

The Lamborghini brand, like other exclusive sports cars, depends on the suggestion of potency, beauty and danger. Its logo is a bull, stamping its feet and snorting, ready to charge. The world has to take notice of its unique design: everything is bigger, louder, faster, edgier, rounder, sleeker. Performance cars exist in another social dimension of marketing – an imaginary space where, free from the everyday constraints of functionality and economic reality, manufacturers can be creative in design and satisfy the desire for speed through the very best in car technology. The performance car itself becomes a form of artistic expression and monumental technological achievement rather than a mechanical tool for transportation. The brand name car is the interface to a dream of the good life as it moves forward in time and space at warp speed. Ultimately, pleasure is derived from your ownership and public operation of the performance car since it is fundamentally a symbol of wealth and luxury. A limited edition sporting car is a form of cultural capital that you can parade on the street in true capitalist style. You can please yourself by showing your good taste to others openly and freely through ownership of a rare commodity. That is why performance cars are collected and pampered, and are considered artefacts or pieces of motor history rather than vehicles used for driving between distances. Some production line cars do incorporate the new technologies and aerodynamic designs of performance cars, but only to the degree where styling and driving ease make economic sense for the manufacturer and the consumer. At the lower price points, power and speed are not as big an issue as fuel consumption. Yes, you want an up-to-date car with all the smooth and curvaceous body contours of a luxury or performance model; it might even have a bit of a kick to get you out of a tight spot. But a small car is still a small car, rumbling away behind performance cars at the lowest end of the car chain, no matter what the brand. You might as well accept the reality and choose a colour that doesn't stand out too much unless you want to be noticed. Is it any wonder most mass-production cars on the road are silver, white, black or grey?

Reviving Reality

Taste now consumes us in the ever-changing choices we ultimately make as members of any culture and community. Yet, it also involves a commitment of interest and time, and the courage to go sometimes where no person would go – except for the sake of good taste. However, it remains a puzzling mystery why the portraits of Elvis Presley painted on black velvet that flooded the United States during the 60s and 70s ended up being so popular. We can only speculate that most of these icons rendered on the California and Mexico border by Latino artisans immortalising 'the King' were just too cheap to resist as pieces of folk culture. What else would look perfect in a mobile home alongside a velvet Jesus, perhaps, or dogs playing poker? Popular culture and the growth of the middle classes has broken down the tradition of relegating things and practices to either high-brow or lowbrow. Mass-production of goods has created mass culture that is both affordable and cheap, and sometimes 'kitschy' in the forms of reproduction it takes – mainly because good taste is no longer the domain of one group or community. We are all consumers now and the idea of elitism and rebellion has been overdone so many times as a marketing strategy that we no longer fully buy into the notion of products making us hip or successful. The images of good taste keep on changing, so our choices merely reflect the sign of the times. There is a definite acceptance of middle or 'nobrow' values that defy categor-isation according to the old systems of classification. The meaning of good taste changes along with the preoccu-pations of the cultures and subcultures populating a society. New values have been easier to disseminate and emulate on a global scale because of innovations in communications media. Machines and the internet have spawned a cyber-sex revolution that has brought 'soul mates' and lovers together, sight unseen, via the bits and bytes of passion exchanged on electronic bulletin boards and chat lines across the world. People have come together regardless of race, class, gender or sexuality. With the advent of modern communications media technologies, there is the promise that the old distinctions between high and low culture will begin to fade.

Only a few hundred years ago, the ruling classes had specific expectations regarding their right to exemplify and develop good taste. The idea of democracy is a lot older than its practice as a system of government. The upper classes and aristocracy who had the money and connections to build private collections were empowered over the lower classes. Historical treasures, fine art, literature and its aesthetic experiences were firmly in the personal domain of the ruling classes. Until the mid to late 19th century, the masses had no access to the refined sensibilities of a 'higher culture'. It was only because of world exploration, colonial expansion and imperialism that public exhibitions and museums were inaugurated and cultural artefacts were put on display so that a general audience could see the conquests of powerful nations. Today things are different. In Western society, all people and classes have potential access to libraries, displays, television and the internet, which offer knowledge, culture and tastes simply by way of their availability. There are educational resources and facilities to help anyone who is motivated and inclined to learn about a subject area of interest. Television, the internet, literature, galleries, museums and libraries provide information that covers how to evaluate modern dance, the history of *haute couture*, Indian philosophy, video art, or even the fine details of stamp collecting. Nothing is out of bounds. Information that is easily accessed nowadays was once almost impossible to come by unless you were born into social circles that allowed you to absorb an elite type of learning under the tutelage of masters as a kind of inheritance or birthright. Cultural insights are no longer 'privileged'; there are no clear-cut class divisions that inhibit our access to artefacts of knowledge and taste, good and bad. All is fair game.

In today's techno-driven society the rich and famous are no longer only aristocrats and royalty, as television programming has created its own prestigious elite. They breeze down the red carpets with an air of true royal status. Catherine Zeta-Jones and Michael Douglas are photographed and paparazzied like a true royal couple – prince and princess. Where Hollywood royalty proves too rare and pricey to continually contract, media producers have devised a way to create a low-grade brand of rags-to-riches celebrities that everyone can identify with. A new set of cultural icons demand an admiration and respect so intense, they have pushed the aristocrats and blue-blooded aside as old-world anachronisms in a media-driven society. The Hollywood royalty live on as the models of our time. Television contests of skill and fantasy play on the ability of the human species to overcome ordinariness in feats of survival, talent, beauty or love. Reality shows are the craze for getting the largest market share of consumers, viewers and advertisers. These gimmick shows allow the audience to live vicariously as celebrities through the 'real people' who are chosen from the mainstream masses to compete for love, fame and fortune. Some might call this display of personal emotions, fears and private moments for entertainment and advertising revenue extremely bad taste. Yet, the shows get the ratings. This lucrative television market that preys on the appeal of *big living on the edge* has brought to us, the common folk, the magical small-screen bubbles of *Big Brother*, *Survivor*, *Temptation Island*, *Fame Academy*, *Pop Stars* and *Pop Idol*. Millions of viewers live out their days and weeks episode by episode, waiting for the ultimate resolution. We, the audience, admire some contestants and dislike others – often cheering for the underdogs. Will our favourite succeed? Contestants, television executives, hosts, directors and programme crews are sworn to secrecy, having signed non-disclosure agreements on pain of litigation. The stakes are high: loads of money, a record contract or true love. The final broadcast of *Pop Idol* solicited viewers to vote on the talent they deemed to be the best. Millions of people took the initiative to contribute an opinion on which of the two finalists they preferred. In the end, Will Young's voice and talent won out over Gareth Gates' equally remarkable singing ability, thanks to a majority vote from the British public. The endearing winner was ushered democratically into stardom. (Although, in the end, Gareth, the runner-up, looks likely to have had the more successful career.) The overwhelming interest in this celebrity sweepstake is somewhat surprising. In the USA version, *American Idol*, 24 million viewers voted during the final broadcast – an astonishing figure for an hour-long television show, considering that in the last presidential election less than 52 per cent of the US population (about 100 million people) made their way to the ballot box to vote George W. Bush into the White House. The power of the media to influence and capture the interest of the population is ultimately staggering. Programmes that raise entertainment to the level of reality allow us to play out our fantasy lives. The public give themselves up to this fantasy far more willingly than to political affairs.

Real-life stories make for compelling, dramatic television: a girl who is kidnapped and kept happy by her captor and his wife to a degree that she willingly does not reveal herself when opportunity arises; or the story of a tycoon bludgeoned to death in his mansion just days before the terms of his divorce settlement were to be finalised, the sudden concern of his estranged wife diagnosed with ovarian cancer while his sister seeks custody of the twin thirteen-year-old heirs. Truth is stranger than fiction. Producers work fast when a story line promises to be a marketable commodity that will incite audience emotions and controversy. After all, isn't real life what stories are made from? Caught on camera in a brawl over money or a cat fight between candidates competing to seduce a bachelor, the dynamics of unstaged human behaviour entertain in a very compelling and yet disturbing way. Coming up with a juicy saga of a deal becomes ever more pressing in the new millennium of television bolstered by the appeal of the reality show that is quickly defining the retrograde good taste of this decade.

There is proof of the longevity of dinosaur cultures: the 70s madman rocker Ozzy Osbourne is still alive, a classic example of the Baby Boomer on his wobbly last legs. Having survived the debauchery of sex, drugs and rock 'n' roll that was the 70s, he is a television celebrity *au naturel*. (A)live and close up – warts and all – Ozzy is the unlikely star of a hit reality television show, *The Osbournes*, based on his foul-mouthed family life. Loving relationships, but X-rated language. 'Semi-retired' from performing in concerts but still at it well into his 50s because the money is good, Ozzy Osbourne is carving out a new career as a television personality and has ironically become the media's patriarch of the nuclear family. Need I say more? The Satanic rocker of Black Sabbath fame has transformed into a man of wealth and highbrow taste refined by upper-class sensibilities. There is no paranoia here. Only contradictions – just cream-coloured taffeta curtains and deep pillowed sofas, plasma television screens and limited edition SUVs. We see him shuffle around his poshly furnished, Spanish-style LA villa cleaning up after the messes of his umpteen dogs and other pets – not to mention 'the kids' and their friends, and the friends of their friends, and the indistinguishable 'hangers-on'. In one episode, he climbs the magisterial steps of the mahogany bannistered spiral staircase, heading to the second floor of the mansion's inner sanctum of private rooms. We think we hear him say, 'I'm tired of this place being a fucking dump', as he mutters unintelligibly to himself or to anyone in his household who will listen. On another occasion, he gives advice to his daughter about the animosity she feels towards her brother for signing a band she had discovered to his record label. We feel for Ozzy and identify with his plight as a father and fellow human being. The rock star becomes all too mortal. He is Us. But it gets even better. We get to see his dirty laundry and he doesn't get to see ours. We feel sympathetic, but ultimately superior. We get to judge the contradictory morality of his behaviour and the quality of his tastes, past and present, as we imagine and visualise them through the camera lens. A Satanic Rocker Baby Boomer? The contradiction between the Osbournes' collective behaviour toward each other as a loving family – the swearing, the back-biting, the daily conflicts, the sibling rivalry, the show of affections, THE SWEARING – and their privileged social standing is what makes the show interesting. It is like watching *The Beverly Hillbillies* all over again. Except this time they have come from hell. The popularity of *The Osbournes* attests to the fascination we have with the living legends of the 70s and the mythology of bad manners and dissipation that has deservedly followed them well past the middle ages of 'Boomerhood'. If it were your family on television, or mine, would this reality show be as popular? I think not! We are compassionate yet critical voyeurs of a walking testament to the need for the tightening of laws governing controlled substances.

Post-Hip: The Generation Gap

Branding is about the corporation transcending the product or service it offers. Nowadays, *a consumer is purchasing an attitude or a lifestyle rather than a material object or a convenience*. A brand defines a corporate philosophy and concepts that consumers buy into, and it in turn defines them within the cultural sphere. The Gap – founded on the cusp of the 70s in 1969 – is only one of a huge number of corporations that places 'vintage' and 'nostalgia' at the centre of its advertising campaign while marketing jeans.

During the 60s, jeans were symbols of rebellion against institutions of authority, 'the Man'. No self-respecting, God-fearing, law-abiding person would have dared wear denim for fear of being called a radical. Coupled with the pursuit of 'free love' and the smoking of some 'righteous weed', jeans represented the essence of the Hippie's life of rebellion. In 60s America, Hippies were on the same social, political and ethical level as those 'Godless Communists' Senator McCarthy feared. Hippies were social outcasts. They lived outside the conventions of lawful citizenship and the dictates of the state. Hippies were easily identifiable by their long hair. And, of course, love beads, tie-dyed shirts, peace signs and faded denim. Jeans were considered the pinnacle of bad taste by the middle classes. They symbolised the filth and physical toil of the labourer or the lawless, not the leisure and disposable income of the white-collar worker. The middle class who supported nation, God, the nuclear family, democracy and capitalism – not necessarily in that order – detested the moral laxity that jeans represented. However, the 60s Hippie rebellion was not about legal and moral prohibitions against sex and drugs. Rather, it was about personal freedom and the problems associated with how the individual citizen fits into society while expressing dissent about the status quo. Jeans allied the Hippies with the working underclass of America: immigrants, the illiterate and the poor – the groups that conservative governments and multinational corporations exploited to get business done. Ironically, the jeans of the working class were a relatively expensive item of clothing due to limited production. But they lasted a long time, so were worth the investment, especially if you had to buy only one pair of trousers. With the deregulation of world economies, the radical mystique of jeans faded as the price dropped dramatically and they entered the mainstream in the 70s.

Exploiting the American love for nostalgia, The Gap uses the tag line 'For every generation' to sell jeans. The campaign builds on the very successful 'Who wore khakis?' ads of 1993 featuring self-destructive idols and beat generation legends James Dean and Jack Kerouac to create a fantasy of brand cool. If The Gap is associated with rebellious celebrities, then it must be 'hip to' rebellious creativity too. At least, that was the marketing angle used to sell khakis as the symbols of the age of the rebel circa the 1950s. Of the peculiarities that have come to represent 60s revolution and counterculture cool, hip-hugging bell bottoms have seen a resurgence in the early 2000s. With a little more emphasis on the sex appeal of the navel and belly than their precursors, the reappearance of low-waisted, wide-legged trousers is considered beautiful and desirable – hip – by all classes.

The cultural superheroes of today are quick to show off the value of retro chic as a counterculture standard of good taste. The leggy mega-model Giselle could sell the vintage glamour of Guess jeans with a flash of fleshy midriff. Other current media stars have also taken to the commercial podium to offer an image to a product. Vince Carter of the Toronto Raptors is shot by Nike in black and white footage with a supersize afro playing schoolyard B-ball against 70s NBAers and high school kids; Led Zeppelin is indirectly featured in a Cadillac promo as the distinctive voice of Robert Plant wails away in the background, singing 'Been a long time since I rock and rolled.' The advertisements are designed to entice you to relive a piece of history and leverage the image of cool by purchasing a running shoe or car. This might explain why in 2002 the top ten bestselling touring musical acts in the world were Paul McCartney, The Rolling Stones, Cher, Elton John and Billy Joel, followed by Bruce Springsteen, Aerosmith, Neil Diamond, the Eagles and Crosby, Stills, Nash and Young. Nostalgia sells. But there is always variation with the theme of rebellion. The names and faces of 60s and 70s countercultures still have the staying power to lead multi-million-dollar marketing campaigns, yet the rich and famous media icons of today are no longer only old money, royalty and the rock and roll aristocracy. New rebels have emerged. Lets face it, if Eminem were walking down one side of a New York boulevard and Her Royal Highness, the Queen, were strolling on the other, odds are that the rapper would draw the bigger crowd. (If the same scenario was to be replayed at a lawn bowling arena in Victoria, Canada – a safe haven for retired British loyalists – chances are the statistics would be reversed in favour of Her Majesty.) The results might have been the same in Soho during the late 60s if Mick Jagger or The Who crossed the Queen's path. There is no denying, however, the effect of counterculture appeal on mainstream media markets and consumer tastes. Everyone from middle-aged weekend bikers to tattoo-sporting teenagers wants to be a rebel.

Counterculture has achieved a marketing integrity in the public sphere that is genuine and influential as the 'cool school' comes of age. Yet again. 'Bad boy' and 'bad girl' celebrities are definitely sought-after media and marketing commodities. Colin Farrell, Brad Pitt, Charlie Sheen, Pink, Courtney Love and Madonna have all fitted the bill in one way or another. Radical or excessive behaviour has given rise to new subcultures that are now the status symbols of the time. 'Divas', 'Goddesses', 'Skaters', 'Bangers', 'Metal

Heads' and 'Hip Hoppers' are examples of groups that draw their identity from countercultures represented by celebrities and media icons. Now subcultures serve to define taste as only the upper classes and aristocracy could in pre-media times. There are 'teens in jeans' who have made their way up to the commercial stratosphere from the lower-income housing of their youth by helping to carve out new directions and priorities for contemporary consumers. These images have been meticulously cultivated. Avril Lavigne plays up the post-AC/DC 'Skater Girl' image of 'frantic youth gone wild', displaying an odd barrage of 70s-style heavy metal hand signs and cheesy school girl outfits complete with tie. Britney Spears has gone from virginal little girl with romantic dreams to sweaty, panting sex kitten in the space of a few bad relationships over two blockbuster albums. Then there is the 'definitely over twenty' crowd that includes Fred Durst of Limp Bizkit, Eminem, Pink, Christina Aguilera, Jennifer Lopez, Kid Rock, Ja Rule, Shaggy and Nelly – ever-maturing idols who have sold millions of albums and moved tons of products this year, setting fads and starting trends for the youth culture of the inner city and middle class alike. 'Hip' and 'cool' now spans ages, races, genders, sexualities and classes as it defines those who move towards and away from counterculture and rebellion.

Body piercing is being adopted by the up-and-coming adolescents, wealthy Boomers, flaky Xers, gazillionaire celebrities and the not so rich and famous alike. It is hard to tell who is radical nowadays with all the hardware dangling from cheek, nipple and jowl. The hyper-sexualised culture of today renders everything pierceable. Skin is skin, isn't it? So, navels, noses, eyebrows, tongues, lips, ears, even sexual organs can be pierced. With a modicum of pain and decency, of course – sterilisation and rubber gloves too! The media age of global tribalism and branding has rendered our sexuality, ethics, social standing, politics and practices visible as our bodies are decorated like the Masai of Africa. We wear logos to show our consumer affiliations with cool brands. Tattoos reflect a low-end, subcultural chic that is radical. Jewellery – of any kind – also reveals pride, as we adorn the natural features we have been graced with. But at the same time it punishes the flesh for the indiscretions of vanity that are supposed to make us beautiful. This tendency to decorate the body in pain has become a universal phenomenon in Western popular culture. When the Masai pierce their ears, though, they do it differently, stretching the hole by using larger and larger ornaments until the holes are so large that you can fit a grapefruit through. The larger the hole the more attractive the style. When seen without an ornament, the five or so inches of hanging skin is, in Western cultural views, not a palatable sight, even a medical emergency. To the Masai, however, who are a very striking people, attractive and ornate in personal presentation, the exaggerated piercing hole represents good taste at its best. In the past, Western cultures were not prone to wearing jewellery from head to toe. Piercing was not an established fashion and lifestyle trend until recently. But now it has become a mainstream counterculture practice, thanks to celebrities and media icons who bear the trinkets and scars of a body's desire sculpted in pain.

Good taste now is not limited to highbrow definitions of quality, but has taken on many radical formations through media icons who have branding strength and currency. Contemporary celebrities hold a surprising amount of persuasion power over the mass migrations of funds from consumers to corporations. But finding a media icon who can set the standards for attitudes, interests and appearance that a marketer wants to express is a tricky business. The chosen idol has to convey the ideals of a brand, and its integrity as a popular choice for consumers: a brand represents not just a product, but a philosophical predisposition, a lifestyle choice and an idea to live by that is sought after by consumers because of its affiliation with a celebrity. No one will question the value of acquiring 'lips' and 'nails' from Estée Lauder when Elizabeth Hurley makes them her own. Achieving even a portion of the appealing effects they have when sported on celebrity models makes the investment seem worthwhile.

Labraun James – a new basketball child prodigy – recently signed a shoe endorsement deal worth over 90 million US dollars shortly after being drafted No. 1 overall in the NBA. Nike did not hesitate to make the offer. Will the kids be able to play basketball like him if they purchase the shoe he is wearing? Not likely many, if any. But the marketing bigwigs at Nike think the investment is worth the cost. There is no way this marketing-savvy corporation would endorse such a deal if they were not relatively sure this gifted teen would be a media icon for kids and so create enough running shoe sales to justify the expense. Manufacturers do not invest millions of dollars producing and shooting commercials with sports superstars like Tiger Woods, Michael Jordan, Rinaldo and Wayne Gretzky if the marketing impact and influence of the ads will not guarantee a profitable return. Corporations want celebrities to sell their likenesses, their voices, their mannerisms and even their bodies. What easier method of advertising could there be than sports and media icons that offer a brand worldwide exposure to millions of consumers over and over again with the flick of a remote control? The proliferation of satellite discs and home entertainment technology has given marketers direct access to the images we see on the big screen 24/7 in our own homes. And since the cachet of the larger-than-life celebrity recalls the brand, the residual exposure and influence has been huge. It is clear that the marketing gurus establish and legitimate many taste choices by coupling the fad or style with a person that creates a desired bond between celebrity status and brand. Pierce Brosnan can act as an effective media spokesperson for Omega watches, convincing many of the trustworthiness of the product brand. 007's sense of good taste offers a classic image of power, handsome looks and intelligence many would like to aspire to. There is no doubt that celebrity advertising affects consumer attitudes and buying habits. The potential of media icons to influence product sales and consolidate brand integrity varies depending on their age, personality, recognisability, race, gender, sexuality, and so on. But there is nothing more crucial to the success of a marketing campaign than the ability of the celebrity to make consumers believe in the good taste of a product. Pierce Brosnan would be an odd choice to promote vintage jeans with a radical edge.

Few celebrities could offer as authentic an image of what previous generations of countercultural rebels did, said and wore as Willie Nelson. The pony-tailed, white-bearded singer is the original Hippie-child bad boy. In Willie Nelson, The Gap has found a counterculture icon that can speak to the present through the words and pictures of a past life. He is the quintessential image of the jeans-wearing rebel of the 60s and 70s. Willie Nelson is just one of 50 denim-wearing celebrities who will proselytise The Gap's message of cultural revolution and individual emancipation, thanks to a New York City ad agency handling the account. If you miss the still on the gigantic black and white billboards, you can watch the MP3 clip in colour online at the corporation web site. Singing a countrified 'Bad to the Bone', Willie is dressed in Gap gear – none of it made from hemp, I presume. He is decked out in the very recognisable accoutrements of 70s counter-revolutionary chic: blue jeans and bandannas are the defining features of the look here. Willie presents a convincing case for historical slumming with a living legend – a relic? – by offering you the chance to gain the bad boy edge with the look of Gap Jeans. The message is clear.

Dressing down has now become a fashion fad that is in good taste, even for the rich and famous. Hundreds of subcultures exist, each developing their own very 'stratified' style priorities. There are so many that it seems as if *almost anything goes*. But within each subculture, there are still rules and restrictions governing what is considered to be good taste. The signature styles for the young and rebellious convey 'attitude'. This serves as a commentary against the restraining element of classical traditions. But although there is a rebellion against the status quo in the appearance of the 'New Age Punk', prerequisites to having an image of good taste still dominate this fashion statement. The 'anti' theme must be carried out in all the components of 'the look': 'anti' colours – black nails, skirts, shirts, socks, shoes. Textures worn must again be symbolic of a rebellious vision – studs, spikes, colourful hair. Even the lines that predominate the 'New Age Punk' look must serve to stir up and agitate in asymmetrical, diagonal, aggressive and less than tidy arrangements. In complete contrast, there are the pro-status-quo cultural styles. The classical traditions of the business-oriented middle classes still set patents for these more conservative young and upcoming individuals who aspire be part of the establishment. The 'Yuppie' cultures of today still strongly follow the 'want to be' mentality of aspiring millionaires through 'quality-name brands matter' to the ideals and living conditions of an upwardly mobile existence. Good taste for this group involves no revolutionary stance, but instead a lot of financial vision about hopeful material gains and an economically sound future.

The so-called 'Yuppie' look is carried through in fashion by way of a careful and clean symmetry of horizontals and verticals, soft edges and hard edges, cottons and khakis that are intended to represent stability in objectives and a sensible aptitude for performance – especially in issues regarding money. Regardless of the many underlying philosophies influencing a group style, good taste reigns through majority approval of choices that best define the personality of a community of taste. Quality is achieved in coordinating a consistency to the image. Those who best accomplish this provide style templates for a cultural image that is constantly challenged by new forms of fashion that express good taste, even though it may be anything but static. An image that pleases enough members in a group usually serves to gain the leading fashion seat. And yet, communally validated aesthetics are continually threatened and altered, always requiring participation in the acceptance of particular idiosyncrasies that arise within a community of taste. There is something exciting and stimulating about this. For those who follow and play with the possibilities, redefining good taste can serve to entertain and please in a big way.

Although the economic downturn of the 70s resulted in a lessening of the consumer boom, advertising was permanently altered. The battle of hip versus square became the central motif in a cultural battle of corporate branding between the Baby Boomers and their parents. Later, Generation X was proclaimed as the next media-savvy counterculture requiring especially ironic and self-conscious advertising that could be called 'Post Hip'. Corporations quickly learned how to pitch goods and services to people who believed themselves too worldly-wise to fall into the marketing trap. Today, nostalgia is the ticket to good taste for Generation X. How ironic is that? Vintage rules today because it sells itself to Gen Xers and Baby Boomers as a way to recapture the essence of a counterculture movement. Nostalgic clothing that harks back to the 60s and 70s offers anyone the chance to live the illusion of being a cultural rebel, while wearing hyper-trendy clothes. Yet there is nothing at all radical about flaunting a fashion everyone is wearing. Vintage perpetuates the fiction of crossing temporal borders and touching the past while living through the present.

The media jockeys call this trip down memory lane 'retro mania', 'retro chic', a 'retro revival'. No matter what hip nostalgia label the spin doctors use to pacify an already unsuspecting public, the beating heart of the 70s has been brought back from the dead to entertain us all – but mostly those unfortunate souls who experienced disco, the pet rock craze and shag haircuts first hand. While the stock traders have lost fortunes on Wall Street after the economic turbulence caused by the post-9/11 trauma, all eyes have been on the Consumer Price Index and the 70s have crept back into our lives like an old aroma. Questioning what constitutes good taste has taken a back seat to recapturing the days of plenty spawned by speculative trading in overvalued internet companies that are now nothing more than registered trademarks. The 70s were an era of conflicting and mixed cultural allegiances, during which time rock music battled disco and was blind-sided by the Punk movement spearheaded by Malcom McLaren's garage band, The Sex Pistols. But now, the second coming of the 70s 'Me' culture has been compressed into readily digestible forms by the media, which have created images of cool for easy consumption among the mass public of a new generation.

Index

Why Do People Hate America?

*Ziauddin Sardar and
Merryl Wyn Davies*

Already considered 'required
reading' (*Independent*) by the
national press, this updated
edition of *Why Do People Hate
America?* sees Britain's foremost
cultural commentators enter the
post-Iraq fray.

Ziauddin Sardar and Merryl Wyn
Davies revisit their best-selling
critique to reflect on the impact the
conflict has had on the world's
already beleaguered view of
America.

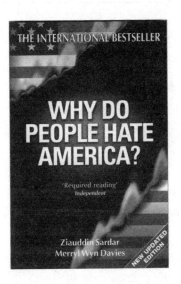

Why Do People Hate America? has sold almost 100,000 copies around
the world and has been translated into every major language – and
some lesser ones too. From French and German to Urdu and Malay,
this is truly an international bestseller.

The authors have toured the globe tirelessly to promote the book,
reinforcing their reputation as the leading British experts on US
foreign policy and culture.

So, why do people hate America? As liberators of the Iraqi people,
shouldn't the US now at last enjoy adoration and respect?
Regrettably, as Sardar and Davies show, the history of this hatred is
long: too often US cultural imperialism has arrived couched in the
language of freedom and democracy. Here is crucial background
reading for everyone concerned about the world of the early 21st
century.

- 'Contains valuable information and insights that we should know,
  over here, for our own good, and the world's' *Noam Chomsky*
- 'Original and thought provoking' *New Statesman*
- 'Packed with tightly argued points' *Times Higher Education
  Supplement*

1 84046 525 5
Icon Books UK £7.99
Canada $19.99

Trust ... from Socrates to Spin

Kieron O'Hara
Introduction by Will Hutton

From Aristotle to Francis Fukuyama, Machiavelli to Naomi Klein, the Book of Job to Blairite newspeak and from Enron to nanotechnology, Kieron O'Hara presents a lively exploration of trust.

Essential for almost all social interaction, trust holds society together and makes co-operation possible. Ubiquitous, and yet deeply misunderstood, it can take years to build up, and after one false move can disappear overnight. Polls show levels of trust in politicians, businessmen, scientists and others to be at all-time lows: a crisis in trust is currently gripping Western culture.

O'Hara moves easily between the great philosophers and sociologists, and the impact of this crisis in our daily lives, animating theory with in-depth case studies, helping us make sense of the daily scares in our newspapers. Is trust declining? Should we be worried? What can we do about it? O'Hara gives few easy answers in this exhilarating ride through politics, literature, philosophy and history.

From Socrates to government spin doctors, *Trust* is a popular, gripping account of the most vital political issue of the 21st century.

1 84046 531 X
Icon Books UK £12.99
Canada $30.00

**Fundamentalist World:
The New Dark Age of Dogma**

Stuart Sim

The collapse of the Argentinian economy, the rise of the far right, 9/11, suicide bombings in the Middle East, campaigns against multiculturalism, anti-abortion terrorism, the militia movement in America, teaching creationism in schools, riots at Miss World: what ties these seemingly disparate phenomena together?

All are products of a fundamentalist mentality, determined to crush all opposing ideas. Belief in these kinds of universal theories was, until recently, assumed to be in decline. Stuart Sim argues that this is far from true.

History, power, security, control, fulfilment, purity, identity and self-definition are key themes of the curiously modern renaissance of fundamentalist thought. And fundamentalism is no fringe enthusiasm, but an increasingly mainstream and powerful influence. Whether it's religious, political, imperialist, nationalist or even market fundamentalism, believe it: we live in an increasingly fundamentalist world.

Fundamentalism is alive and well and will affect every one of us if we don't fight it now, argues Stuart Sim.

1 84046 532 8
Icon Books UK £12.99
Canada $30.00

1 84046 277 9

1 84046 280 9

Postmodern Encounters

Pocket-sized despatches from the cutting edge of thought, *Postmodern Encounters* is a series of small books, each discussing a key figure or idea in contemporary philosophy, psychology, science and beyond.

UK £3.99 (unless stated otherwise)

1 84046 093 8

1 84046 237 X £4.99